Contents

Kinsmen and Clansmen

R. W. Munro

I luif justice, and wald that everie man
Had that quhilk richtlie dois to him perteine
Yet all my kyn, allya, or my clan,
In richt or wrang I man alwayis mantene.

Alexander Arbuthnot
(Principal of King's College Aberdeen), 1569

JOHNSTON & BACON
London & Edinburgh

First published 1971

SBN 7179.4550.2

Johnston & Bacon
(A Division of Geoffrey Chapman Ltd)
Edina Works · Edina Place
Edinburgh EH7 5RW

Filmset by Keyspools Ltd., Golborne, Lancs.
Printed by Lowe & Brydone (Printers) Ltd., London

The cover illustration of the family tree of the Campbells of Glenorchy, ancestors of the Earls of Breadalbane, was painted in 1635 by George Jamesone and is reproduced here by kind permission of the Scottish National Portrait Gallery, and with the assistance of Tom Scott, Edinburgh.

Preface

THIS book is meant for anyone who is curious about surnames in general and their place in Scottish life in particular, as well as for those who are interested in one family or clan. It is written in the belief that the story of one name is better understood by having some knowledge of others, and that family or clan loyalties can suffer by being too exclusive.

Apart from giving facts of general interest and importance, the aim has been to focus attention on occasions when people of the same name acted in concert because they bore that name—whether by agreeing to settle disputes among themselves, promising mutual support, or being 'out' together in 1689, 1715 or 1745. It is remarkable how many instances of solidarity are to be found on record.

Not too much distinction has been made between clans and families, although the first is by custom used mainly of groups in the Highlands and Borders. The term 'chief' is used sparingly, although not perhaps sparingly enough for some readers. General usage agrees with the late Dr W. Mackay Mackenzie's Highland viewpoint that 'all chiefs were heads of families, but not all heads of families were chiefs or chieftains of clans'; but I have not forgotten the interchangeability which is implicit in the 17th century Lord Advocate Sir George Mackenzie's dictum that 'with us the chief of the family is called the head of the clan.'

I have avoided the subject of family origins, partly because any statement would have to be hedged about with 'ifs' and 'buts' and other elaborations quite unsuitable to a book of this size, and partly because I am not convinced that the result would have much meaning for the general reader. Further information on this and other aspects of the subject will be found in the sources listed on page 192; those with only a slight knowledge of Scottish history may find some help in the notices of the Royal Stewarts (page 176) and the Clan Donald (page 86).

Any choice of names for inclusion in a book of this kind must to some extent be an arbitrary one, and the method of treatment a matter for individual taste and judgment. No offence is intended by the omission of any name, and none should be taken. Too much significance should not be read into the fact that one family is said to have had an acestor killed at Flodden, for example, or to have produced a famous inventor or explorer, or to have a clan or family society, while the notices of others make no mention of such items.

The importance which the Scots still attach to surnames, and the strength of family feeling among us, is a legacy from the past. This sense of kinship and clanship is part of the background of Scottish history, and it colours many of our thoughts and actions to this day.

R. W. M.

ARMSTRONG

ARMSTRONG

On the western marches of the Borderland, the 'sturdy Armstrongs, who were for ever riding' held the wide haughs and gently-rolling hills of Lower Liddesdale in the days before the Scottish and English crowns and parliaments were joined. It was wild and hard of access even when Sir Walter Scott, in his vacation raids into the valley, examined the ruined peel towers and explored the hidden retreats of this once numerous clan.

Gilbert Armstrong, steward of the household to David II, was sent on an embassy to England in 1363, and there were Armstrongs at Mangerton in Liddesdale thirteen years later. By the 16th century they occupied a large part of the 'debateable lands' between the two kingdoms, and had spread into Eskdale, Ewesdale, Wauchopesdale and Annandale. A descendant writes of 'the honourable profession of moss-trooping', for they counted themselves leviers of tribute rather than plunderers, and prided themselves on the good rule they exercised over a lawless set. The Border ballads testify how in the process they defied the wardens of the marches and even the king himself.

One of the most notorious was Johnnie Armstrong of Gilnockie, who encountered James V during a royal progress designed to restore order in 1530. John had ridden out gaily with a score or so of well mounted and apparelled henchmen to meet the king; he had an angry reception, and tried to bargain for his life with offers to keep himself and forty gentlemen always ready for the king's service, never to rob Scotland or the Scots, and to produce on a given day any English subject dead or alive, however high his degree. But all in vain: Johnnie was summarily hanged on the spot with all his followers, an example of rough justice which was fine material for the chroniclers and balladists, and long remembered on the Borders. Less picturesque is the fact, attested by contemporary records, that only a few years before John had signed a 'bond of manrent' promising personal service and support to one of the Scottish wardens, and that later in the same century an Armstrong of Arkilton and others of his 'branch, kin and friends' submitted their quarrel with some Elliot neighbours to the Privy Council's arbitration, accepting their decision in advance.

In what Scott—no mean judge in such matters—called 'one of the last and most gallant achievements performed upon the Border', another Armstrong known as 'Kinmont Willie' was rescued from prison in Carlisle castle by Scott of Buccleuch and a raiding band which included Willie's four sons. He had been taken by the English while returning home from a warden court, and Buccleuch had failed to secure redress for this unsportsmanlike act. As King James had reached an understanding with Elizabeth by the time this happened, in 1596, and it was a period of official Anglo-Scottish friendship, uproar and diligent inquiry followed; but a year later we find 'Will of Kinmonth' named among the leaders of a band of Armstrongs called 'Sandie's bairns'.

Away in London, James and his son Charles must have had many a laugh from their court jester, Archie Armstrong, whose nimble tongue 'jested him into a fair estate'. But the last laugh was with the clan, when Gilnockie's descendant 'Christie's Will' kidnapped one of the king's judges in Edinburgh and kept him out of harm's way in Annandale while a friend's case was decided in his favour; and as late as 1629, King Charles was issuing a pardon to Armstrong of the Ash, Edward Armstrong alias Kinmond, Hector alias Stubholme, and John Armstrong called John-with-one-hand.

In the course of securing peace on the Border, however, leading Armstrongs were brought to the scaffold, their strongholds razed to the ground, and their estates given to others, until hardly a single landowner of the name was left throughout the extensive districts they once possessed. Mangerton lost his life and lands after a single raid in 1610; Armstrong of Whitehaugh was executed two years later, though his branch survived in Liddesdale for a further 200 years. The clan found other outlets for their energies: some were distinguished in medicine (one pioneered research into poliomyelitis), others in engineering (from motor cars to ordnance); an Armstrong discoverer of the North-West Passage wrote the name on an island in the Canadian Arctic; and we can be sure that some of the sturdy Armstrong blood flows in the veins of the first man to walk on the surface of the moon.

BRUCE

BRUCE

It is no accident that the name of Bruce means to most Scottish people a person rather than a family, and that King Robert I is as often known in common speech by his surname as by his royal title.

The first Robert Bruce of Annandale was an English landowner of Norman origin, who was granted this important border zone by David I in 1124. When Alexander III died, and succession to the Scottish crown was left in doubt with the death of his grand-daughter the 'Maid of Norway', the Bruces had already been for five generations a Scottish landed family. The Lord of Annandale (grandfather of the future king) was then an old man; almost half a century earlier, owing to his mother being the second daughter of David, Earl of Huntingdon, and therefore niece of William the Lion, he had been acknowledged as heir-presumptive when Alexander II expected to die childless. When the question of succession was submitted to Edward I of England as arbiter in 1291, Robert Bruce was one of the two chief competitors; but as there were now descendants of the Earl's elder daughter the crown was awarded to her grandson John Balliol. Although failing in this vital contest, Robert the 'competitor' was a magnate of importance in various parts of Scotland; from his mother he also inherited a northern barony including the Garioch in Aberdeenshire, and his son married the heiress of Carrick in Ayrshire. So young Robert, born of this marriage on 11th July 1274, is justly described as 'a Scotsman, born amongst Scots' by his latest biographer, Professor G. W. S. Barrow. How through 'toil and weariness, hunger and peril' (in the words of the Arbroath declaration of 1320) he won the independence of his country as well as his own right to the throne is a story and an achievement which has made the name of Bruce dear to the Scottish people. He had many loyal supporters in the struggle whose names are famous in Scottish history, and no doubt many obscure kinsmen and others from the Bruce lands in Annandale and Nithsdale, and Highlanders from Galloway and Badenoch, fought in the armies which he led.

The old lordship of Annandale was made over during the king's lifetime to his friend Thomas Randolph, Earl of Moray, and it eventually passed to the Douglases. In the next two reigns the name of Bruce became associated with a more central part of Scotland, lying on either side of the River Forth where it widens out above the modern bridges to form the Firth of Forth. Soon after Bruce's son David II returned from a long captivity in England he granted the castle and barony of Clackmannan to his 'cousin' Robert Bruce, whose exact relationship to the king is not known. That was in 1359, and the family continued in possession until 1791, when the last Mrs. Bruce of Clackmannan died, leaving the great two-handed sword of the hero king (with which incidentally she had 'knighted' the poet Burns) to another Bruce of the Clackmannan line, the Earl of Elgin. The head of yet another cadet house, Bruce of Kennet, inherited the title of Lord Balfour of Burleigh through the female line.

Meantime on the south side of the Forth a family 'claiming the nearest descent of any of that name to the blood-royal' had taken root and spread out branches. Sir John Bruce of Airth, who probably built part of the castle on its rock above the river, was murdered in 1483 by a neighbour and brother-in-law Menteith of Karse; and when the Lords of Council tried to make peace between the two families we find on record a family group consisting of the new laird Robert, his uncles Alexander and Lucas, another Robert Bruce, 'and others their kin and friends'. Among the many offshoots of this branch were two famous Bruces of Kinnaird, the one a churchman and reformer, and the other the Abyssinian traveller and writer.

Holders of the name of Bruce may not be as 'clannish' as some others in every sense of the word, but they have a special right to pride of race. Even in the prosaic 20th century a Lord Elgin, who gave the authority of his great name as well as personal support to movements for preserving the site of the battle of Bannockburn, and setting up economic and cultural bodies such as the Scottish Development Council and the National Trust for Scotland, found occasions for showing the king's great sword in public, and invoking the inspiration of his memory.

BUCHANAN

BUCHANAN

Of all the many islands which diversify the scenery of Loch Lomond, Clairinch opposite Balmaha is of special interest to the Buchanans. Less than half a mile long by one-eighth of a mile broad, it was given by an Earl of Lennox to his seneschal, Anselan or Absalon, 'son of Macbeth', by a charter of 1225 confirmed by Alexander II. This was the first of the family on record, and the island's name became the *slughorn* or war-cry of the Buchanans, bringing all able-bodied clansmen to the island or other rendezvous set by their chief.

According to clan tradition, the chief's surname was originally M'Auselan, from the founder of the family, a patronymic form retained by the eldest cadet while those of the main stem adopted a territorial designation. In the reign of David II, Maurice of 'Buchquhanane' had from Lennox a charter confirming him in the lands of that name, and this the king confirmed in 1370. For 300 years the family spread out in a succession of cadet branches such as Leny, Carbeth, Drumakill, Arnprior, Spittal and Auchmar, and in various sept families. But they have never been quite the same since, with the death of John Buchanan of that Ilk, the house and lands of Buchanan were sold to the Montrose family in 1682.

Although his branch had come off the main stem 135 years before, the nearest cadet was William Buchanan of Auchmar, who was steeped in the genealogy of the name and had hoped to inherit the lands. In 1723 he published an inquiry into Scottish surnames in general, and the origin and descent of the Highland clans, and an elaborate 'historical and genealogical essay upon the family and surname of Buchanan' which he intended principally for clan reading. Auchmar, who lived until 1747 (his own line died out in 1816), remembered perhaps with sadness the day when the name was so numerous in the district that the laird of Buchanan could, in a summer's day, call fifty heritors of his own name to his house, upon any occasion, and all of them might with convenience return to their homes before night, the most distant being not above ten miles from Buchanan. He lists them carefully—ten, himself included, immediately descended of the laird's family, and their dependants; seventeen of the Drumakill line, headed by Craigievairn; Buchanan of Leny and nine others of his line; fourteen of the Carbeth line; besides others of the sept names of MacAuselan, MacMillan, MacColman and Spittel.

The clan has produced some notable men, of whom the most illustrious was George Buchanan of the Drumakill line, accounted the finest Latin scholar of his time, tutor to James VI and historian of Scotland; Alexander Buchanan of Arnprior boasted that even if James V was King of Scots, he was 'king of Kippen'; and Walter of Boquhan, a branch of Carbeth, was found guilty in 1729 of housebreaking and sheepstealing, as well as being accused of blackmail and fire-raising, and was banished to the American plantations. Walter's son Hugh was one of three Buchanan lairds who agreed to pay 'watch-money' to the Grahams (really MacGregors) of Glengyle for the protection of their lands, according to a formal contract drawn up and signed before witnesses in 1741.

The Buchanans played no corporate part in the Jacobite risings; but there was a Buchanan on the ship which brought Prince Charles Edward to Scotland in 1745; Buchanan of Arnprior, though not 'out', was executed in 1746; and Buchanan of Drumakill was blamed for giving up Lord Tullibardine and others who surrendered to him at his Lochlomondside home. The Buchanans were dispersed as other men replaced Auchmar's flock of heritors. One, of Ulster Scots ancestry, became fifteenth President of the United States of America. Many of them settled and prospered nearer home, and in Glasgow they established a charitable society in 1725 to provide support for needy clansfolk, and to assist boys of the name in school, university and trade apprenticeships, 'so as to put them in the way of advancing themselves in life'. Surviving the upheaval of 1745, it was eight years later erected into a legal corporation, comprising 'the said name, the reputed septs, and branches thereof, owning themselves to be such', as recorded in Auchmar's book. The Buchanan Society is now the oldest clan society in Scotland; it registered arms in 1919, and in 1939 a wealthy clansman bequeathed to it, to be kept as an animal and bird sanctuary, the island so long associated with the name, so that Clairinch is now once again in Buchanan ownership for all time.

CAMERON

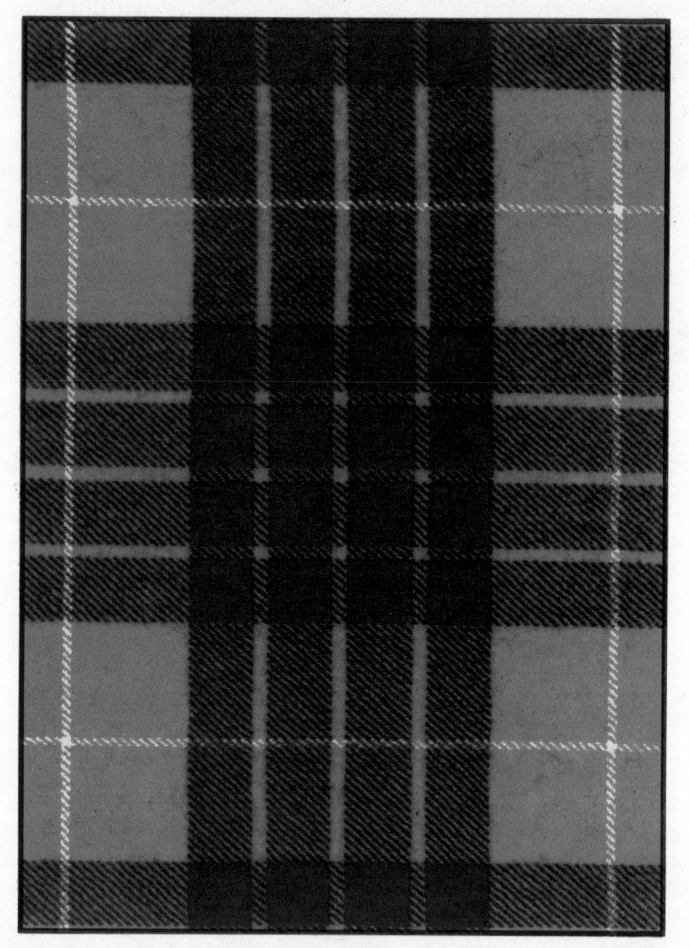

CLAN CAMERON

In the wild country of Lochaber, among the hills which surround Loch Lochy, Loch Arkaig and Loch Eil, there grew up a clan which was described by Drummond of Hawthornden in the 17th century as 'fiercer than fierceness itself'. They were the Camerons, who were so constantly harassed from without that they were virtually compelled to live by the sword. Holding their own for centuries without a legal title to much of the land they occupied, they earned a reputation for valour which clung to the name even in the great wars of recent times.

Donald *dubh*, the chief from whom the Camerons of Lochiel derived a Gaelic patronymic, was a formidable warrior who is believed to have led the clan in the army of the Lord of the Isles at Harlaw in 1411. There is a tradition that the family were descended from the marriage of a MacMartin heiress in Lochaber with one of the Cambruns or Cambrons, who held land in Fife, Perth, Angus and Aberdeenshire. When the Lord of the Isles rebelled against James I in 1429, the Camerons supported the crown; and in revenge, when he was restored to power, their lands were granted to others (although some were later returned), and earlier Mackintosh claims to territory occupied by the Camerons were ratified. These remained a subject of bitter dispute for more than two centuries, and the Camerons' survival as a clan is an extraordinary instance of tenacity.

After the fall of the island lordship in 1493, James IV confirmed Ewen Cameron in his lands of Loch Eil, and in 1530 they were erected into a barony and he was given 'half the bailiary of Lochaber'. He had further charters of lands in Lochaber, including Inverlochy, Torlundy and Letterfinlay, but the Mackintoshes maintained a legal claim to Glen Loy and Loch Arkaig, although they could never establish anything like a lasting occupation. The patriarchal rule of a clan chief inevitably clashed with the feudal rights of a superior, and in 1616 Allan of Lochiel forcibly prevented Mackintosh as superior from holding courts in Lochaber. Sir Ewen of Lochiel, 'the Ulysses of the Highlands' as Macaulay called him, became chief in 1647, and was one of the last royalists in the field before the Commonwealth grip on Scotland tightened. Monck's garrison at Inverlochy, forerunner of Fort William, was established primarily to daunt the Camerons, and Lochiel defended his tenants and estates from Government troops before submitting with his clan on honourable terms.

After the Restoration the Mackintoshes renewed their claims, and with Privy Council backing invaded the Cameron lands. But as a result of negotiations Lochiel was able to purchase Glen Loy and Loch Arkaig in 1665, with Argyll paying the purchase money on condition that Ewen and his successors held the lands as his vassals. The clan was spreading beyond its old bounds; after the call to arms for Dundee's rising in 1689 they only mustered 240 men at first, 500 more arriving from the outlying districts three days later. Sir Ewen made over his estates to his grandson Donald; this left his son John free to take the clan 'out' in 1715, for which he was attainted and went into exile. Donald, the 'gentle Lochiel' of the Forty-Five, was a man of peace interested in the welfare of his people and the good of his estates. Although his judgment warned him not to join Prince Charles when he landed without support, his opposition gave way before the prince's personal appeal, and the Camerons' initiative which caused others to follow made the early Jacobite successes possible. The clan fought in every major engagement in the campaign, with the chief at their head, and suffered losses estimated at 300 out of a strength of about 800. Lochiel himself was wounded at Culloden, Achnacarry and his tenants' houses were burned, but the Camerons were 'still in the hills with full arms' six months later. Lochiel went into exile with the prince, and his estates were forfeited, not being restored until 1784.

Many Camerons joined the Highland regiments which came into being from 1757 onwards, and Allan Cameron of Erracht raised the 79th Highlanders (later Queen's Own Cameron Highlanders) in 1793. The military tradition learned in centuries of fighting has continued ever since, and Camerons from Lochaber distinguished themselves in the two world wars of the 20th century.

CAMPBELL OF ARGYLL

CAMPBELL OF ARGYLL

In telling the story of clans smaller than the Campbells, it is natural to record the public honours and rewards won by their chiefs. But if one were to do so with the Campbells, the details of their progress from baron to earl (1457), marquess (1641) and duke (1701) would leave no room to speak of their impact on the clan as a whole and on the country where theirs is the leading name.

The Campbells were established around Loch Awe, with the castle of Inchconnell as headquarters, before Inveraray was built in the heart of what became 'real Argyll'. From Colin, who died at the end of the 13th century, the heads of the clan became known as *MacCailein Mor*, and their power was founded on the grants of land and keeping of castles with which Robert Bruce rewarded his supporters. This growth owes much also the the loyalty of innumerable cadet families, such as Campbell of Loudoun who in 1430 resigned his rights in certain lands on account of friendship shown and to be shown by his kinsman Duncan of Lochawe as 'chief to all his kin and surname'.

By supporting the crown against other clans the area of Campbell influence widened—Macdonald lands in Knapdale in 1476, later the valuable Kintyre estate, and then the vast and scattered Maclean territories in Mull, Morvern, Tiree and Coll (1674–80). Friends were rewarded, a military following ensured, and order preserved in the annexed lands by a policy of settling Campbell kinsmen and allies on them. Meantime too the house of Argyll received a series of commissions (as many as twenty-five during the 16th century alone) with powers of varying extent, most of them against other Highland clans, but some in connection with the Lothians, Merse, Teviotdale and Lauderdale.

But civil war brought doom as well as power in the century that followed, and two Argylls went to the block, one of them for open rebellion against James VII. With the Revolution the heir of Argyll returned in triumph—'the head not only of a tribe but of a party', as Macaulay put it. In the Jacobite risings which followed, the Campbells with few important exceptions fought on the Government side, although according to one Jacobite writer in 1715 Argyll's own clansmen were 'to the extent of one half in favour of the Scottish rising, against the Union, more than actually in favour of a Stuart king.' By 1745 they were reckoned 'the richest and most numerous clan in Scotland' —the duke could raise 3,000 men on his own property and his kinsmen's lands, Breadalbane more than 1,000, and the great Campbell barons such as Ardkinglas, Auchinbreck (one of the few Jacobite lairds), Lochnell and Inverawe at least another 1,000. In fact, some 2,700 Argyll men were in arms during the '45, and there could have been more if there had been enough arms for them. In some of the more recently acquired territories, such as Mull and Morvern, Jacobite sympathies were openly avowed and Government recruitment resisted.

Before the Union of 1707, the nine Earls of Argyll were Gaelic-speaking Scots, with practically none but Scottish blood in their veins; but the dukes tended to be more English in outlook as well as in blood, and to concern themselves with matters affecting Great Britain as a whole. As landowners, however, they were not afraid of change: the second duke abolished the tacksman system and gave leases direct to the men who worked the land, and the fifth issued a remarkable series of orders for the betterment of his lands and tenantry, using a statistical basis which produced what was probably the earliest Scottish census giving names, ages, status and occupations of all the inhabitants on his vast estates in 1779.

Such power and prosperity as the house of Argyll enjoyed, and some of the means by which it was acquired, naturally aroused jealousy and even hatred. In March 1746, for example, Lochiel and Keppoch wanted Prince Charles Edward 'to hang a Campbell for every house that shall hereafter be burnt by them' (a policy of destruction which the duke himself condemned on political and economic as well as humanitarian grounds). To the accusations so often levelled at the clan as a whole it has been replied: 'Because the Campbell chiefs nearly always trod a path of level-headed common sense, must they be declared cunning and unscrupulous?'

CAMPBELL OF BREADALBANE

CAMPBELL OF BREADALBANE

ALTHOUGH descended from the house of Argyll, the Campbells of Glenorchy, Earls (1677) and Marquesses (1831) of Breadalbane, are regarded not so much as a branch of the main stem as heads of a separate house with cadets, clansmen, and a distinctive character and history of their own. Under their protection, too, gathered many sept families and 'broken men' of other clans and names, who chose to acknowledge Glenorchy as their chief, accepted written agreements between landlord and tenant, and added to his strength in war and prosperity in peace. So wide were their territories that, from Aberfeldy in Perthshire to Easdale off the coast of Argyll, it was true to say 'the land was all the Markiss's', for he could travel nearly 100 miles from east to west without leaving his own property.

Founder of this potent family was Sir Colin Campbell, who received the lands of Glenorchy from his father (Sir Duncan of Lochawe) in 1432, and acquired a third of the great lordship of Lorn by marriage. In a few generations they extended their authority eastward along the line of access to the highlands of Perthshire, and built castles in Loch Dochart and at Finlarig near the head of Loch Tay, repaired Kilchurn on Loch Awe, and built towers at Achallader on the way to Glencoe and at Barcaldine in Benderloch. The site of Balloch castle, later known as Taymouth, is said to have been recommended as a means of inducing the laird's successors to extend their property eastwards, as they eventually did.

Sir Duncan was one of the first great Highland landowners to improve their estates by making roads, planting trees, and building houses and churches. Records of his vigorous and methodical administration from 1583 to 1631 throw a flood of light on clan affairs and estate management. His register of bonds of friendship, homage and maintenance show a striking mixture of feudal and patriarchal elements; formal deeds of child adoption are so common that it was evidently an approved way of transferring property. The baron court was a local council with wide authority, often acting with the advice and consent of 'the whole commons and tenants', and having a role that ranged from laying down that all stock should be kept at the mountain shealings between 8 June and 15 July to punishing wives found drinking in the public brewhouse without their husbands. In Sir Duncan's time the family chronicle known as the 'Black Book of Taymouth' was written, and his son commissioned George Jamesone to paint the family portraits, and the genealogical tree which appears on the cover of this publication.

It was Sir John of Glenorchy, 'as cunning as a fox, wise as a serpent, but as slippery as an eel', who raised the family to an earldom. He lent money to the bankrupt Earl of Caithness, foreclosed on the title and estates, married the widowed countess, and fought a battle against the Sinclairs near Wick (with several hundred Breadalbane men under his cousins of Glenlyon, Glenfalloch, Lochdochart and Achallader) to establish his claim; and when deprived of the title he got a new patent from the king as Earl of Breadalbane with the original precedence. He was given £12,000 to win over the chiefs to King William—'The money is spent, the Highlands are quiet, and this is the only way of accounting among friends', he wrote—but was at heart a Jacobite. In 1715 a detachment of 500 Breadalbane men under Glenlyon and Glendaruel invaded Argyll, and were met by about 700 under Campbell of Fonab at the head of Lochnell; but 'to spare the effusion of Campbell blood' a parley was arranged, and they were allowed to march off and join Mar in Atholl.

Lieut.-General John Campbell of Carwhin, who became fourth earl on the failure of the senior line, was made a marquess. His son and successor, although a champion of civil and religious liberty at the time of the Reform Bill and the Disruption, allowed many long-established families on his estates to be cleared to make way for sheep. Queen Victoria and Prince Albert were given a 'princely and romantic' reception by him at Taymouth in 1842, with the Breadalbane Highlanders 'all in Campbell tartan'. The title passed, after prolonged litigation, to the Campbells of Glenfalloch, but shortly before their line ended in 1923 Taymouth and the eastern portion of the estates were sold, and nearly all of what remained was disposed of thirty years later.

CARNEGIE

CARNEGIE

The lands and barony of Carnegie, from which this surname is derived, lie between Carmylie and Panmure, in south-east Angus, and the name has spread through the district where the rivers North and South Esk divide Strathmore from the Howe of the Mearns.

In a charter by David II confirming the original lands in 1358 to John de Carnegie, he is described as John son of Christian son of John de Balinhard, but he took the name of the lands as his own and his line continued for two or more generations as the Carnegies of that Ilk. James, the last of these in the direct male line of descent, resigned the lands of Carnegie into the hands of his superior Maule of Panmure in 1527; less than forty years later they were acquired by the Carnegies of Kinnaird, near Brechin, one of whose sons revived the style of Carnegie of that Ilk and appeared under that name in a special Act of Parliament in 1581.

The Kinnaird family, which was apparently the next senior branch, held their lands on the tenure of 'keeping the king's ale cellar within the sheriffdom of Forfar', so that the king should be supplied when he happened to reside there. In 1452 'Wat of Carnegy' of this line took up arms with the king's forces under Huntly against the Earl of Crawford, and had his mansion-house and family records destroyed for his pains.

David of Kinnaird (better known from his estate of Colluthie in north-west Fife) was one of the 'Octavians' appointed to administer the royal finances in 1596, and two of his sons were created earls—David with the title of Southesk in 1633, and John of Eathie (later changed to Northesk) in 1647. A sidelight on family life in the period is that, when the great Marquess of Montrose married one of the future Lord Southesk's six pretty daughters in 1629, the contract stipulated that her father should 'entertain and sustain' the couple 'in house with himself' for the first three years, and two of their four sons were born at Kinnaird. The Southesk family proved strong partisans of the Stewarts, and Kinnaird was visited by James VI, Charles I, Charles II and the Chevalier. The 'brave Southesk' of Sheriffmuir was hero of the Jacobite ballad 'The Piper o' Dundee', and his estates lying in seven counties were forfeited for rebellion. At his death the succession passed to the baronets of Pitarrow in Kincardineshire, who later repurchased a large portion of the property, and from this line sprang several influential families of the name. One younger son, who had joined Prince Charles Edward at 18, escaped to the Continent after Culloden, and was so successful as a merchant at Gothenburg in Sweden that he returned to Scotland with a fortune about twenty years later.

Of the Earls of Northesk the seventh, an admiral and the son of an admiral, served under Duncan, St Vincent and Nelson, and was third in command at Trafalgar; even more remarkable was the confidence shown in him by the fleet in mutiny at the Nore in 1797, when the 'delegates' chose him to take their petition to the king. Cadets of Northesk include the Carnegies of Finavon, Lour, Boysack and Balnamoon: James of Boysack was an ardent Jacobite and private secretary to the Prince in 1745, and Alexander of Balnamoon was forfeited for his part in the Rising of 1715.

Probably the most famous modern holder of the name was Andrew Carnegie, the Dunfermline weaver's son who became one of the richest men in the world. All he had to say of his ancestry in an autobiography was that he was born 'as the saying is, "of poor but honest parents, of good kith and kin" '; he was a staunch republican, with an inherited distate for hereditary power and titles, and could not feel much interest in 'any who occupied positions not by merit, but by birth'. It is worth noting that the Carnegies had a share in starting the handsome series of volumes enshrining the genealogies, letters and charters of Scotland's noble and landed families which are a lasting monument to competitive family pride in the 19th century; their compiler, Sir William Fraser, knew the Carnegie history from having helped to substantiate the claims to the Southesk peerage, and put it on record that the earl to whom it was restored in 1855 was one of the first to propose the publication of such a family history.

CLAN CHATTAN

CLAN CHATTAN

THERE were two Clan Chattans, one traditional and the other historical, both named after an ancestor Gillichattan Mor. The dividing line may be drawn in 1291, the date assigned to the marriage of the heiress of the traditional clan to the chief of the Mackintoshes, by which the historical clan was founded. This became a confederacy of lesser clans or families, and membership remained remarkably constant from the earliest written evidence in the 16th century and probably long before that, until the mid-18th century.

Members of the historical clan fell into two categories—those 'of the blood' which included descendants of the traditional clan like the Macphersons, Cattanachs and Macphails, and the Shaws, Farquharsons and MacCombies whose founders were originally Mackintoshes; and the independent small clans which voluntarily placed themselves within the confederacy, such as the MacGillivrays from upper Strathnairn, the Davidsons from Badenoch, the Macleans of Dochgarroch near Inverness, and the Macqueens. Protection was the keynote of their association, and this could involve them in episodes such as the defeat of Cameron invaders at Invernahavon (1370) and support of Donald of the Isles at Harlaw (1411). Dwellers in the plains must have come to fear the Clan Chattan, for in 1528 the Earl of Moray and others in the northern sheriffdoms were authorised to 'pass upon the Clanquhattan and invaid thame to thair uter destructioun be slauchter, byrning, drowning and uther wayis, and leif na creatur lewand (living) of that clann except priestis, wemen and bairns'.

A series of 'bands' or agreements give some idea of the purpose and effect of the confederacy. In 1543, Mackintosh signed an alliance with Huntly for himself and 'his kin of Clan Chattan', and the leading members agreed to renounce their dependence on him if he broke it. At a great gathering at Termit in Petty (near Inverness) in April 1609, arising out of 'controversies, quarrels, questions and hosts' within the clan, the members bound themselves to assist and defend Mackintosh their chief and to stand by each other on all occasions. In 1664 there was a band directed solely against the Camerons, and in 1756 the clan gave formal consent to certain transactions over land. There is a reference in the 1609 band to 'the King of Scotland's gift of the chieftainrie of the Clan Chattane', and such grants by David II and Robert II are on record elsewhere.

Mackintosh was generally acknowledged as chief of Clan Chattan, on the ground that the chiefship had been passed by the heretrix Eva's father to his ancestor; but at various times the Macphersons of Cluny claimed it by virtue of descent in the male line from the old Clan Chattan. This was then a practical matter, and not merely one of status, as chiefs were held answerable for the good behaviour of their clans. In 1622, Mackintosh was authorised to use the military services of 'all and sindrie persones of the Clan Chattan . . . quhairever they dwell'. So when Cluny secured armorial bearings in 1672 as 'the only and true representer of the ancient and honourable family of Clan Chattan', Mackintosh at once objected, and the Privy Council considered it important enough to hear five days' legal debate on the issue. Finally the council ordered each to answer for those descended of his own family, his men, tenants and servants, and the Lord Lyon found Mackintosh to be the undoubted chief not only of his own name but also of Clan Chattan, comprehending the Macphersons, MacGillivrays, Farquharsons, Macqueens, Macphails, Macbains and others.

In 1745 the Clan Chattan regiment was led by MacGillivray of Dunmaglass, as Mackintosh was not 'out' and the Macphersons acted independently. An unsuccessful move was made in 1727 to recast the clan in modern form, by employing lawyers to watch and defend its interests, and an attempt to have the ownership of some lands in Inverness-shire limited to heirs 'of the Clan Chattan allenarly' (i.e. only) in terms of a tack of 1632 was thrown out by the Court of Session in 1862. After the death in 1838 without a direct male heir of the last Mackintosh chief to own the Clan Chattan estate of Glenspean, the Lord Lyon held that the chiefship of Clan Chattan had become separate from that of Mackintosh as there was no ascertainable mention of it in the late chief's settlement.

CHISHOLM

CHISHOLM

THERE is both a Lowland and a Highland section of the Chisholms, descended from a common ancestor, and it is because of their non-Gaelic origin that the chief of the clan is referred to as 'The Chisholm'. This highly prized distinction is regarded as strictly correct in his case, whatever it may be in others.

The early Chisholms owned land near the English border, and the first of the name known in Scotland is Alexander de Chesholme, witness to a charter in 1249. One of the family married a daughter of Sir Robert Lauder, who went North in David II's reign and did good service as justiciar and constable of Urquhart castle; their son Robert Chisholm succeeded to his grandfather's lands near Elgin and Nairn and eventually to his offices as well. In the next generation Alexander acquired Strathglass by marriage with a descendant of the Bissets, and founded the Chisholms of Comar or Strathglass, later known as 'Chisholm of Chisholm'. James V created the barony of Comarmore, to be held direct from the crown, and this remained almost continuously in the family from 1538 until 1937. From a younger son of Robert came the Border Chisholms, first called 'of that Ilk' and later 'of Stirches,' and the Chisholms of Cromlix in Perthshire who produced three successive bishops of Dunblane.

The Highland clan occupied a compact piece of country among the hills to the west of Inverness, in the valleys of the rivers Glass, Affric and Cannich. In those days Strathglass lay on important routes from Inverness to the west coast through Glen Affric, and to Fort Augustus by Invercannich and Guisachan. Surrounded by powerful clans like the Frasers, Mackenzies and Grants, the Chisholms yet managed to remain secure and independent in their fertile and sheltered valleys.

At no time did the clan grow to very large numbers, and the highest estimate of their fighting strength was 200 men. There are no acknowledged sept names, and only three main cadet families—the Chisholms of Kinneries and Lietry, of Knockfin, and of Muckerach. From as early as 1514 we find Chisholm of Comar being held responsible to the king and council, like other chiefs, for the good behaviour of all living within his bounds, and this practice of using the clan in the defence of law and order continued for another 150 years; but when a party of Maclean tenants in Strathglass were accused of witchcraft in 1662, their own chief in Mull was appealed to and the case was tried outside the Chisholm jurisdiction.

Roderick Chisholm brought 200 of the clan under his cousin John of Knockfin to Sheriffmuir. His estates were forfeited, but he was pardoned in 1727 and they were bought back and came eventually to his son. The clan were 'out' again in 1745, and thirty were killed at Culloden, where the chief's youngest son led his clansmen while two brothers fought on the other side as officers in the 21st Regiment. Prince Charles found refuge in Strathglass during his wanderings, and three of the 'seven men of Glenmoriston' who guided him were Chisholms.

With the spread of a money economy, and increasing sub-division of land, younger sons and later whole families began to leave Strathglass, as they left other parts of the Highlands. By the 1780s Alexander Chisholm had tempting offers from Lowland sheepfarmers, but urged by his daughter Mary (ancestor of the present chief) he resisted them. His brother William later began evicting tenants from the Chisholm estate, and as men gave way to sheep those that were left treasured the memory of well-peopled glens where at a wedding in the Knockfin family they could gather five generations to dance a reel together. Later hydro-electric and forestry development brought new activity, centred on the modern village of Cannich.

Meantime in the Borders the old Chisholme estate (as the name was spelled there) near Roberton in Roxburghshire remained in the family until 1624, and Stirches near Hawick became the home of the elder branch of that family. A junior branch, through a fortune made in Jamaica, began to buy back some of the family properties, including Chisholme itself, but it was only for a time, and now in both Highlands and Lowlands the clan thinks less in terms of ancestral acres than of old loyalties and modern kinship.

COLQUHOUN

COLQUHOUN

JUST as Dumbarton is one of the western gateways to the Highlands, so Loch Lomond and the Vale of Leven form a natural route between them and the low country. And the Colquhouns, with possessions lying on that route, were constantly and often seriously involved in holding the gate.

Robert de Colechon, on record in 1259, was apparently the first to take his surname from the family's lands in Dunbartonshire. About the mid-14th century Sir Robert Colquhoun married the heiress of Humphrey de Luss, and became the lord of both Colquhoun and Luss. His successor, as keeper of Dumbarton castle during the minority of James II, was active in suppressing Highland depredations, and he met his death with many of his clan at Inchmurrin on Loch Lomond in 1439, when men from the Isles invaded the

Lennox. There were feuds also with the Buchanans and MacFarlanes, in one of which Sir Humphrey Colquhoun was killed, but as his brother was beheaded at Edinburgh for his murder it would be unfair to put all the blame on their neighbours. A hint that other motives were not wanting is the rumour that one raid was instigated by the Duchess of Lennox, 'seeking the wracke of the Laird of Luss, who held (his lands) of the king and not of the duke'.

But the chief enemies were undoubtedly the MacGregors, and the Earl of Argyll seemed to be quite unable to prevent their raids. After the women of the clan, it is said, had appeared before the king at Stirling each carrying the bloodstained shirt of a murdered husband or son, the Luss tenants were allowed to carry arms for their own protection, and the chief was given a commission of fire and sword against the MacGregors. But the worst was yet to come. Accounts of what led up to the massacre of February 1603 are conflicting, and traditions speak of wrongs done by either side. Anyhow, to meet an expected incursion Alexander Colquhoun of Luss assembled all his 'dependers and friends', to the number it is said of 300 horsemen and 500 foot; and when a detachment of MacGregors cornered them in Glenfruin only 12 miles from Dumbarton they were routed with great slaughter, while the invaders suffered little loss. The chief just managed to escape, but about 200 were killed, and the clan were made poorer by 600 head of cattle, 800 sheep and goats, 280 horses, and the 'haill plenishing, goods and gear of Luss'.

For the Colquhouns, Glenfruin was a crippling blow, and as if it were not enough they continued to suffer further murders and oppressions. They were given some cash compensation for their losses, and the next chief was one of the first baronets of Nova Scotia created by Charles I. The clan remained firmly royalist, but it was not again seriously reckoned as a military force; after the Restoration the chief was made responsible like others for the behaviour of his clan, and he was expected to call out 100 men in the event of an invasion by Argyll. Sir Humphrey was a member of the last Scottish parliament, in which he strenuously opposed the Union, and the clan must have recalled former days during the so-called 'Lochlomond expedition' in 1715, when their task, along with a party of fully armed and plaided Grants, was to deny the MacGregors boats with which they could forage on behalf of the Jacobite army.

In the years that followed, a Colquhoun might have been excused for not being sure who was his chief. Sir Humphrey's only child was a daughter Anne, 'heretrix of Luss', married to a second son of Grant of Grant. The marriage contract and a deed of entail provided that she and her husband and children should succeed, provided they took the name and arms of Colquhoun of Luss and never allowed the estates to be conjoined. The chief's death in 1718 led to something like a game of musical chairs, until finally there had to be a lawsuit by one brother to force another to part with Luss. But it did ensure that the old link between the name and the lands should not be broken.

Much of the credit for preserving the beauty of Loch Lomond and his clan country belongs to the late Sir Iain Colquhoun, who realised a twentieth century landowner's double responsibility in allowing the public a reasonable right of access to the countryside. If he had entertained a twentieth part of the applications he received for building on the shores of the loch, the pleasure of millions would have been spoilt for the benefit of a few. As it is, the heritage which the Colquhouns share with the people of Scotland and her visitors was saved from some of the worst encroachments.

CUMMING

CUMMING, HUNTING

THERE can be few more striking illustrations of the fate of those who back the wrong side in a national struggle than the story of the Comyns, or Cummings as most of their present-day descendants spell the name.

Of Norman descent, the Comyns figured prominently in Scotland up to the war of independence, and were identified with the leadership of the patriotic and anti-English faction among the nobility. They operated from a position of great strength, for by the time of Sir John, Lord of Badenoch and justiciar of Galloway, who died in 1274, the Comyns were the most powerful family in Scotland; he was nephew of the Earls of both Buchan and Menteith. His son John was one of the six Guardians of the kingdom after the death of Alexander III; when the throne became vacant with the death of the Maid of Norway in 1290 he was one of the thirteen claimants, and he later gave his support to the successful competitor, John Balliol, who was his brother-in-law. The next John, his son, known as the 'Red Comyn', had estates in Nithsdale, Tweeddale, Atholl and elsewhere, as well as the two Highland lordships of Lochaber and Badenoch; the Earl of Buchan, Constable of Scotland, was his cousin. John supported Balliol's rising against Edward I, headed resistance to the English after Wallace's defeat at Falkirk, and was Guardian of Scotland from 1298 (with a short interval) to the general submission of 1304, which followed an invasion that brought Edward into the heart of his territory at Lochindorb. This, then, was the man to whom the Comyns looked as their chief, and whose rivalry with Robert Bruce led to his murder at Dumfries in 1306. The wrath of the Comyns and their relatives was not the least penalty which the new king paid for that rash act.

King Robert struck hard and quickly at those who were irreconcilably opposed to his rule. The 'herschip' or harrying of Buchan was not the only tale of uprooted Comyn families that was to leave a long and bitter memory. By the forfeiture of the Lord of Badenoch and the Earl of Buchan, large tracts of land were available to reward the king's supporters. Badenoch was included in Randolph's new earldom of Moray; Lochaber was given to Angus of Islay; and the Buchan earldom was dismembered, the Keiths and the Hays (who also got the office of Constable) being among the families that rose on the ruins.

It has been said, however, that King Robert had no intention of exterminating the Comyns, or pursuing a clan vendetta against them. Families of the name were still occupying a respectable, if no longer dominant, place in the north of Scotland during the later Middle Ages. Half the Buchan earldom went to Margaret Comyn, the earl's niece, and through her husband Sir John Ross to the earls of that name, as the barony of Kingedward. The Cummings of Inverallochy, and their cadets of Culter, were a remnant of the old house. From a son of the first John of Badenoch came the Cummings of Altyre, in Moray, who were made answerable as Highland landlords to the Privy Council from the 'General Band' of 1587 onwards Robert, who was required to find caution for his whole name and clan in 1664, also took part in a curious experiment in inter-clan mediation at Inverness. In a dispute over lands between the Camerons and Mackintoshes, the two chiefs, with several hundred followers each, lay on either side of the river during a three-day parley, while the bishop of Moray and the laird of Altyre as arbitrators were rowed backwards and forwards for consultation until a settlement was reached. To help him answer for the conduct of his own clan, a 'bond of relief' was signed at Altyre in 1672 by his friends and vassals promising obedience to the laws by 'the whole persons of their name descended from their families, wherever they may dwell'. Now also representing the Gordons of Gordonstoun, the chiefs still own part of their ancient property, of which portions were parcelled out to cadet branches such as Earnside, Auchray and Relugas.

In other parts of the old Comyn lands, too, the name was not wiped out. A Comyn who occupied Nairn castle and had the lands of Meikle Geddes and Rait was able to hang several Mackintoshes as late as James I's time, showing that they still had power in Badenoch; and in Lochaber there were Cumming landowners in recent times.

CUNNINGHAM

CUNNINGHAM

Taking their name from the old northern division of Ayrshire, the Cunninghams were originally settled in that district, where they held great estates and founded families whose descendants still live there. Richard de Cunningham appears as a witness in a grant of lands at Stevenston in the first quarter of the 13th century, and from a nearby estate the Cunninghames of Kilmaurs —from whom all of the name are sometimes said to be descended—took their designation before being made Earls of Glencairn in 1488.

As landowners in Cunningham, this family became the centre of a group of lairds of the name. Sir Alexander of Kilmaurs, the first earl, was the king's bailie of Cunningham, and when the office was bestowed by James II on their neighbours and rivals the Montgomerys of Eglinton a century-long feud began which gives some idea of the clannishness of both sides. Lord Eglinton was waylaid and shot in 1586 after dining at a kinsman's house of Langshaw near Stewarton, and according to a Montgomery account the chief perpetrators of the deed were Glencairn's brother John, Cunninghame of Robertland, Cunninghame of Corsehill, Cunninghame of Aiket, and Cunningham of Clonbeith—all living within a five-mile radius. It was reported that the signal to these neighbours, most of them within sight of Langshaw, was a white table napkin hung over the battlements by a Cunningham accomplice, perhaps the lady of the house herself. The Montgomerys showed their resentment by killing every Cunningham they could come by, without distinction: Aiket was shot at his own door, Robertland and Corsehill escaped, and Clonbeith (who had fired the fatal shot) was hunted down and cut to pieces.

A less unpleasant example of family solidarity is to be found in the Reformation period. The 'good earl' of Glencairn was a staunch supporter of the reformed faith, and a bond signed by many of the Ayrshire barons and gentry in 1562 'professing the true doctrine of the Evangel' bears not only his signature but those of his two brothers, his brother-in-law John of Caprington and his son William, Robert of Auchenharvie, William of Cunninghamhead, and two other William Cunninghams. Typical of these old cadet families were the Cunninghams of Cunninghamhead, who branched off early in the 15th century and acquired large possessions in Lanarkshire and Midlothian as well as Ayrshire; but from about the end of the 17th century these lands were sold off parcel by parcel until at last Cunninghamhead was alienated in 1724 and the male line of the family became extinct. There were many other cadets with lands in Ayrshire and farther afield in Stirlingshire and as far north as Caithness to carry on the name and add to its distinction.

In the civil wars Glencairn took up arms for King Charles II and raised a large following in the Highlands, and after the Restoration he was made Chancellor of Scotland. In more peaceful times one of the first Ayrshire lairds to recognise the genius of Robert Burns was Sir William Cunninghame of Robertland; William of Annbank and Enterkine and Sir William of Milncraig are mentioned in his poems; Alexander (eldest son of James of Hyndhope) was his friend and correspondent; and the earl himself was the patron and friend of Burns, who wrote a haunting lament on his death—

> And I'll remember thee, Glencairn,
> And all that thou hast done for me.

The family honours have been in abeyance since 1796, although claimed by more than one collateral, but the name of Cunningham is still to the fore. At one stage during the Second World War the three senior British service chiefs in the Middle East were Admiral Sir Andrew Cunningham (later Viscount Cunningham of Hyndhope), his brother General Sir Alan Cunningham, and Air Marshal Sir Arthur Coningham. It is a symptom of the disappearance of the old feuds that the representative of Cunninghame of Corsehill married a Montgomery heiress and took her name in addition to his own. On the spelling of the name, it has been explained that generally speaking the west-coast lairds spell it Cuninghame, the east-coast Cunyngham, and the Irish branch of the family Conyngham, while the Earls of Glencairn usually spelt it Cunningham.

DALZELL

DALZELL

A 'fertile little haugh beside the Clyde', one of the many places in Scotland called *dail ghil* or white meadow, gave a name to the lands of Dalzell and to the family which owned them. A 'baron of Daliel' appears on record in 1259, and it has been listed in 220 different forms ranging from 'Alidiel' to 'Thial', and including the abbreviation 'D.L.' which perfectly expresses the most common correct pronunciation. Spelling is now generally confined to the forms Dalzell (favoured by the Earls of Carnwath), Dalyell (by the famous cadet branch of Binns in West Lothian), Dalzel, Dalziel and Dalziell.

The whole lands of Dalzell in Lanarkshire were held by the family by 1397, and from the same century Elliok on the banks of the Nith near Sanquhar was a Dalzell property. From this time they seem to have been as much

Dumfries-shire men as Clydesiders; William Dalzell of that Ilk was killed in a fray at Dumfries in 1508 between Lord Maxwell and Lord Crichton of Sanquhar—but his grandson received a solemn and humble apology from Maxwell twenty-five years later. An earldom was bestowed on the laird, already Lord Dalzell, in 1633; but 'there was a curious wildness in the Carnwath family, conspicuous even in a wild age', wrote John Buchan. In Montrose's campaign of 1644, it was reported, a Mrs Pierson rode at the head of a troop of Carnwath's horse, and passed as his daughter, with a commission made out in the name of Captain Francis Dalzell. The second Lord Carnwath is best known for having seized King Charles's bridle at Naseby when he was about to lead a charge, and urged him to leave the field.

The earl and his brother, Sir John of Glenae and Newton, were both taken prisoner at Worcester in 1651, and so was the most remarkable man of the name, their cousin Thomas Dalyell of Binns, already a major-general of foot. 'Tam' managed to escape and reached the Continent, returned to Scotland for the campaign of 1654, and after ten years in the service of the Czar of Russia returned in time to command the royal forces in Scotland during much of what the Covenanters bitterly remembered as 'the killing times'. He lives in popular tradition as a rough soldier of fortune and oppressor, but inventories of the plenishing of Binns in his day reveal a man of some taste and refinement. One of his sons was made a baronet on account of his father's services, another fell at Blenheim, and a grandson was captain of the city guard when Prince Charles Edward entered Edinburgh in 1745. Although Lord Carnwath was chief of his name, the two families seem to have had little to do with each other, except that in 1704 the earl was appointed one of the guardians of the second baronet of Binns.

Meantime the Carnwath title had been going through some vicissitudes. The Dalzell estate, with its old peel-tower, had been sold in 1647 to a Hamilton cousin, and the Carnwath estate to a Lockhart in 1684, but Lord Carnwath was still a laird in Nithsdale. When the main line died out in 1703 the earldom passed to the head of the Glenae branch, and it was reckoned in 1715 that he could muster 300 men, 'most, with their chief, against the Government and in the rebellion'. He was one of the leaders when the Chevalier was proclaimed at Lochmaben, marched with the Jacobites to Hawick and Jedburgh and then into England, and was taken prisoner along with his brother at Preston. Impeached in the Lords, he pleaded guilty and was sentenced to be executed, but was respited and then pardoned. His title and lands were forfeited, and although he recovered the estates (except Elliok which reverted to the Duke of Queensberry as superior), it was not until 1826 that the earldom was restored to his grandson, a lieut.-general in the Army. It became dormant when the last earl died in 1944 without known heirs male.

No doubt many of the name are descended from the Dalzells of that Ilk, but the family has had relatively few cadet branches. The Binns baronetcy is one of the few that can descend (as it has done more than once) through the female line to successors in the family estate. The house was the first in Scotland presented under the 'country house scheme' to the National Trust for Scotland, to whom Mrs Eleanor Dalyell of the Binns granted a charter in 1944 so that it should be 'preserved in all time coming for the benefit and enjoyment of the nation', with all its history and legend, and memories of the family of Dalyell.

DOUGLAS

DOUGLAS

DOUGLAS is a name that resounds through Scottish history like the call of a trumpet. The services of the 'doughty Douglases' in Scotland's struggle for independence were second only to those of Wallace and Bruce, and in later times the formidable power which they acquired, added to their military skill and daring, made them the family 'whose coronet so often counterpoised the crown'. And behind every Douglas magnate one could name there must always have been a strong group of kinsmen and a host of Douglas followers.

William de Douglas flourished in the last quarter of the 12th century, but the rise of the family began with lavish grants of lands and powers to the 'good Sir James', one of Bruce's chief lieutenants and trusted councillors. Said to have loved better to hear the lark sing than the mouse squeak, he won renown by exploits such as the thrice-repeated attack on his own castle of Douglas while it was held by the English, and the capture of Roxburgh by disguising his men as black oxen. His nephew was made Earl of Douglas and added the earldom of Mar by marriage; the second earl was the dead man who won a fight at Otterburn, through his death being concealed from the Scottish army; and the fourth played a leading part in warfare with England, both on the Border and in France, where he was made Duke of Touraine. At the height of their power the Earls of Douglas held the whole of south-west Scotland as well as lands in the north and east, and it was said they could call on 30,000 to 40,000 men. 'None durst strive against a Douglas nor yet a Douglas man'. The 'black dinner' at Edinburgh castle when the young earl and his brother were beheaded in 1440, and the assassination of a Douglas by the king himself at Stirling in 1452, were deeds of shame; but the forfeiture of their title and estates in 1455 were acts of policy against an 'over-mighty subject' who threatened the peace of the kingdom.

But another Douglas rose to power on the ruins, for the man who led the royal forces against the last Earl of Douglas was his kinsman of a junior branch, George Earl of Angus. Because one line was swarthy and the other fair, it was said that 'the Red Douglas had put down the Black', and as reward Angus was granted the Douglas estates. Archibald, the earl known as 'Bell-the-Cat', was a leading man among the nobles who opposed James III; his two sons fell at Flodden with 200 other Douglases; and his grandson married James IV's widow Margaret Tudor and virtually ruled Scotland until the 'Red' Douglases were forfeited in their turn. The fame of the family so impressed James VI's youthful mind (perhaps thanks to his Douglas grandmother) that he persuaded the tenth earl to undertake a family history based on record evidence and tradition, which was written by David Hume of Godscroft.

The head of the Douglases in Dumfries-shire was created Earl of Morton in 1458. The fourth earl, who was in command of operations against Queen Mary's partisans during the so-called 'Douglas wars', was Regent of Scotland for eight years during her son's minority. He was executed in 1581, when the earldom of Morton passed to Douglas of Lochleven, and the earldom of Angus (after some opposition from James VI as heir of line) to Douglas of Glenbervie. Power such as they once knew had passed from the Douglases, but honours still accumulated: the Douglas Laird of Drumlanrig was advanced to Earl (1633), Marquess (1682) and Duke (1683) of Queensberry, and Angus to Marquess (1633) and Duke (1703) of Douglas. The glamour of the name had something to do with the intense excitement over the 'Douglas cause' to decide the fate of the vast family possessions after the death of the Duke of Douglas without immediate heirs in 1761. When the Court of Session's decision against his young nephew (and in favour of the house of Hamilton) was reversed by the House of Lords in 1769 the news was received with public rejoicing and windows in Edinburgh were illuminated, while a mob broke those of the judges who had been hostile to the young man.

After seven centuries and more than twenty generations, Douglasdale still remains in the family. The Douglases and the Homes, who had many encounters in the old Border times, are united in a line which has produced a Prime Minister of Great Britain. If the cry 'A Douglas! A Douglas!' is heard no longer, there can be few places in the south of Scotland at least where some bearers of that mighty name are not be found.

DRUMMOND

DRUMMOND

DRUMMOND is a surname derived from the parish of Drymen in what was the Lennox, now the western district of Stirlingshire, but it achieved its greatest strength in a different gateway to the Highlands, where the Grampians form the northern edge of the rich and populous valley of Strathearn. This move resulted from a compact entered into in the 14th century with the Menteiths; later the Drummonds spread farther east with the acquisition of Stobhall on the River Tay through one of those marriages with the 'best families' which steadily increased their power and possessions. By this means, two grandsons of one of Bruce's great barons brought to the Drummonds the stewardship of Strathearn and the Perthshire lands of Concraig, Auchterarder and Kincardine in Menteith, while in the next generation marriage with another heiress founded the families of Carnock, Meidhope, Hawthornden (made famous by its poet laird), and others, and gave a queen to Scotland as the wife of Robert III.

Such ramifications were not without their added responsibilities and dangers. During James IV's reign Perthshire was divided by a great feud between the Drummonds and the Murrays, which began with a dispute over jurisdiction and an attempt to disperse a court held by Sir John Drummond of Concraig at Crieff, the capital of Strathearn. The head of the house, created Lord Drummond in 1488 and Earl of Perth in 1605, eventually became chief of a considerable number of Drummond barons and gentlemen in the low country, and about 300 Highlanders in Glenartney and other Perthshire glens. He mustered over 500 men for the so-called 'Highland Host' sent to harry the Covenanters of the south-west in 1678, and in the later Jacobite risings the Drummonds 'more than any other clan' signalised themselves by fidelity to the Stuart cause.

As Chancellor of Scotland under James VII, the fourth earl had the chief administration of the kingdom in his hands. He went into exile after the Revolution, was created Duke of Perth in 1693 (his brother being made Duke of Melfort), and was made governor to the young Prince James. Right from the famous 'hunting party' on the braes of Mar which preceded the '15, when the clan strength was put at 1,500, until the second duke left Scotland with the Chevalier after his attempt had failed, the Drummonds were in it. During both risings their territories were a centre of political and military activity; Crieff was burned in January 1716, and after an interval of repairs and improvements narrowly escaped the same fate in 1745/6. James the third duke was named as joint Commander-in-Chief along with Lord George Murray, and gracefully withdrew from an impossible role; his brother Lord John brought over a contingent of troops from France; Viscount Strathallan, a Drummond of the Madderty line, fell at Culloden. It is impossible to say how many Drummonds fought under these leaders, but one of the clan who is known as a zealous Jacobite was Robert Drummond, an Edinburgh printer, who during the occupation of that city printed the Prince's proclamations and manifestos, and was later jailed for vilifying the civic authorities led by his illustrious namesake, Lord Provost George Drummond (whose part in founding the new town of Edinburgh is better known than an earlier Drummond's share in the development of Crieff).

But whatever part the Drummonds took in war, they were well to the fore in more peaceful pursuits. As far back as 1672 an Earl of Perth was confirmed in the right to hold a yearly fair at Crieff, and by 1723 the number of cattle sold there was 30,000. At the 'tryst' Highland drovers met Lowland buyers in a sort of frontier atmosphere, under Drummond control and patronage. The earl held a court to regulate disputes and keep order, and was assisted by certain of his tenants under the terms by which they held their lands. By the time the great cattle market moved south about 1770, the Commissioners, appointed to administer the forfeited Jacobite estates, had been active in fostering industries such as bleaching, tanning and paper-making, and later the arrival of the railway combined with a healthy climate and beautiful scenery to bring further popularity and progress to the Drummond country. The lands, and later the earldom of Perth, were restored to the family, but an heiress carried the old Drummond estate to the Earls of Ancaster with whom it remains.

DUNBAR

DUNBAR

FROM a starting-point in East Lothian, where they took their name from the lands and earldom held by the family for nearly 400 years, the Dunbars sent out powerful branches which extended as far as Galloway and Caithness, and established themselves strongly in the earldom of Moray.

The name first comes into prominence when the earldom of Dunbar was granted to Cospatrick, Earl of Northumberland, whose descendants adopted it as their surname. He was granted Dunbar with adjacent lands in Lothian by his cousin Malcolm III in 1072, after being deprived of his English earldom by the Conqueror and seeking refuge with the King of Scots. The family soon acquired lands in England as well as in Scotland, where their territories included Cumnock in Ayrshire and Mochrum in Wigtownshire. The ninth earl married a daughter of Thomas Randolph, Earl of Moray, famous as 'black Agnes of Dunbar' for her defence of the castle in 1338; her sister Isobel married another Dunbar, Sir Patrick, grandson of the seventh earl. Randolph's two sons being killed in battle, the Moray estates were divided between the two sisters and ultimately went to Isobel's children; her son John had a regrant of the earldom of Moray in 1372, without the districts of Lochaber and Badenoch.

This was the foundation of the Dunbar influence in the North. It was further strengthened about the mid-15th century by the appointment as heritable Sheriff of Moray of Sir Alexander Dunbar of Westfield, in Spynie parish, son of the last Dunbar Earl of Moray, and ancestor of a host of important cadet houses of the name. In the next generation two of the Sheriff's sons married the co-heiresses of Dunbar of Cumnock and Mochrum. Later Mochrum passed to the descendants of a third son, and it remained with them as heirs male of the earldom of Dunbar and sheriffdom of Moray; other descendants acquired Hempriggs and other estates in Caithness.

As 'settlers' in Moray, the Dunbars had to find their level. Even after they had become substantial holders of property in the western portion, there was friction between them and the Inneses, who were predominant in the east. In 1554 the prior of Pluscarden and the dean of Moray, who were both Dunbars, and some laymen of the name were attacked by eighty Inneses in Elgin cathedral. A feud smouldered for thirty years, and was only ended by outside arbitration; to keep the two sides separate while a decision was being reached, it was agreed that no Dunbar should go east of the cairn of Kilbuick (between Forres and Elgin), and that no Innes should enter the burgh of Forres. Some years later the Dunbars were in trouble with the Roses and had to ask Huntly for support, and before this feud ended a Dunbar laird's son had been killed and their houses of Dunphail, Sanquhar and Mundoll burned.

Dunbars played an important role among the great families of northern Scotland. The name is still a common one in Moray, but its influence has dwindled. Of the many wealthy and influential landowners only two or three families remained by the end of the 19th century, and only one whose forefathers had held land continuously since the Dunbars settled in Moray 500 years earlier. When Westfield wanted to raise money by selling the hereditary office of Sheriff, his Dunbar kinsmen objected and one of them, a clergyman in England, was deeply shocked at this affront to 'all that bear the name of Dunbar, or have the remotest connection with it'; but sold it was, for £2000, to the Stewart Earl of Moray (who got £3000 compensation for its abolition twenty-five years later).

How the name has spread throughout Scotland is shown by the six baronetcies held by Dunbar families—Baldoon (Wigtown), Mochrum (Wigtown), Durn (Banff), Northfield (Moray), Hempriggs (Caithness), and Boath (Nairn), all of which survive, most of them still with some of their original property attached. Remembered with pride, too, is William Dunbar, supposed from an allusion in one of his poems to have been born in East Lothian, who was the chief among Scotland's 'makars' and the first poet in Britain, if not in Europe, to emphasise the dignity of the common man.

DUNDAS

DUNDAS

ALTHOUGH the chiefs of the name never rose higher in rank than laird or minor baron, the Dundas family produced a remarkable series of men who rose to the highest public offices, and whose record throws some light on family influence in Scottish life.

The name first appears in a charter of the lands of Dundas in West Lothian, probably dating from the late 12th or early 13th century. In 1424 James Dundas of that Ilk had a licence to build a battlemented tower at Dundas in West Lothian, and towards the end of the century a charter of Inchgarvie in the Firth of Forth gave the family the right to build a castle there for the protection of shipping. Sir George took the parliamentary side in the civil war, and in 1638 he and other members of the house of Dundas in the Lothians subscribed the National Covenant; the Inchgarvie garrison surrendered to Cromwell, who dated several letters from Dundas Castle. After the Restoration Dundas took sufficient interest in his status as a baron and chief of his name to join in (if not to lead) a protest by some of the barons that they had not been given 'supporters' in the arms recorded in the new Lyon Register set up in 1672. The greater part of the Dundas estate remained in the family until 1875, and in selling it they reserved Inchgarvie, a portion next the lands of Hopetoun, and the Carmelite monastery in Queensferry.

The family's interests were not confined to the shores of the Forth. In the 14th century the barony of Fingask in Perthshire was acquired so that it could go to the chief's eldest son by a second marriage, from whom the United Kingdom Earls (1838) and Marquesses (1892) of Zetland are descended. Similarly to provide for the issue of a later laird's second marriage the Arniston estate in Midlothian was bought in 1571, and settled on a branch which was to have a unique record of judicial office. In the century after the Revolution, for all but a dozen years, some member of the house of Arniston was either a judge, Solicitor-General, Lord Advocate, or Lord President; and although there were two Lords Arniston, and two Lords President Dundas of Arniston in addition, 'each succeeding heir was the rival of his father in capacity for affairs', and the second Lord President was one of the greatest who has filled that office; not only that, but his son, already Lord Chief Baron, was invited (but declined) to become the third of the family to occupy the President's chair.

Founder of the Melville branch of the Arniston family was Henry Dundas, a half-brother of the second Lord President, who rose higher in the public service and wielded more political influence than any of them. As 'manager' for Scotland for forty years, with the task of ensuring a Tory majority in Parliament, he exercised control partly through family influence and personal friendship, partly through dispensing state patronage, and partly through simple bribery. Apart from his own family and official acquaintances, the Dundases were related by marriage to people of influence in every part of Scotland. Always at the head of some great public department, and with the indirect command of places in every other, he could cajole or reward the landed gentry who were the only voters in pre-Reform days with posts, pensions and promotions for themselves and their families. As president for its first sixteen years of the board set up by Pitt to govern British India, Dundas was able to find many new openings for Scots overseas, to the benefit of both. Patronage on a lesser scale was demonstrated by Sir Robert of Beechwood, law agent and factor for both Arniston and Melville, whose Dundas clients all held sinecure offices, it is said, with him as their 'depute'.

It was typical of the later 18th century in Scotland that Henry Dundas (created Viscount Melville in 1802) sprang not from the great aristocracy, but from one of the increasingly important smaller landed families with strong legal and administrative backgrounds. It is known from his correspondence that he himself was no enemy to the 'principles and consequences of clanship', but very much the reverse, and his sympathies were shown by his Act for the restoration of the forfeited estates and by the repeal of the ban on wearing the Highland dress.

ELLIOT

ELLIOT

THE Elliots share with the Armstrongs the doubtful honour of being named first in the lists of unruly Border clans drawn up during the century or so before the Union of the Crowns. Their home was chiefly in Upper Liddesdale, on the benty uplands around and above the Liddel and Hermitage waters, where from the 15th century they rose rapidly in numbers and influence.

Robert Elliot of Redheuch, who had a charter in 1476 from that bold Earl of Angus remembered as Archibald 'Bell-the-Cat', was the first of a succession of his name, some of them captains of Hermitage castle, from whom the leading branches of the clan presume descent. Throughout the 16th century in particular Liddesdale had the reputation of being the most unruly section of the Scottish Borders, and a dozen punitive expeditions were made into it, sometimes with English co-operation. These culminated in two major raids in 1569, and the sixty or so promises of good behaviour given during the second—for which the Lords of Council were careful to choose a 'moonlit nicht'—give some picture of the clan as it was then. Martin Elliot of Braidley (uncle of the young chief) went surety for himself 'and the haill branch of the Reidheuch that dwells within the Swyres' (watersheds), while Ade Elliot called Cowdais did the same for the branches of Burnheids and Weschaw, John of the Park and 'eld Will Elliot' for their two branches, 'Arche Keen' for the Gorrumberry branch, John of Thirlishope for that branch ('except Hob Elliot and his brother Will of the Steill'), Lancie Elliot for his branch, and Ninian called the 'Porter of Ewis durris' for all the Elliots dwelling in Ewesdale (to which his name suggests that he held the door). But in spite of such pledges we find that in 1574 the head of the Redheuch family was one of the three Border potentates brought to task for failing to keep order in his district.

War has been the trade of every frontier area at some time, and the Regent and lords of council had various other ways of trying to sort out clan disputes. One was for them to name friends on either side as arbiters before the council, and in 1575 such a method was used to end the 'deidlie feud and inymities' between the Pringles and the Elliots. A day was named for twelve Pringles and six Elliots to appear, but only two of each turned up and the attempt seems to have failed. A few years later the Elliots of Ewesdale and a group of Armstrongs took the more unusual course of submitting their quarrel to the Privy Council and promising in advance to abide by its decision. In 1587 parliament decreed that 'notorious thieves' in the Borders should be returned to their native places such as Liddesdale, where their chiefs could be responsible, unless their immediate landlords would become surety for them; significantly, the Elliots stood at the head of the list of 'broken clans' in the Middle March.

An Elliot would probably say that his clan were neither more nor less lawless than their neighbours. The clan system on the Border began to decay as a new order was forcibly established by James VI—from 1603 King of England as well as of Scotland—and as numbers were reduced by wholesale executions and other severities, banishment, enlistment for foreign service, and compulsory removal. The property of the Elliots of Redheuch, or of Larriston as they became, passed in the female line to a younger son of Eliott of Stobs, one of many cadet houses that had sprung up. A junior branch of Stobs are the Elliots of Minto, whose line has included two notable policy-making rulers of India—Sir Gilbert, created Earl of Minto on his return, and the fourth earl, remembered for the Morley-Minto government reforms.

With as many as seventy different spellings of the name, the following rhyme directs attention to the chief modern variants:

> The double L and single T
> Descend from Minto and Wolflee;
>
> The double T and single L
> Marks the old race in Stobs that dwell;
>
> The single L and single T
> The Eliots of St Germains be;
>
> But double T and double L
> Who they are, nobody can tell.

ERSKINE

ERSKINE

THOUGH not a clan in the ordinary acceptation of the word, the Erskines are of Celtic origin, and have been closely united by marriage and interest to some of the principal Highland families. John Erskine, the Earl of Mar who led the Jacobite Rising in 1715, believed firmly that clanship ought to be kept up and encouraged, and wrote to his son: 'You are to be at the head of one which, though not so numerous as those in the highlands, is perhaps as old, and has not been inconsiderable in Scotland'.

The Erskines have again become mainly a Lowland house, as they began. The name seems to derive from the lands of Erskine on the lower Clyde, which one of the family owned in the reign of Alexander II. The 'worthy, wyse and lele' Sir Robert Erskine of that Ilk, for some years High Chamberlain of

Scotland, helped to secure the release of David II and the succession of Robert II, and his rewards included a grant of the lands of Alloa on the north side of the river Forth in 1368. Sir Robert, the first Lord Erskine, claimed the ancient earldom of Mar in right of his mother, who was descended from the old Celtic earls of which the senior line failed in 1435; but when he took Kildrummy castle by force the crown retaliated by confiscating his rich estate and tower of Alloa, and he had to consent to an exchange. The Erskines of Dun in Angus and of Pittodrie in Aberdeenshire, founded about this time, were the first of many long-descended cadet branches, and four of the Dun family died with Lord Erskine at Flodden.

The boy heirs to the throne were entrusted to the Erskines through five generations, and this led incidentally to the settling of the long struggle with the crown over the earldom of Mar. 'Moved by conscience', on her marriage with Darnley in 1565, Queen Mary granted the earldom to the Lord Erskine whose father had been her early guardian, and in doing so left a problem which puzzled the peerage lawyers and finally produced two earldoms of Mar. The estate comprised Strathdon, Braemar, Cromar and Strathdee, and the lordship of Garioch, but it was not until 1626 that the Erskines entered fully into their ancient inheritance. Mar was given the care of Prince James in 1567, and guarded him through the rule of Moray and Lennox before undertaking his own short and uneventful regency. After his death the family still retained a say in the king's education, and the young earl began a long friendship as his playmate. Members of the family were created Lord Cardross (1610), Earl of Buchan (1617) and Earl of Kellie (1619), while Mar himself, made Lord High Treasurer, worked for the final recovery of the earldom.

At Braemar the earl built a 'new strong castle' near the ruins of Kindrochit, and visitors were amazed at the extent of his hunting-grounds. It was still reckoned in 1715 that Lord Mar could bring out a personal following of up to 800 or 1000, but debts were already making necessary the sale of estate after estate, till the family possessions were reduced to little more than the lordship of Alloa, apart from Mar which remained in the family until 1731.

The Rising of 1715, though short-lived, was of course disastrous. Some Jacobite clansmen, like Lord Lyon Sir Alexander Erskine of Cambo, escaped with imprisonment, but the earl himself was attainted, and his estates forfeited. Family solidarity, however, led to their being bought back on behalf of the heir in 1724 by his uncle, Lord Grange, and Lord Dun, head of the senior cadet branch. Given the empty title of duke by the exiled King James, Mar was fully aware of how much he was obliged to 'several of our name'; he advised his son 'to keep them united, which is the way to make them considerable', but not to let 'fondness for those of your own clan and kindred make you neglect those of merit who shall deserve well of you'.

Not all Erskines were Jacobites, and 1715 was not the first or the only time they diverged in opinion. The laird of Dun was one of the chief leaders of the Reformation in Scotland; Ebenezer and Ralph Erskine, leaders of the secession movement against patronage in the church, came of a Roxburgh family (Lady Mar was Ebenezer's godmother and Lord Grange Ralph's groomsman); the Mar line produced a tulchan bishop of Glasgow; and Cambo (cadets of Kellie) had a Roman cardinal, who corresponded with his 'Scotch cousins' the brilliant brothers Lord Buchan, Harry Erskine and Lord Chancellor Erskine. There was a clannishness about the Erskine which could make light of all barriers.

FARQUHARSON

FARQUHARSON

ONCE described as 'the only clan family in Aberdeenshire', the Farquharsons are a branch of the Clan Chattan who established themselves as a formidable power in upper Deeside and the adjoining glens at the crossing with the north-south route which skirts the Cairngorm mountains.

Descended from the same ancestor as the Mackintoshes, the clan is named after Farquhar, a son of Shaw of Rothiemurchus in Strathspey. Finlay mor, first Farquharson of Invercauld, fell at the battle of Pinkie in 1547, and from his grandson Donald there sprang a large number of cadet houses, including several barons of 'competent fortunes' such as Monaltrie, Inverey and Finzean. Each remained largely independent of the others, but when the occasion demanded it they were ready to act together in a common cause. At various times the head of one line or another took the lead, or gave surety for the good behaviour of the whole name. Frequently they acted along with the Mackintoshes, who had the chief place in the Clan Chattan confederacy, and a bond of manrent from a group of Farquharsons in Braemar dating from 1595 survives among the Mackintosh muniments. During the 'troubles' of the 17th century, Sir Robert Farquharson, a prosperous Aberdeen merchant and politician, much enhanced the fortune and position of the Invercauld family, while men of the Inverey and Monaltrie families led Farquharson contingents in Montrose's battles.

In 1666, John Farquharson of Inverey, 'a mettled independent gentleman' known as the Black Colonel, had the misfortune to kill a Gordon neighbour in a skirmish. Gordon had been acting for the town of Aberdeen after some Farquharsons and their tenants had caught fish in the River Dee during a close season, and the skirmish was in reprisal for a raid in which sixteen or eighteen horses had been seized. When Inverey was hailed before the judges in Edinburgh to answer for his crime, Mackintosh himself intervened both as his chief and in gratitude for services rendered him in Lochaber. As a result no accuser appeared, but the Gordons seem to have got their own back when Huntly and the laird of Grant caught the Farquharsons between two attacking forces and something like a massacre followed. The Black Colonel escaped, and lived to fight in Dundee's rising of 1689, and carried on a guerilla warfare after the defeat at Cromdale.

Some time before this the Privy Council had required bonds of good behaviour from the Highland chiefs, and Alexander Farquharson of Invercauld bound himself and his successors on behalf not only of his own tenants and servants, but of 'all persons of his name, descended of his family, wheresoever they dwell'. Such undertakings were buttressed locally by 'bonds of relief' given to their chief by 'branches of clans and heads of families', and Invercauld had one of these in 1683 from Donald Farquharson of Balfour, son to Finzean. The Mackintosh link remained strong and Invercauld brought 300 Farquharsons to the chief's aid in an expedition to Lochaber.

When the royal standard was raised on the Braes of Mar in 1715, the local Jacobites were slow to rise in spite of the earl's threats. Later, however, 100 men from Braemar were put under Inverey, and several other Farquharson lairds were 'out', presumably with a following of clansmen and tenants. Along with Mackintosh, Invercauld joined the Prince at Perth and fought at Preston, but he later declared that he was forced out by Mar as his feudal superior. In 1745, 200 of the clan fought under Balmoral and Monaltrie, but the clan hero was Invercauld's daughter, the wife of Mackintosh, who raised some of her father's as well as her husband's men for the prince, though both chiefs were for the Government. Monaltrie was restored to the 'Baron ban' in 1784, but shortly after that the high steep-roofed house of Balmoral went back to the Gordons, from whom the Prince Consort bought it in 1848 and built the present 'castle' as a royal residence.

Deeside lairds were among the great 'improvers' of the 19th century, and Invercauld planted sixteen million fir trees and two million larches, besides building twenty miles of roads on his estate. Huge logs of timber from various Farquharson properties went sweeping down the Dee, to the peril of the new bridges which were opening up the countryside. But Deeside was not allowed to lose its rural beauty, and Queen Victoria could write of her beloved Balmoral: 'The view of the hills towards Invercauld is exceedingly fine.'

FERGUSSON

FERGUSSON

ALTHOUGH the Fergussons never looked on themselves as a single clan, nor were they so regarded by others until recent times, there was for many generations a feeling of community within several groups of the name, and between some of the groups a 'clannish' feeling existed.

Landed families of the name were already established in Dumfries-shire, Ayrshire and Perthshire by the mid-15th century, and had been there for some generations. The name means, of course, the sons of Fergus, but the ancestor may not always have been the same person. In modern times families from Ayrshire, Dumfries-shire, Argyll and Perthshire have generally retained the double 'ss', while those of Aberdeenshire, Fife and Angus have preferred the single 's'; but the difference is not really significant, and cannot always be a sure guide to the origin of any family before spelling became standardised.

The Fergusson family with the longest recorded history is that of Craigdarroch in Dumfries-shire. Their oldest charter granting lands in Glencairn dates from the reign of David II (1329–71). These Fergussons and their branches were more law-abiding than the Border clans to the east of them, and in the 17th century they were mostly staunch Covenanters like the Galloway men of the west. In Ayrshire there was a whole group of Fergusson families who looked to Kilkerran as their chief, spread over the southern part of Carrick from Maybole to the borders of Galloway. The Kilkerran family had held lands there since the days of James II at least, and according to tradition since the days of Robert Bruce; since the mid-17th century they produced four M.P.s, two Lords of Session, a general and an admiral, as well as more than one notable estate improver.

The principal group of Fergussons who lived in the style of a clan under their own chiefs were the Fergussons in Atholl. The Dunfallandy family, previously designated of Derculich, can be traced before 1489, and were influential over a wide stretch of country from the banks of the Tummel to Strathardle and Glenshee. Like other clans in the central Highlands, they were a source of constant trouble to the Government, as their lands gave shelter to wandering bandits and other 'broken men'. In 1591 'Baron Fergusson', as Dunfallandy was informally known, had to find caution for the good behaviour of those living on his lands. Another Highland group, although not such an extensive one, were the Fergussons in Cowal and Kintyre, where the name is often recorded in corrupted forms of Gaelic such as McKerras. One family at the head of Lock Eck held lands from the Argyll family along with a hereditary office as their representatives in Strachur on Loch Fyne. There were other Fergusons in the east and north-east, where the Badifurrow family with lands near Inverurie had by the 18th century several flourishing branches including Kinmundy and Pitfour.

The Fergussons as a whole were not Jacobite sympathisers. Several of the lairds were active on the Government side in both Risings, and the 'black captain' John (of Badifurrow descent) scoured the Hebrides in the *Furnace* in search of the Prince and other fugitives. Dunfallandy was 'out' in 1745, with at least one of his cadets and no doubt a following of clansmen, and was only acquitted of treason through the efforts of James Ferguson (later Lord Pitfour), who defended some of the prisoners tried at Carlisle. This was not the only nor the first contact made between separate groups, for in 1727 Kinmundy and Pitfour had appealed to the future Lord Kilkerran to settle a dispute, and later the poet Robert Fergusson (whose father hailed from Tarland in Aberdeenshire) had presented a copy of his book to Sir Adam of Kilkerran. As the old clan system came to be replaced by an informal family bond the barriers of geography were more easily stepped over, and the head of the Ayrshire group came to be regarded as chief of the whole name. A 'very clannish' Fergusson of the Perthshire group, anxious to help any of the name who might benefit by a liberal education, gave a start in life to a minister of Logierait whose son became Professor Adam Ferguson, the 'father of modern sociology'. In his *Essay on the History of Civil Society* the philosopher insisted that mankind should be studied 'in groupes, as they have always subsisted', which seemed only natural to a former chaplain to the 42nd Highlanders brought up in a group united by ties of name and blood.

FORBES

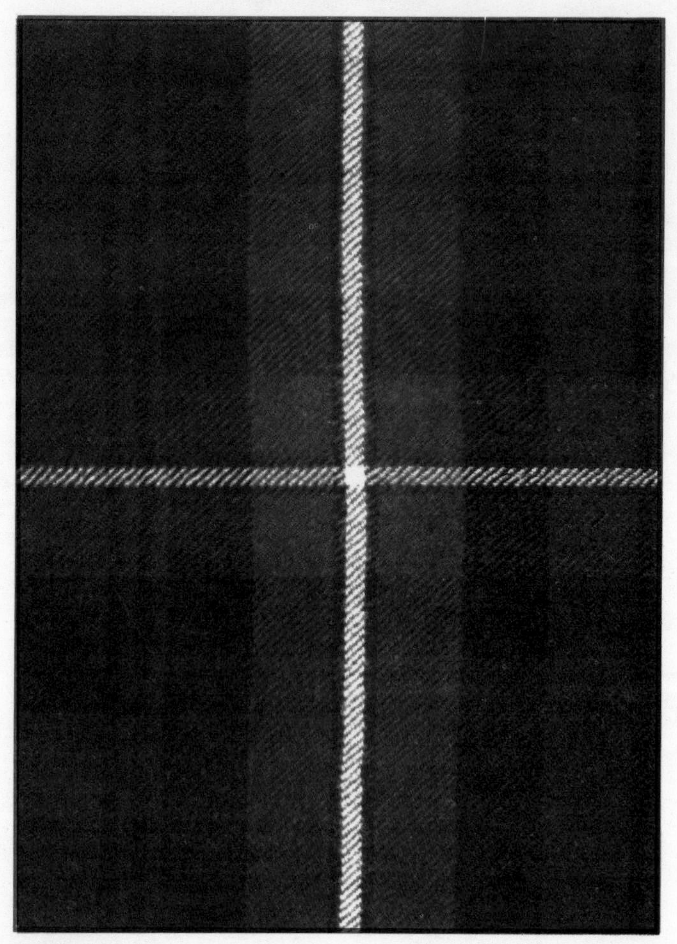

FORBES

If we can believe a 17th century writer on the family of Lord Forbes, the premier baron of Scotland, 'all the Forbes's in or out of Scotland are branch'd forth from that only root'. By the 14th century this family was well established in Aberdeenshire, in the valley of the Don. Their original castle was near Rhynie, on the Braes of Forbes, and the name of Castle Forbes was later transferred to Putachie, on the banks of the Don below Bennachie, where a modern mansion stands on the old site.

Any map of this part of Aberdeenshire showing the castles and estates now or at one time in Forbes ownership is studded with a bewildering cluster of names. This proliferation began in the time of Sir Alexander Forbes of that Ilk, who is known to have been building (or rebuilding) his house of 'Drumynour' in 1440, about five years before being made a Lord of Parliament. In his generation the family branched into four great divisions through his three younger brothers, Sir William of Pitsligo (from whom came the family of that name and those of Boyndlie, Newe, Culquhonny, Callendar, Castleton, and Rothiemay), Sir John of Tolquhon (from whom also Forbes of Culloden, Waterton, Thainston, Pitnacalder and Foveran), and Alister of Brux (from whom also those of Skellater, who produced a field-marshal in the Portuguese army, and of Ledmacroy, Belnabodach, Kildrummy, Towie, Inverernan and Echt).

The Forbeses were often at feud with their neighbours, including the powerful house of Huntly. One quarrel with the Gordons over the possession of certain church lands went on for more than ten years, until composed by arbitration at Perth in 1582, and during it the chief and forty-six other Forbeses were specifically exempted from Huntly's jurisdiction. After a brush with the Irvines in 1605, in which one man was murdered and two others wounded, Lord Forbes with Pitsligo, Tolquhon and another local laird took burden on themselves 'for the whole clan and name of Forbes and their friends' (the only time the family are officially called a 'clan') to pay Irvine of Drum £4,000 for killing his servant and the attempted murder of some of his name. The Forbeses could raise 1,000 men for the king in 1594, and in 1628 Lord Forbes agreed to furnish 800 for foreign service; his son served under Gustavus Adolphus and rose to the rank of lieut.-general in the Swedish army, and a militant chaplain named 'William Forbesse' (the spelling illustrates the old pronunciation) earned praise for having more 'courage, discretion and good conduct' than some captains.

While spreading through Europe and beyond, new branches continued to settle on the rich acres beside the Don and its tributaries. From two brothers, sons of the second Lord Forbes, came the houses of Corsindae, Balfluig, Monymusk, and Leslie, and those of Corse, Craigievar, Granard (earls in the Irish peerage). Among their finest monuments are some of the characteristic tower-houses of the north-east, built first for defence but now among the glories of Scottish domestic architecture. Plundered by Highland caterans, Forbes of Corse vowed to build 'such a house as thieves will need to knock at ere they enter', and Corse castle near Lumphannan (1581) was the result; the power and wealth of the Tolquhon family are shown by the massive ruins of their castle near Tarves (1584–89); and Craigievar itself, the 'most cultured, scholarly and refined' of Scottish castles, was completed in 1626 by a Forbes laird, 'Dantzig Willie', a merchant and man of taste typical of those who had turned their backs on the 'old wild life of sturt and strife'.

The more peaceful pattern was briefly shattered by the Jacobite risings, in which the name was prominent on both sides. Lord Forbes of Pitsligo was 'out' in 1715 and 1745, and his influence led to others joining him although he was a man of small estate with 'no vassalage or following to his family'; he was forfeited and remained hidden in his own neighbourhood for four years. Lord President Duncan Forbes, a wise lawyer and politician, whose ancestors had been lairds of Culloden since 1625, was the mainstay of the Government in the north, and kept many of the Highland lairds and chiefs from joining Prince Charles. The battle which took place on his doorstep in 1746 ended the last attempt to restore the Stuarts to the British throne.

FRASER

FRASER, DRESS

Not all the Frasers in Scotland belong to the Highland clan of that name. The first on record was Simon, who gave a large tract of land to the monks of Kelso in 1160, a Fraser bishop was one of the guardians of Scotland after the death of Alexander III, and several were prominent in the war of independence. The family spread through Tweeddale and the Lothians, Stirlingshire, Angus and Kincardine to Aberdeenshire, and later obtained large possessions around Inverness. The senior line, who obtained Philorth in Aberdeenshire in 1375, are now represented by Lord Saltoun.

Founder of the clan was Hugh Fraser, mentioned as Lord of 'Loveth' and portioner of the Aird (at the head of the Beauly firth) in 1367, who still owned lands in Peebles-shire ten years later. Kinship with the Frasers of

Philorth was so near that the heads of the two families made mutual entails of their properties in 1464, although succession by direct heirs made them inoperative. The clan chief, by now a Scottish peer as Lord Fraser of Lovat, also owned Stratherrick to the east of Loch Ness; his descendants extended the family estates, including some properties in Aberdeenshire bought from Fraser kinsfolk. What became known as the 'Fraser country' proper, extending about twenty-eight miles from east to west, and averaging about eight miles from north to south, comprised the low-lying fertile portion first acquired, and also some peculiarly Highland territory in Stratherrick, part of Strathglass, and Strathfarrar.

While Philorth was busy building a harbour of refuge which became the nucleus of Fraserburgh, the manpower of the clan was seriously reduced in 1544 by one of the bloodiest clan fights in Highland history, followed by a succession of minorities. Competition arose in 1577 between the child chief's uncle, Fraser of Strichen, and a great-uncle who had been tutor in the previous generation, as to who should lead the clan, and it was only after 'a great heat of unbecoming altercations' at a general meeting of the leading men of the name (numbering 300 with their followers) that the elder man withdrew. By the time of the civil war, when the clan had recovered and indeed had reached the summit of their influence, there were twenty-six cadet branches living on their own properties in the clan country, compared with only five a century before. In Montrose's first campaign Sir James Fraser of Brae brought the clan into the field against the king's general, and the Fraser lands suffered in consequence, but by 1650 they had returned to their royalist allegiance and fought for the king at Worcester. Sir Alexander of Philorth, who was there also, inherited the Abernethy title of Saltoun. Fraser of Muchalls, in Aberdeenshire, made a peer in 1633, had his right to the simple title of 'Lord Fraser' (now extinct) confirmed by Act of Parliament.

The Frasers were divided after the death in 1696 of Hugh Lord Lovat, leaving a daughter Amelia but no sons. Lord Saltoun planned a match with his son, put forward as 'a true Fraser and a man of a handsome fortune that would support their whole name'; but the heir male, Fraser of Beaufort, and his son Simon warned the leading men of the clan against him. When Saltoun ventured into the clan country, he and his followers were seized and threatened with hanging unless he promised to go no further. The impulsive Simon put himself outside the law by his actions, and for Amelia a Mackenzie husband was found who took the name of Fraser of Fraserdale. Some of the leading men sent to France for Simon, who returned just in time to withdraw 300 Frasers from Mar's army before Sheriffmuir, and did such useful service in ousting the Jacobite garrison of Inverness that he was pardoned for his past crimes while Fraserdale was attainted. Having eventually obtained the title and estates Simon lost them and his own life by his notorious double-dealing in and before 1745.

Fraser's Highlanders, raised by the Master of Lovat mainly in the clan country, took part in the capture of Quebec in 1759, and two more battalions followed after the family estates were returned in 1774. The succession passed to the Strichen line in 1815, and later the title too was restored. Lord Saltoun, chief of the name, was present when the clan mustered at Beaufort castle in 1951 on the invitation of Lord Lovat, war-time commando leader and chief of the Frasers of Lovat.

GORDON

GORDON

WHETHER or not the Gordons were 'no claned familie' (as an 18th century writer maintained), it was a true saying over a long period and a wide area in the north-east of Scotland that 'the Gordons hae the guiding o't'. This area consisted of three main portions—a western section, comprising Strathbogie and Enzie (with Huntly Castle on the Deveron and Gordon Castle at the lowest crossing-place on the Spey) and stretching southwards into the mountains; a section on Deeside, including Aboyne, Glentanar and Glen-muick, acquired by marriage with an heiress; and a section in the Aberdeen neighbourhood where many cadet branches settled and prospered.

The first of the name recorded in Scotland was lord of the barony of Gordon in the Merse (Berwickshire) in the late 12th century, and it was after the wars of independence that Sir Adam Gordon received the lands of Strathbogie in Banffshire from King Robert. The fall of the Comyns and later the crown's annexation of the earldom of Mar enabled them to become the most powerful family in the north-east. Early in the 15th century an heiress married Sir Alexander Seton, but the family remained Gordons. The Earls (from about 1445) and Marquesses (1599) of Huntly and later Dukes of Gordon (1684), along with a large number of cadets including the Earls of Aboyne (1660), dominated the region; they were the leaders of 'a very considerable and powerful name' in the low country of the north-east, able to raise up to 3,000 men with 'a great posse of gentlemen on horseback', as well as a Highland following from their upland territory. The Gordons of Lochinvar in Galloway (Viscounts of Kenmure from 1633) and Gordons of Haddo (Earls of Aberdeen from 1682) branched off the main stem before the Seton marriage.

Aberdeenshire and Banffshire became dotted over with Gordon cadets. Some of the lesser gentry—and even great magnates like Atholl and Argyll—bound themselves to Huntly by promises of protection and support, useful in an area where so many different clans and families were inextricably mixed up together. In 1462 Huntly even undertook to preserve the freedom and property of the citizens of Aberdeen in return for hospitality and such help as the Gordons might need in their own defence. Such a combination of man-power and resources enabled the earls to take a prominent part in national politics, and also provoked a certain amount of resentment and jealousy. On at least six occasions between 1475 and 1557, as the King's Lieutenant in the north, Huntly was given sweeping powers of control over an area which might stretch from the Forth to the Orkneys; the second earl was Chancellor of Scotland, an office later held by the first Earl of Aberdeen. When the family fell on evil times, solidarity among the Gordons themselves remained unshaken.

After 1603 Huntly lost his commanding position in Scotland, although steadily advanced in the peerage. The second marquess supported Charles I (Gordon cavalry fought with distinction at Auldearn and Alford), and shared the king's fate in 1649; the duke kept the flag flying for James VII over Edinburgh castle for a year after the Revolution; the heir was 'out' in 1715, raising 500 horse and 2,000 foot from a sometimes reluctant tenantry, but with the enthusiastic Gordon of Glenbucket in command; and thirty years later 'the terror of Glenbucket's name brought out half Aberdeenshire and Banffshire'. But the dukes themselves remained uninvolved, and later raised two regiments of infantry which made the name of the Gordon Highlanders famed and feared far and wide.

When the last Duke of Gordon (subject of a famous 'Cock o' the North' portrait) died in 1836, the chiefship and Huntly titles passed to his cousin Lord Aboyne, and the greater part of the Gordon estates to his nephew the Duke of Richmond. Some of the old family grandeur can still be glimpsed in the stately shell of Huntly Castle, and the remains of Gordon Castle, where the dukes exercised a princely hospitality. Aboyne Castle is now the chief's home; at the annual gathering on the Green of Charlestown his great square banner and many Gordon ensigns are displayed; and 'the House of Gordon' aims at bringing together all those connected with the name.

GRAHAM

GRAHAM OF MONTROSE

Few names or families in Scotland, it has been said, can boast such illustrious heroes as the 'gallant Grahams'. One of the results is that their history is apt to be overshadowed by the deeds of Montrose and Dundee, not to mention a comrade-in-arms of Wallace and one of Wellington's commanders in the Peninsula, to go no farther than the leadership of men in war. It is only by remembering those behind the heroes, as well as the heroes themselves, that the clan can be seen in any depth.

The earliest holder of the name on record in Scotland was William de Graham, a magnate at King David's court in the first half of the 12th century, who received the lands of Abercorn and Dalkeith. Sir John de Graham fell gloriously at Falkirk in 1296, and Sir David, whose name appears on the

Arbroath declaration of independence in 1320, exchanged with Bruce the lands of Cardross on the Clyde for those of Old Montrose on the east coast. But the heart of the Graham country is in central Scotland, the districts of Menteith and Strathearn, where they lived the anxious life of Lowland lairds on the edge of the Highland hills. The founder of the Montrose line, who in 1237 obtained Dundaffmuir and Strathcarron in Stirlingshire, Mugdock near Glasgow, and Kincardine near Auchterarder, was Sir David, whose descendants became Lord Graham (before 1445), and Earl (1503), Marquess (1644) and Duke (1707) of Montrose. The first earl fell at Flodden, his successor at Pinkie, and another became Chancellor and then Viceroy of Scotland when James VI went to London.

A cadet, on marrying the heiress of the ancient Earls of Strathearn, was created Earl of Menteith in 1427, and Grahams enjoyed that title for nine generations. In Charles I's day the earl was Justice-General of Scotland and President of the Scots Privy Council, and was said to have boasted that he had the reddest blood in Scotland and a better right to the crown than the king himself. Graham 'clannishness' is illustrated by the anxiety of his grandson to convey his titles and estates to someone of the name able to preserve them both (which led to some rivalry between the third Marquess of Montrose and Graham of Claverhouse), but on his death the lands passed to Montrose, his personal estate to Graham of Gartmore, and the title went into abeyance.

James Graham, fifth earl and first Marquess of Montrose, whose character and campaigns won him lasting fame, used to write to other Grahams as 'your loving chief'. Patrick Graeme younger of Inchbrakie, known as 'black Pate', was his sole companion when he joined the clans in Atholl at the start of the campaign, and other clansmen were among his most devoted followers. After the Restoration, when his remains were gathered together for honoured burial, David Graham of Gorthie took the head from the iron spike on the Edinburgh Tolbooth in the presence of the Graham barons of Morphie, Inchbrakie and Orchill, and places were allotted in the funeral pageant to the heads of the cadet houses of Balgowan, Cairnie, Deuchrie, Drums, Duntroon, Fintray, Killearn, Monzie and Potento. It was a family as well as a national occasion.

In the Highlands especially the memory of the 'great marquess' was held in honour. There can be little doubt that the belief that 'fortune and success was entailed on the name of Graham' (as the Estates were told in 1689) helped John Graham of Claverhouse, Viscount of Dundee, in his short campaign for James VII, which ended with his own death at Killiecrankie. His was the most 'clannish' troop in a regiment of horse which he raised in 1682, with three Graham officers out of four, and a Graham as his aide-major, and there were probably some Grahams among the brave company who set out with him on his last campaign. A century later, when Lieut.-Colonel Thomas Graham of Balgowan (later Lord Lynedoch) raised the Perthshire Volunteers, the head of his branch of the family, Robert Graham of Fintray, recruited for him in the principal towns, and his son joined as senior subaltern.

To note the 'clannishness' of these great men is not to imply that their interests were limited. It was the third Duke of Montrose who, as Marquess of Graham, M.P., secured the repeal of the prohibition enacted after the 'Forty-Five against wearing the Highland dress.

GRANT

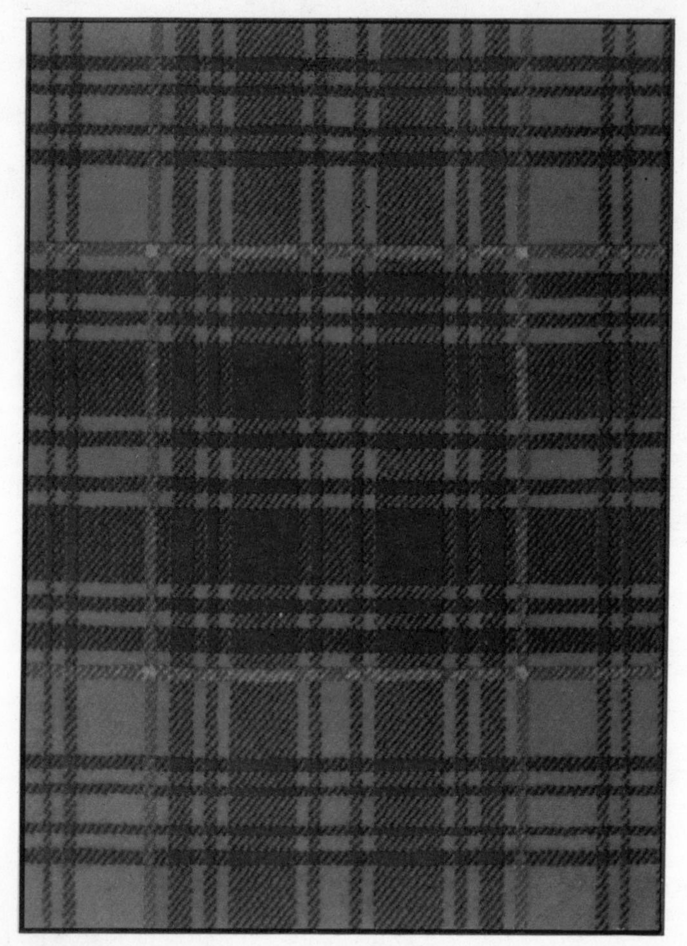

GRANT

GRANT territory lies chiefly on Speyside, between the two Craigellachies—one above Aviemore and the other where the river enters the coastal plain of Moray. It includes the district of Rothiemurchus on the slopes of the Cairngorms, and the straths of Glenurquhart and Glenmoriston on the other side of Loch Ness.

There have been Grants in the north since at least the 13th century, when Laurence (also on record as sheriff of Inverness) and Robert 'called Grant' witnessed a transaction in the bishop of Moray's court. But the real history of the clan begins from the time when they became landholders in Strathspey in 1434. The first chief on record, Sir Duncan, acquired Freuchie near the modern Grantown by marriage, and it was erected into a barony in 1494. A castle was built there in 1536, known first as Bellachastle and later as Castle Grant. From the outset the laird was supported by his kinsfolk in consolidating his property; the barony of Strathspey, for example, was feued by himself, his three sons, and his kinsmen Grant of Culcabock, Grant of Ballindalloch and his brother, and another Grant. By the end of the 16th century he was being styled Laird of Grant or Grant of that Ilk, and the surname was being widely adopted; two lists of the inhabitants of Duthil in the Grant country, separated by only about thirty years, show a change from Gaelic patronymics to the name of Grant. The barony of Urquhart was given to the chief by James IV in 1509, two of his sons receiving the neighbouring lands of Glenmoriston and Corriemony. By the time of the civil war the Laird of Grant had built up 'ane great huge estait', and in 1694 all his lands and their outlying portions were formed into the regality of Grant.

This progress was relieved by a traditional kinship with the MacGregors, for whom the Grants were ready to defy established authority. When that clan was proscribed and many fled for refuge to Strathspey, the Grants were not too active in hunting them down; they were repeatedly admonished, and had to pay a fine of 16,000 merks in 1614. Although they suffered at the hands of both armies in the Montrose campaign, the clan as a whole gave no support to the Stuart cause. They gave some help in suppressing the Rising of 1715 (Glenmoriston was 'out' with the Jacobites), but held back in 1745, when Sir James in London advised his son whom he had left in charge 'to stay at home and take care of his country, and join no party'. They thought the whole man-power of the clans whose chiefs were loyal to the house of Hanover should be called out to serve under their own chiefs, instead of raising Independent Companies with Government-appointed officers.

The Grant chiefs' relations with their clan and its leaders were sometimes unusual. In 1584 the ailing chief, who had lost his son and heir and found himself 'mishandlet' by his neighbours, sent his surviving son and grandson to ask 'his maist speciall freindis and kynnis men' if they had any fault to find with him so that it might be amended (the gentlemen of the clan met in the church of Cromdale and sent a reassuring answer). Although clan tartans as such were still unknown, a baron court in 1704 enacted by order of the young laird that all able-bodied tenants and cottars should provide themselves with 'Highland coats, trews and short hose of tartan of red and green sett'. In 1710 the chief resigned all his estates to his son, and handed over the chiefship to him before the whole clan assembled in full dress at the gathering place of Ballintome. In the next generation the councillors of clan Grant caused the young laird to be imprisoned on account of misbehaviour and prodigality, which would have imperilled the estate.

After 1745 the Grant estates were reorganised by Sir James, and the interests of the lesser tenants safeguarded. Grantown was established in 1766 as a small agricultural and industrial centre, the village of Lewiston founded in Glen-urquhart, timber from the Rothiemurchus forests was floated down the Spey, and planting pushed forward. After some family adjustments to ensure that the chief's marriage with a Colquhoun of Luss would not result in the two estates being united, the chiefship was held along with the earldom of Seafield from 1811 to 1915, after which (while remaining in the same family) it became separated from the wide estates which the Grants had done so much to improve.

GUNN

GUNN

ALONG with the Sinclairs, Sutherlands and Mackays, the Clan Gunn made a considerable noise in the story of the far north of Scotland. Of Norse descent, they seem at first to have occupied the highland portions of Caithness, and were described as 'ancient possessors' in Strathy and Strathhalladale in the Mackay country; but later they moved to Strathullie in the Sutherland parish of Kildonan. There is no evidence of them holding land before the mid-17th century, and what they had must have been kept by the sword. As their latest historian puts it, they 'preferred the full sail of valour to the ballast of deed and parchment'.

The name comes into prominence in the 15th century with Crowner or Coroner Gunn (his name is generally supposed to have been George), 'a great commander in Cattenes in his tyme, and one of the greatest men in that countrey'. He lived in a castle at Harberry in Clyth, on the sea-coast some miles south of Wick, and represented the royal authority in Caithness at a time—if we are to believe Sir Robert Gordon's account—when the earldom was in the king's hands before being granted to the Sinclairs in 1455. The clan was already one of some local importance, but the 'Crowner' himself was apparently killed with several of his sons and principal kinsmen during a feud with the Keiths, just when a meeting of reconciliation was about to take place.

This incident was followed by the first of several 'flittings' known from traditional sources, but it is not always easy to date them or to know whether the accounts refer to different occasions. After the 'Crowner's' death, which may have been in or about 1464 or 1479, his eldest son James removed with his family to Sutherland, where he settled under the earl's protection, making his home at Killernan in Strathullie, and founding a line known from him as *MacSheumas* or MacKeamish. The other sons included Robert, ancestor of the 'Robson' Gunns of Braemore and other families; John, ancestor of the Gunns of Dalemore and Dale, and others; Henry, traditionally the ancestor of the Caithness Hendersons; and William, from whom the Caithness Williamsons and Wilsons.

Various clashes with one or other of their powerful neighbours continued, and the Gunns were blamed for the troubles and commotions that disturbed the North. In 1585 the Earls of Sutherland and Caithness resolved that some of them, 'chiefly such of that tribe as dwelt in Caithness', should be made away with. The plan failed, however, for the Gunns and their friends made good use of their bows and an advantage of ground at Altnagown, 'below the Glutt of Strathmore', where they united for the last time in battle for existence.

The Gunns were listed officially in 1594 among the 'broken clans' of the North, and their connection with Caithness as a distinct community came to an end soon after. In 1618 the head of the 'Robson' branch, having fallen out with the Earl of Caithness and Mackay, sought refuge in Sutherland. Sir Robert Gordon, the young earl's uncle and tutor, settled one group among their own kin in Strathullie, and others wherever they could most conveniently be placed. Of the Gunns' record in Sutherland, Caithness and Strathnaver, he wrote: 'They are very courageous, but more desperate than violent. They have such intelligence and correspondence amongst themselves that they all run one course when any of them is persued in any of these countries.'

Captain Alexander Gunn, who had a commission in the Independent Companies in 1745, was the last *MacSheumas* to live in chiefly style in Strathullie, both his sons having died abroad on military service. In 1800 the Countess of Sutherland was looking for a chief of the Gunns to 'recognise and promote' in recognition of the clan's ancient service and support of her house, but she noticed that the Gunns were among the 'refractory' tenants when the Sutherland estate's removal policy reached their glen. Lower Kildonan was cleared in 1814 and upper Kildonan in 1819, and with that the story of the Gunns as a clan may be said to have ended. It continues mainly as that of individual Gunns, such as those who founded a new Kildonan in Canada and another who helped to choose the site of New Zealand's capital, but in the 20th century the clan have found a new unity and have set about trying to find a chief.

HAMILTON

HAMILTON

PEOPLE are named after places more often than places after people in Scotland, but the name of Hamilton not only gives the highest title to the premier peer of Scotland, but is also attached to an ancient burgh and to the parish in which it lies. The earliest known ancestor of the princely house of Hamilton was Gilbert, father of the Walter FitzGilbert who handed over Bothwell Castle to Bruce after Bannockburn and received valuable estates in Lanarkshire and West Lothian; but it was not until his grandson's day that Hamilton was adopted as a surname. The territorial designation Hamilton of Cadzow was used until 1445, when a charter creating its owner a lord of parliament ordained that the principal place in his lordship (hitherto called 'the Orchard') should in future be styled Hamilton—a change reflected also in the renaming of Cadzow parish.

Lord Hamilton was the first of the family to play a prominent part in Scottish history, and ever since one or other of his descendants has figured in its pages. By marrying the Princess Mary, sister of James III and widow of Thomas Boyd, Earl of Arran, he made the house of Hamilton the nearest family to the throne, with a lasting impact on the history of Scotland. Hamilton was a supporter of the Douglases, but escaped being involved in their ruin; and in 1503 on the occasion of James IV's marriage to Margaret Tudor his son was made Earl of Arran. For virtually the whole of the period from 1536 to 1594 the direct Stewart line depended on the life of the reigning monarch, and a Hamilton was heir apparent to the throne. The second earl was Regent of Scotland during Queen Mary's minority, and Duke of Chatelherault in France, yet it has been said of the family that 'they were loyalest to the queen when they were nearest to the throne'. Mary of Guise called the Regent 'a simple and inconstant man who changed purpose every day', and a wavering nature has been put forward as the explanation of the family's relative lack of political success. They were not so prone to violence as some others, but quarrels between powerful factions brought trouble to their dependants as well as to themselves. During James VI's minority, for instance, a raid known as the 'harrying of Bothwell Muir' led to 400 cattle and 600 sheep besides other animals and goods being carried off from the Hamilton tenants, whose lamentations were loud enough to 'make ane stane-hearted man to greet and bewail'.

Involvement in the political sphere meant honours as well as power, and the 'haughty Hamiltons', as people called them, rose from Earl of Arran to Marquess (1599) and Duke (1643) of Hamilton. Some of the oldest branches died out or sank into obscurity during the 17th century, but the Abercorn line, descended from a younger son of the Regent, became earls in the peerage of Scotland, marquesses of Great Britain, and Irish dukes. One of the senior cadets, sprung from the Hamiltons of Innerwick, was made Earl of Haddington, and a Hamilton of Dalzell was also raised to the peerage.

In 1656 Anne, Duchess of Hamilton in her own right, married William Douglas, Earl of Selkirk, and (while the Abercorn line became heirs male of the house of Hamilton) their descendants eventually came to hold that position in the house of Douglas. The fourth duke unsuccessfully led the opposition to parliamentary union between Scotland and England, and fell in a duel with Lord Mohun in 1712; the fifth commissioned William Adam to design a remarkable building at Chatelherault (near the old castle of Cadzow), in pleasing contrast to the 'disagreeable pile' of Hamilton palace. The sixth duke married one of the beautiful Gunning sisters, and the seventh inherited the Douglas name and honours but failed to add their estates to his own. After the Napoleonic wars the tenth duke created the short-lived glory of a new Hamilton palace, but as mine-shafts spread beneath it and smoke-stacks crept nearer it was abandoned 100 years later, and all that remains is the magnificent family mausoleum which the burgh bought in a 'moment of sentiment'. The eleventh duke married a cousin of Napoleon III, who confirmed the French dukedom on their son; and the fourteenth, who carried the crown of Scotland before Queen Elizabeth during her coronation visit to Edinburgh, had piloted the first aircraft over Mount Everest in 1933. Spreading across the world, the name has gained fresh laurels far beyond the place on the Clyde on which it was conferred more than 500 years ago.

HAY

HAY

HISTORIANS and heralds have not always seen eye to eye about the story of Hay and his two sons having saved the day for the Scots in the battle with the Danes at Luncarty. On the one hand it has been dismissed as one of Hector Boece's fables; yet the farm implements which are said to have been the trio's only weapons figure to this day in the coat of arms of two Scottish earls and several other families of the name.

We are on firmer ground with Sir Gilbert Hay of Erroll, trusted companion of Bruce, whose family had owned lands in Perthshire since the 12th century. The king rewarded him with the fortress and lands of Slains, on the rocky coast fifteen miles north of Aberdeen, and the office of Constable of the realm. The Hay sphere was in southern Buchan, but later marriage brought a scion of the family into possession of the great barony of Delgaty around Turriff, and an early cadet extended it westward beyond the Findhorn to Lochloy. The earldom of Erroll was created in 1453, and when the fourth earl fell at Flodden it is said that eighty-seven gentlemen of the name of Hay, besides other followers, died with him. Also killed was Lord Hay of Yester, whose family had the same origin and were later Earls (from 1646) and Marquesses (1694) of Tweeddale, with lands there and in East Lothian. Other Hays, of the Megginch line, were Earls of Kinnoull from 1633.

The Lord High Constables were the first men in Scotland after the blood royal, but as Hays of Erroll they could be unchancy chiefs to follow. Arising out of the eighth earl's second marriage, his three brothers were so anxious about the influence of the new countess that they entered the Place of Slains by ladders 'under silence of the night' in 1576 and held Lord Erroll prisoner until he signed documents satisfying them over the inheritance. James VI intervened personally, entrusted the estate to another Hay who was Lord Clerk Register, and saw that the succession was fixed on the rightful heir. He may have regretted his decision when the new earl became one of the leaders of the Catholic cause in the north. After Queen Mary's execution Erroll entered into correspondence with the Spanish court, then busy preparing the Armada for an attack on England (by a strange coincidence, one of that unlucky fleet was wrecked near Slains); he threatened Aberdeen with fire and sword in 1594, for which he had the old castle of Slains thrown down, but was allowed to keep his vast possessions. Later, when a quarrel between the earl's cousin and a Gordon ended in the Gordon being shot dead, and Hay being whisked before a Gordon sheriff-depute in Aberdeen, convicted and summarily beheaded, there was an uproar which 'almost put all Scotland in a combustion'. Erroll and Huntly went to Edinburgh 'with all their friends on either side' to see fair play, but in the end it was left to King James to bang a few Hay and Gordon heads together when he came to Scotland again in the next year (1617).

The Erroll lordship in Perthshire was sold in 1633, and with old Slains in ruins a new castle was built about five miles farther north in 1664. This clifftop eyrie was an excellent place of entry for Jacobite agents, and although the earl was abroad in 1715 and his sister was countess in her own right in 1745, some of the clan were 'out' in both Risings. The next sister was wife of the Earl of Linlithgow and Callendar, who was attainted in 1715, and their son-in-law Lord Kilmarnock was executed in 1745, but the Erroll earldom survived and in the next generation went to one of the 'handsome Hays', who as Constable at George III's coronation struck Horace Walpole as 'the noblest figure I ever saw'.

On Tweeddale the Hays built Neidpath Castle about the end of the 14th century, and a canopied Hay pew survives in the little church of Lyne. Their East Lothian seat, Yester House near Gifford, was begun by the marquess who was Secretary of State for Scotland when the office was abolished in 1746. Of the Hays of Megginch and Kinfauns, Sir George (later first Earl of Kinnoull) was made Chancellor of Scotland in 1622, and two of his successors held the office of Lord Lyon King of Arms for seventy years before it was put on a more professional footing in 1867. John Hay of Restalrig, a cadet of Kinnoull, was for a short time right-hand man to 'James VIII' in Rome, and was created Earl (1718) and Duke (1727) of Inverness in the Jacobite peerage.

INNES

INNES

In the coastal strip of Moray, between the rivers Spey and Lossie, lay the barony which gave its name to this northern clan or family, and formed the nucleus of the estates they held for 600 years. The name Innes was probably derived from the Gaelic word for an island or a riverside meadow, but the exact meaning was easily lost sight of in an area where a local proverb advises, 'Speak weil of the Highlands, but live in the Laigh'.

First of the name on record was a Fleming named Berowald (a name still in use), who had a charter from Malcolm IV in 1160 of the lands of Ineess and Etherurecard (Innes and Nether (?) Urquhart) in the district of Elgin. A grandson, Walter de Ineys, had a charter from Alexander II in 1226. By 1490 the family's earliest home had been replaced by a fortalice or tower of

Innes, where Sir James of that Ilk ('James of the beard') entertained the young James IV, in whose father's household he had served. Generally speaking, the lairds were 'brave and worthy' men, under whose care the family estates became 'vast'; but they came to have such a high opinion of themselves that they were 'uneasie and ungratious' to their relatives. In 1522 one misguided laird was whisked away by his brother and some others from his own house to Caithness, where he was consigned to Girnigoe castle on the ground that he had 'waistit and destroyit his landis and gudis'; an appeal to the Lords of Council led to his being interdicted from alienating any of his lands, in order to save 'ane auld honorable hous quhilk hes done the kingis grace grete service and mony honest folkis cummyn of the samin'.

It was seen as a judgment on the family that this line died out with two unhappy brothers. Alexander lost his temper with a clansman, stabbed or shot him at the cross of Edinburgh, and was beheaded by order of the Regent Morton in 1578; and John, 'having neither children nor discretion to manage a fortune', resigned his birthright to the nearest heir male (Innes of Crommey), who at once took possession. Although the Inneses were then at deadly feud with the Dunbars, one of the other cadets (Innermarkie) murdered the new laird in Aberdeen with the connivance of his predecessor and others of the clan. John was reinstated, and changed the disposition of the estate to Innermarkie, but two years later Crommey's son Robert appeared and with official authority displaced laird John and disposed of his rival. In 1587 Innermarkie's heir renounced all pretensions to the lairdship of Innes and acknowledged Robert as 'principal and chief of the name'.

Robert's son, a prominent Covenanter, was one of the first baronets of Nova Scotia, and welcomed Charles II when he landed at Speymouth in 1650. To remove any lingering doubts in the clan, Sir Henry, fourth baronet, obtained a formal certificate from the Lord Lyon King of Arms declaring his right to the chiefship, after an elaborate proof prepared by his uncles Duncan Forbes of Culloden (also his father-in-law) and David Forbes of Newhall. Their full account of the origin and succession of the family ended with the statement that they regarded themselves as notable and happy on three counts—their inheritance never went to a woman, none of them ever married an ill wife, and no friend ever suffered for their debt. In 1767 a rash scheme brought to an end the connection of the Innes chiefs with their ancestral estates, which were somewhat encumbered with debt. Sir James sold them to Lord Fife, apparently with some idea of speculating with the proceeds (perhaps in the way of heiresses) and repurchasing them. But the buyer had other ideas, and a crown charter in 1770 completed the transaction. Other possibilities opened up with the death of the Duke of Roxburghe in 1805 without a direct heir; Sir James's great-grandmother was an heiress in this family, and against strong competition his claim to succeed to the title, fortune and estates was allowed by the House of Lords in 1812. The former Laird of Innes became fifth Duke of Roxburghe, but he did not forget his Innes ancestry, and Duncan Forbes's account of the family was privately printed at his expense in 1820 'to show those proud Kers that he was of as good blood on his father's side as on his great-grandmother's.'

JOHNSTONE

JOHNSTONE

JOHNSTONE or Johnston is one of those names that can be found arising independently in different parts of the country. It is derived from the place-name 'John's town' (of which there are still about a dozen in Scotland), and is found in four main groups of which the leading families were the Johnstones of Annandale in Dumfries-shire; of Westerraw in Lanarkshire, who later moved to Westerhall, Dumfries-shire; of Elphinstone, East Lothian; and of Caskieben, Aberdeenshire.

By far the largest group were based on Annandale, where a secluded hollow in the hills at the very head of the river, now called the Devil's Beef Tub, was once known as 'the beef stand of the Johnstones'. Of them Sir Walter Scott wrote: 'They were a race of uncommon hardihood, much attached to each other and their chieftain, who used to sally [out] as from a fortress, and return to its fastnesses after having accomplished their inroads.' John, founder of the family, gave his name to his lands in Annandale, from which his son Gilbert took his surname; Gilbert appears in charters between 1195 and 1215 both as 'son of John' and as 'de Jonistoune'.

First of the name to take an active part in public affairs was Sir John, who is said to have won a victory over the English at the Water of Solway in 1378. James of that Ilk, who received a charter in 1509 from James IV of the lands of Johnstone, Kirkpatrick and Wamphray, was held responsible for his increasingly powerful clan. His tower of Lochwood in the heart of upper Annandale was a natural centre from which strategic routes led up the Annan, Evan, Moffat and Wamphray waters, and was also convenient for operations to the south and on the Border. By the 16th century the Johnstones were to be found in all four valleys—Raecleuch guarded the chief's interests in the Evan Water, the men of Moffatdale followed Johnstone of Craigieburn, and Johnstone lairds led the lads of Wamphray to the fray.

The clan was a power to be reckoned with on the Border by the time of John, described as 'ane greit man, and havand ane clan of the cuntre at his command', who had a crown charter of the Barony of Johnstone in 1543. He was active in catching marauders, and agreed to assist Douglas of Drumlanrig in his wardenship of the west march. In 1552 he helped in arranging an important treaty which divided the 'debateable land' between the two kingdoms. As his own clan had not changed their habits, he secured the support of the leading men in hunting down those who had committed any crime (one such obligation was signed by twenty-three Johnstones in 1555). When Craigieburn died in 1581 he charged his sons to serve the laird of Johnstone 'even if he be unkind to you' and to rally round their nephew as head of their own branch under the laird's leadership. Besides Johnstones, the chief became bound for keeping good rule among Dinwiddies, Latimers, Grahams, Bells, Irvings, and the people of Lochmaben and Moffat, and one list of 414 names includes more than a dozen heads of landed Johnstone families and their followers.

The Johnstones' growing influence was a challenge to the power of the Maxwells, and it led to 'the greatest of all Border feuds'. This began with the killing of a Maxwell ally known as 'meikle Sym Armstrong', and an attempt at a settlement by the Privy Council had no permanent effect. Johnstone of that Ilk was appointed warden of the west march in 1579, and after a brief Maxwell interval was reappointed in 1582; in 1585 their rivals plundered and burned Lochwood. In an open battle at Dryfe sands near Lockerbie in 1593 Maxwell was killed while holding the wardenship, but Johnstone was absolved of the crime, reappointed warden, and killed by Lord Maxwell in 1608. At last King James managed to bring about a reconciliation, and the principal men on both sides solemnly 'choppit hands' at Edinburgh in 1623.

Freed from this disastrous feud, James of that Ilk became one of the most extensive landowners in southern Scotland, and was created Lord Johnstone of Lochwood (1633) and Earl of Hartfell (1643), a title later changed to Earl of Annandale (Marquess, 1701). The title has been dormant since 1792, in spite of attempts to revive it, but the family still own large estates in Annandale and a local proverb has it that 'They have been there a thousand years, A thousand more they'll bide'.

Many families stemmed from the chief house, but the Johnstons of Caskieben took their name independently from lands in the earldom of Mar.

KEITH

KEITH

As the dominant family in Buchan after the war of independence, the Keiths rose from the position of small landowners to immense territorial and political influence, until towards the close of the 17th century they started to decline. They had a special place among the Scottish nobility through the office of Great Marischal of Scotland, which the chiefs of the name held for something like 700 years. An office which involved their presence in every battle attended by their friends might be expected to reduce the family's manpower, but cadet branches spread into most corners of Buchan, and at the height of their power the earls Marischal owned property in so many Scottish counties that it was said they could travel from Berwick to John o' Groats eating every meal and sleeping every night on their own estates.

The Keiths began with small possessions in the south of Scotland. The surname is evidently derived from lands in East Lothian, and even in the 12th century the earliest authentic ancestor is described as 'Marischal of the King of Scotland'. Grants of land in Buchan moved the main centre of the family's interests to the north-east; Sir Robert the Marischal, whose cavalry routed the English archers at Bannockburn, and his brother were given the biggest share of the forfeited Comyn estates in that region. Towards the end of the 14th century Sir William Keith acquired the lands of Dunottar in exchange for others in Fife, and built a new tower on the high crag which juts into the North Sea near Stonehaven. His grandson was made a Lord of Parliament by James II and created Earl Marischal in 1458; as one of the four great Officers of State it was his duty to maintain internal order in the Scots Parliament, and he also had his place in the royal army. The standard which rallied the Keiths at Flodden is still preserved, but at least one of the earl's sons did not return.

Later in the 16th century the family moved into a new 'palace' on the rocky plateau at Dunottar, with more room for guests and retainers. James IV had visited the earl in 1504, and James VI was at Dunottar in 1580. One earl is chiefly remembered for founding Marischal College at Aberdeen in 1593, but in his younger days he had been involved in the slaughter of his kinsman, the 'knight of Ludquharn'. Dunottar could serve as a prison as well as a home—Keith of Craig and Keith of Harvieston were warded there for debt in 1629 and 1630, and when they broke out the earl was authorised to apprehend them with the support of four Keith lairds. In 1651 Parliament ordered the Earl Marischal (a Covenanter) to remove the 'Honours of Scotland'—crown, sceptre and sword of state—to his castle to save them from Cromwell's clutches, and when Dunottar was besieged they were smuggled out and buried in Kinneff church. The earl's brother, who had some part in the stratagem, was appointed 'Knight Marischal of Scotland' at the Restoration and later Earl of Kintore, and the Marischal himself attended Parliament in state to hand over the regalia. In 1707 the earl acted by deputy when they were lodged in Edinburgh castle, and his protest against the Union referred to the office of Great Marischal of Scotland as one 'which my ancestors and I have possessed and exercised as rights of property these 700 years'.

The brothers George and James Keith, one the last Earl Marischal of Scotland and the other a Field Marshal of Prussia, were 'two of the most remarkable men that were ever banished from their native country'. Both ardent Jacobites, they were 'out' in 1715 as young men and again in the 'attempt' of 1719; in the long exile which followed they played honoured roles in France, Spain, Germany and Russia ('never was there a reproach on the Keiths'). James was killed in battle in 1758; his brother, pardoned in 1759, fell heir to the Kintore estates, and revisited Scotland in 1763. Joyfully received by his 'numerous vassals and friends' (no doubt many Keiths among them), he was broken-hearted by the sight of his boyhood home at Inverugie in ruins. Most of the forfeited estates which he had bought back were allowed to pass out of the family, but he sold Dunottar to Alexander Keith of Ravelston, an Edinburgh lawyer, whose son Sir Alexander had the keeping of the regalia as Knight Marischal of Scotland during George IV's visit in 1822. The ruins and the regalia are now safe, but the hereditary Great Marischals have disappeared. 'Keith sleeps far from bonny Inverugie', wrote Carlyle: 'the hoarse sea-winds and caverns of Dunottar singing vague requiem to his honourable line in the imagination of some few'.

KENNEDY

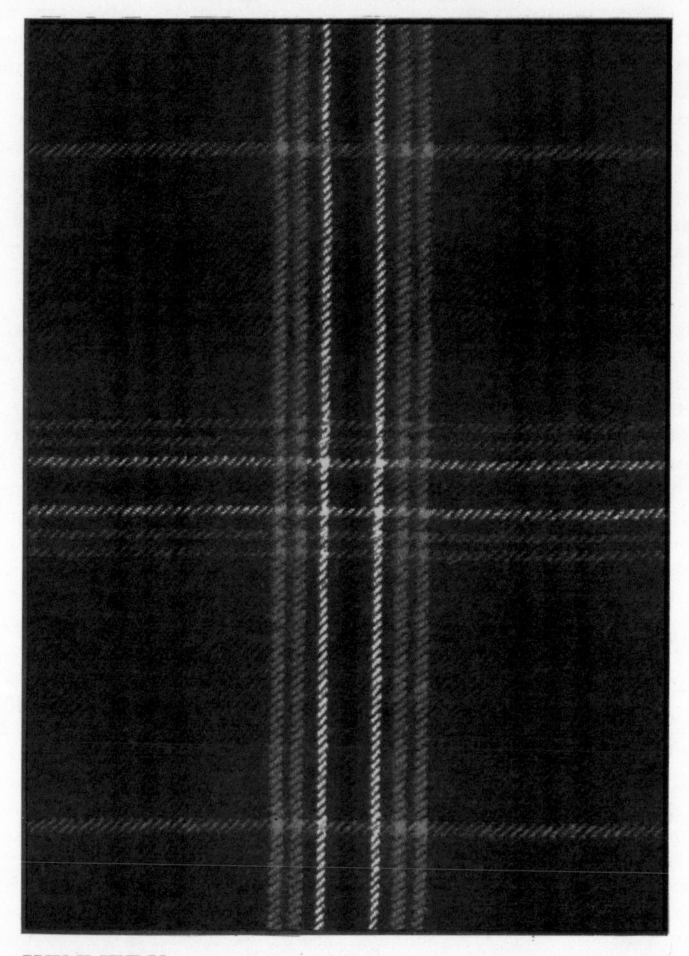

KENNEDY

In the south-west of Scotland, and particularly in the district of Carrick which was the farthest south of the three ancient divisions of Ayrshire, the power and influence of the Kennedys became proverbial.

The name first emerges into the light of authentic history in 1263, the year of the battle of Largs, when Gillescop MacKenedi is on record as steward of Carrick. Just over a century later John Kennedy of Dunure had a grant from Robert II of the chiefship or 'kenkynol' of the clan and the right to lead the men of Carrick in battle. From John's son were descended most of the landed Kennedy families in Carrick, the senior of which became successively Lord Kennedy (1458), Earl of Cassillis (1509) and Marquess of Ailsa (1831). The century after Flodden was the great period of Kennedy power, when the clan were numerous and strong throughout the southern part of Ayrshire, Wigtownshire, and part of the Stewartry of Kirkcudbright—

'Twixt Wigtoune and the town of Aire,
And laigh down by the cruives of Cree;
You shall not get a lodging there
Except ye court wi' Kennedy.

The Carrick earldom, with which the Kennedys had such close associations, had been in the royal family since Bruce's day, and in 1405 James Kennedy of Dunure married a daughter of Robert III. One of their sons was the statesman Bishop of St Andrews, James Kennedy, a man of peaceful and moderate counsels described by Scott as 'one of the wisest men of his time', who at a critical moment advised James II how to deal with his unruly nobles by showing him a sheaf of arrows bound together which could easily be broken if taken one by one. To be of 'the Kingis blude' brought dangers as well as rewards, and during the troubled years of the Stewarts a Kennedy chief fell with James IV at Flodden, and four lairds and others of the clan fell at Pinkie.

But the clan found themselves involved in private quarrels as well as in the nation's cause. The worst of all was the great feud between the two principal families, the Kennedys of Cassillis and of Bargany, which lasted for two generations and ended with the extinction of the latter in the early years of the 17th century. One of the early incidents in it was the attempt by Cassillis to secure the abbey lands of Crossraguel after the Reformation by cruelly 'roasting' the layman who held them over a fire in the castle vaults at Dunure, from which he was rescued by Bargany. Sir Thomas Kennedy of Culzean, tutor of Cassillis during the minority of his nephew the fifth earl, paid with his life for the active part he took in the family feuds, for he was murdered in 1602.

In the social and economic upheavals caused by the religious wars, John, sixth Earl of Cassillis proved a staunch leader in the Covenanting struggle for religious freedom, raising a regiment of foot which suffered in the defeats at Alford and Kilsyth. The resulting fines, bankruptcies and enforced sales of estates led what had been 'the great and almost only name amongst the gentrie' to find itself by 1700 or thereby 'under great decay in comparison of what it was ane age agoe'. But in the meantime the name was making its mark in the world beyond, with side-effects in the old Kennedy country as well. For example in the Kirkhill family (an offshoot of Bargany) Sir Thomas Kennedy, after being Provost of Edinburgh by King James's influence in 1685–86, bought the estates of Dalquharran and Dunure, and built a fine new house on the one and a harbour on the other. There were lawyers, soldiers and business men among his seven sons: the eldest, who followed him, had a successful career as M.P., law officer, and judge on the Exchequer bench, while the youngest began as a rolling stone by going to Sumatra, Virginia, Spain and the Jacobite shadow court in Rome, before returning to Scotland in 1727 and living for nearly forty years at Dalquharran, first as manager for his elder brothers and latterly as laird.

The chiefship of the name passed in 1759 to the Kennedys of Culzean, who became Earls of Cassillis and later Marquesses of Ailsa. But their chief glory was the castle by the sea created for the family by Robert Adam in the 1780s, since 1945 under the care of the National Trust for Scotland and a place where every Scot can share in the pride of the Kennedys.

KERR

KERR

If this warlike Border family were ever so crabbed and contentious as to deserve their popular description as 'the cappit Kerrs', it was no doubt because of the long contest for supremacy between the two great houses of Cessford and Ferniehurst. Family tradition relates that they were descended from two brothers, without settling the important point of which was the senior. Although for many years the heads of each line alternated in the office of Warden of the Middle March, their rivalry brought death and disorder more than once to the Border. The centre of the family's power lay in lower Teviotdale, but various Kerrs acquired lands in the counties of Peebles, Haddington, Dumfries, Lanark, Stirling and even Aberdeen in the reign of David II. While probably of the same stock, all families of the name in Scotland do not necessarily descend from the two contending houses.

First of the name in Border history was John Kerr, 'hunter' at Soonhope near Peebles, who emerges towards the end of the 12th century. John Kerr of the forest of Selkirk acquired Altonburn in 1358, and the second Andrew of that place had a crown charter of the lands and barony of Cessford in 1467. The castle of Cessford—impressive even in ruin—stood on the bank of a hill stream running into the Kale water near Morebattle, on the northern edge of the Cheviots. Meantime Thomas Kerr of Smailholm, apparently a younger son of Cessford, got Ferniehurst by marriage, with its castle (now replaced by a later building) on the wooded banks of the Jed. They were only six miles apart and about the same distance from the English Border.

Family quarrels were not the only cause of trouble among the Kerrs. A few years before Flodden three Englishmen killed Sir Robert Kerr, a former warden of the middle march, while he was attending a march meeting across the Border, and his son tracked down one of the murderers and gave him what was known as 'Jeddart justice'. After Flodden some of the Liddesdale clans put themselves under Ferniehurst's protection, but in 1523 his castle was taken by the English after a bold defence. Cessford, who had worked as warden for peace and co-operation with England, was killed by a follower of Scott of Buccleuch in the attempt to rescue James V from the Douglases. The two Kerr houses sank their differences then, and again in 1545 so that their feud should not weaken the defence of the Border against the English. But Scotts and Kerrs continued to raid each other's lands, and in 1552 Buccleuch was murdered in Edinburgh by Cessford and some others. The Privy Council managed to patch up the quarrel, with Cessford promising to 'bury the past in oblivion and live in amity in the future' with the Scotts, and a solid phalanx of lairds of both names agreed to ride together against trouble-makers, 'Scot with Ker and Ker with Scot'. Not until two more Kerrs had been killed, including a laird of Ancrum 'expert beyond others in the laws and customs of the Borders', was the feud settled by a humble apology from Cessford and payment of 10,000 merks, followed by 'letters of slains' in forgiveness from the murdered man's sons. As the long-standing national rivalries also came to an end, one of the last of the 'general bands' against Border thieves and aggressors was signed in 1602 by five Kerr lairds in Jedburgh and two more in Peebles.

Union with England under one crown reduced the importance of Border clans and groups, but by now the principal Kerrs were influential magnates. Two of them followed the court to London, and royal favour was reflected in a series of honours—Cessford was made Lord Roxburghe (1600), earl (1616) and duke (1707), while Ferniehurst became Lord Jedburgh (1622) and through a cadet branch Earl (1631) and Marquess (1701) of Lothian. They had a long struggle in Parliament for the right of precedence; the old Border towers were abandoned, and Floors Castle and Newbattle Abbey grew in rival magnificence. The Roxburghe estates and peerages were inherited successively by the Drummonds of Perth, Bellenden of Broughton and Innes of Innes, but the Lothian honours continued in the male line and the family remained simply Kerrs. Though short of a dukedom, they gave a Kerr to Lord Salisbury's administration as Secretary for Scotland, and another was Ambassador to the United States in the Second World War—and as a bank governor (a clansman proudly noted), the former had his portrait for years on one of these typically Scottish products, the £1 note. Perhaps honours were even, at last.

LAMONT

LAMONT

CLAN Lamont's historian has described its chief characteristics as compactness at home, accessibility, obedience to law and order, and capacity for emigration and colonisation. It is an unusually well-documented record, because this clan, although never powerful, has a line of chiefs vouched by charters at a time when most other Highland families can rely only on verbal tradition.

They made their home in the district of Cowal, almost surrounded by water, with the Firth of Clyde on the east and Loch Fyne on the west, and a small detached portion in Glassary to the north of Loch Gilp. There the Lamonts must have been established by the reign of Alexander II, for between 1231 and 1241 Duncan son of Ferchar and his nephew Lauman son of Malcolm bestowed on the monks of Paisley some lands which the donors' ancestors had possessed at Kilmun, on the Holy Loch. Lauman's home was at Inveryne, on Loch Fyne, and his lands and those of a cousin Angus were included in the new sheriffdom of Kintyre carved out of Argyll in 1293. There is little doubt that the decline in fortune and possessions which overtook them was because, like the MacDougalls of Lorn, they opposed the claims of Robert Bruce.

John Lamont of that Ilk, whose ancestors had held appointments under the Stewarts before they reached the throne, was bailie of Cowal, and he received a charter of the family's lands from James III. By this time Toward castle had been built, nearer the centre of affairs, although Inveryne continued to be the chief's territorial designation. A surviving relic of more peaceful pursuits is the Lamont harp, still preserved among the nation's treasures in Edinburgh, which is said to have been taken from Argyll in the mid-15th century when a Lamont married a Perthshire laird. The clan made little stir during the critical years when the young James VI was tightening his grip on the outlying parts of his kingdom, although 'the Laird of Lawmont' was listed among the landlords made answerable for any 'broken men' harboured on their lands.

During the civil strife of the 17th century, Sir James of Inveryne brought ruin on himself and his clan in an attempt to regain the lordship of Cowal from the encroaching Campbells. After many vacillations he backed Montrose, and carried fire and sword into the Campbell country. In 1646 he and his followers were besieged in Toward and Ascog; surrendering on a promise of life and liberty for the garrisons, he was seized along with 'the whole gentlemen of the name of Lamont'. According to his account, 'not any of the name of Lamont that were past seven years of age' was spared, about thirty-six of his people (most of them 'special gentlemen' of the name) were taken to Dunoon and hanged on a single tree, and two more Lamonts were hanged after a summary trial at Inveraray. Sir James was held in Dunstaffnage and then Inchconnell for nearly eight years; at the Restoration all these complaints were set out in detail among the charges for which Argyll suffered death, but the Lamonts were never the same again, and some of their estates were never recovered. The chief took over Ardlamont from a cadet, and it became the family's home until 1893.

One important branch had for long been settled in Glassary, where they were known as Clan Sorley or Somhairle, before adopting the surname Lamont. A cadet of the chief's family owned Monydrain until 1873, but its heir had emigrated to Australia and to that line the chiefship passed on the failure of the main stem in 1929. The last of the Lamont lairds with lands in Cowal were the Knockdow family, who from 1431 to 1958 owned their estate on Loch Striven.

The scattering of the tartan had an unexpected result. With the formation of a Clan Lamont Society in 1895, it was early intended to produce a history of the clan. The researches of Sir Norman of Knockdow laid a firm foundation, and in 1927 two wealthy American members, impressed with the good fellowship and ideals of the society, offered to find four-fifths of the sum required if the society would raise the rest and members contribute any traditional or other knowledge they possessed. When in 1938 the sumptuous story of *The Lamont Clan* appeared, it bore the proud sub-title 'seven centuries of clan history from record evidence'.

LESLIE

LESLIE, HUNTING

LESLIE influence has from earliest times been divided between the north-east of Scotland and Fife, and the details of family relationship are not always certain. But 'a chronic and adventurous poverty' is noted by one historian as a characteristic shared by them all, and it seems natural that in the various branches of a prolific family they should have proved themselves to be born soldiers of fortune. At one time, indeed, three Leslies were generals in three kingdoms—Alexander Earl of Leven in Scotland, Sir Alexander of Auchintoul in Russia, and Walter Count Leslie in Germany, 'besides many colonels and other inferior officers'.

The Leslie homeland in the north-east lies 'at the back of Bennachie' and in fact on all sides of that distinctive hill. The family is traced back to the 12th century, when gifts of the Lessele lands in the Garioch from David Earl of Huntingdon gave them their patrimony and their name. In the centuries which followed they planted offshoots in Moray and Fife, with a Leslie being first styled 'of Rothes' in 1392, and another changing the designation to 'of Fythkill' after receiving a royal charter of that Fife barony (later to be called Leslie) in 1398. The Aberdeenshire lands of the Leslies of that Ilk went in 1439 to a cousin, Leslie of Rothes, whose son was created Earl of Rothes in 1459, but the old line continued though reduced in importance. A quarrel with the Forbeses kept large parts of Mar and the Garioch in an uproar, and in 1525 three Leslie lairds—Leslie, Wardes and Balquhain—raided the town of Aberdeen. Nearly a century later the family seat passed to a Forbes, but the family continuity was unbroken, and in 1632 George Leslie of that Ilk could trace his forebears back for ten generations, and was served heir to Malcolm Leslie, the great-great-great-grandfather of his father's great-great-great-grandfather.

Meantime, the Leslies of Balquhain, one of the longest-lasting and most distinguished branches, had become the leading northern family of the name. At nearby Harlaw in 1411, at least six sons of 'red Sir Andrew' of Balquhain are said to have fallen, and later he himself set Strathdon at defiance from the old hill-fort on Bennachie. The family prospered, with younger sons carving out fortunes for themselves, and in 1562 the tall square tower of Balquhain gave the Queen of Scots a night's entertainment on her northern progress. But the next two lairds 'dilapidated' the estate, and their successor sought military service in Russia and fell at the storming of Ingolwitz in Poland in 1655. Thereafter, when a Leslie of Balquhain became a Count of the Austrian Empire, with estates in Germany and Scotland, he made an entail to ensure that they would be kept distinct and separate among his heirs. One of the Balquhain line, a Jesuit priest whose brother was a field-marshal and nephew of the count, compiled a genealogy in Latin with an elaborate title beginning *Laurus Leslaeana explicata* which was published at Gratz in 1692, and has preserved many details of a complicated family tree.

Although without a recognised head, and their senior branch in decline, the Leslies had a period of unusual distinction in the 17th century. Alexander, a field-marshal in the service of Gustavus Adolphus, 'that old, little, crooked soldier' whose wisdom and authority commanded obedience, came home and took command of the Covenanting army, and was made Earl of Leven in 1641; David Leslie, who defeated Montrose at Philiphaugh but was routed by Cromwell at Dunbar, became Lord Newark in 1651; and John Earl of Rothes rose from one office of state to another to end as Chancellor of Scotland in 1667 and a duke in 1680.

Most of the old Leslie estates are now in other hands, but in some cases a link has been retained. Rothes was sold to a Grant in 1711, but the earl (the dukedom died with its first holder) still owns the castle-hill in Strathspey. Another of the family is keeper of the ancient castle of Leslie in the Garioch, and a Baron of Balquhain still owns the ancestral castle below Bennachie.

LINDSAY

LINDSAY

WHAT a literary Lord Lyon King of Arms, Sir David Lindsay of the Mount, called 'ane surname of renown', appears first in Scotland in the 12th century, at the close of which a Lindsay owned the lands of Crawford near the head waters of the Clyde. Families of the name are now spread all over Scotland and abroad, and many of them have gained distinction.

Sir David Lindsay of Crawford, who put his seal to the declaration of Scotland's independence sent to the Pope in 1320, was the ancestor of the Earls of Crawford (premier earls of Scotland, 1398), of Lindsay (1633), and of Balcarres (1651). There were six Lindsay knights—Froissart called them the *'enfants de Lindsay'*—in the host which invaded England before the battle of Otterburn. The family remained chiefly in Clydesdale until the death of

Sir James of Crawford in 1397, but lands in Angus had already been acquired by marriage, and they made their home there with Finavon at the mouth of the Angus glens as their principal residence. The estates which were united to form the earldom of Crawford spread over about two-thirds of the modern county, and have been identified by a local historian as 'the land of the Lindsays'.

They were a clannish people even then, with a reputation for buoyant cheerfulness which earned them the soubriquet 'the lightsome Lindsays'. When in 1421 the earl settled the Crawford estates on his heirs male for ever, he stipulated that they should pass only to heirs 'bearing the name and arms of Lindsay' (probably the first strict entail under which anyone not complying would forfeit the succession); and when the 'Tiger Earl' submitted to James II after joining the Earl of Douglas in rebellion in 1452, he told the king (according to Lindsay of Pitscottie the historian) that what moved him to appeal for mercy was the prospect of 'the decay and falling of our house' and the fact that the lives, lands and goods of the noblemen of Angus and the rest of his adherents were in danger 'for my cause and surname of Lindsay'.

It was a wide community of which he was the head. The earl had his own petty parliament, consisting of the great vassals who held their lands for services rendered to him; lesser men had undertaken to assist him when occasion arose; he and his more immediate dependents had a following of tenants and servants and in addition he could rely on the support in general 'of Lindsays of high and low degree'. Within three or four centuries after their move north, about a hundred minor houses or families of Lindsays were flourishing in Scotland, most of them settled in Angus and the surrounding counties, and all acknowledging the Earls of Crawford as chiefs of their blood.

Standing between the old age and the new, and in a middle place within the clan, was Sir David Lindsay of the Mount, whose *Satyre of the Thrie Estaits* was performed before James V and his court in 1540. A man of gentle birth known to Scots of all degrees, he was an influential courtier who spoke to and for the common people. In his poetry, written for 16th-century audiences but still acclaimed by their 20th-century successors, he attacked corruption in the church and state, and even ventured to ridicule female fashions. He was the most widely read and frequently printed of the Scots 'makars', and as the leading Scottish herald was one of the great men of his day.

The last of the original line of Crawford earls, a royalist, was forfeited by Parliament in 1644. Homeless and destitute, he had arranged for the title to pass to his distant relation the powerful Earl of Lindsay. But in Angus the laird of Edzell was now the principal man of the name, and when bonds for peaceable behaviour had to be renewed he, and neither of the Lindsay earls, was named in 1669. The last of this family died abroad in 1744, leaving the Earl of Balcarres in Fife as next heir male of the house of Crawford; and about a century later, Lord Balcarres's claim to the earldom of Crawford was established by the researches of his son, author of *The Lives of the Lindsays*. Once again the scattered families of Lindsays could look to Scotland's premier earl as their chief, with feelings not so much of pride as of affection in a family where 'the meanest felt himself akin to the highest, and the feudal bond was sweetened by blood'.

MACALISTER

MACALISTER

UNDER a patronymic of its own, the Clan Alister (or Allaster) of Kintyre are the senior cadet branch of the great Clan Donald, earliest of all the offshoots from the parent stem. The Alexander in the 13th century from whom they are descended was a son of Donald—grandson of the mighty Somerled, and great-grandfather of John first Lord of the Isles. From the first their possessions appear to have been in Kintyre, and they were never very extensive. Being a small clan, they cultivated friendship with their powerful neighbours, the Macdonalds of Islay and the houses of Argyll and Hamilton, and survived long after the Campbells became dominant in Kintyre.

The chief family of the name held the estate of Loup on the south shore of West Loch Tarbert, near its mouth, and they also had leases or tacks of other holdings in Kintyre. Next in importance were the MacAlisters of Tarbert, who became constables of the strategic castle on the isthmus between Kintyre and Knapdale. Members of the clan who had settled in Arran formed with their descendants a group sometimes known as the Clan Allaster *beg*. After the submission of the Lord of the Isles in 1475, when James III was allocating some of the confiscated lands in Kintyre, he formed the Stewardry of South Kintyre and appointed 'Tarlach (Charles) MakAlexander' as steward, with headquarters in Dunaverty castle and the liferent of certain lands. When the Lordship of the Isles finally disappeared in 1493, the chief was probably John *dubh* MacAlister, whose son is on record as 'Angus Johne Dowisoun of the Loupe' (1515).

The MacAlisters supported the Clan Donald in their great feud with the Macleans, and the laird had a charter of his lands from the Earl of Argyll. Unfortunately for the clan, towards the end of the 16th century there was an internal dispute in which the Tutor of Loup was killed; when his sons took refuge with Macdonald of Dunyveg at Askomull in Kintyre the young laird joined a party of Macdonalds who surrounded the house at dead of night, and set fire to it when the MacAlisters refused to surrender themselves. Three years later, in 1600, there was more trouble when the late tutor's son Alister, with some of the clan seized the house of Knokransay in Arran belonging to Montgomery of Skelmorlie, took his wife and children prisoner, and spoiled his goods. A report to the Privy Council says that Alister was delivered up 'by his clan' to Montgomery in security for reparation and good behaviour. In 1602 Tarbert's son was concerned in a large-scale raid into Bute in which several Campbell lairds and a following of about 1,200 men were involved.

When the king sent an emissary to Kintyre in 1605 to receive the obedience of 'the principal men' of the South Isles (which included Kintyre), only Angus Macdonald and a few local lairds, including the MacAlisters, bothered to appear. Two years later Ranald tutor of Loup bound himself and 'all others of his kin and clan of M'Alaster' in a bond to the Marquess of Hamilton that they would do no hurt to his Isle of Arran. When the Macdonald lands in Kintyre fell into Argyll's hands the MacAlisters, although they had taken part in Sir James Macdonald's abortive rebellion in 1615, were engaged along with others in maintaining law and order. But Alexander of Loup fought for James VII at Killiecrankie and Cromdale, escaped with the remnant of his followers, crossed to Ireland and took part in the battle of the Boyne. The family kept their lands in Kintyre until early in the 19th century, when they acquired an estate in Ayrshire by marriage.

Many of the old name are still found in Kintyre and the neighbouring districts, and there was an echo of older times when the bankrupt Tarbert family had to sell their castle and estate soon after 1745. The Duke of Argyll managed to secure a judgment in the Court of Session that his vassal was bound to keep up at his own expense a six-oared boat, with six rowers and a steersman, to transport the superior and his family across Loch Fyne or up the coast as far as Lochgair; he was excused from keeping the old castle in repair so long as a mansionhouse lately built on the estate was kept wind and watertight. The family survived, however, and in later days produced a principal (later chancellor) of Glasgow University, Sir Donald MacAlister of Tarbert, who was one of the ornaments of the name.

MACAULAY

MACAULAY

ON the eastern shore of the Gareloch, stretching from about Cardross to Garelochhead, was an estate which for nearly five centuries belonged to a family first known as Ardincaple from their lands, and later as Macaulay. Their castle, built on the crest of the coastline marking the old sea-level, faced across the Gareloch to Argyll's castle of Rosneath, and towards Greenock on the other side of the Clyde; and as their possessions and numbers grew the Clan Macaulay took an important place in events on the south-western fringe of the Highlands—'of good account, though not numerous', as Sir Walter Scott put it.

The name appears early in the Lennox, where Duncan the son of Auleth witnessed a charter about 1285. The barons of Ardincaple are said to have been proprietors there during the wars of independence, when Wallace found the Earl of Lennox 'bydand at defence' in Faslane. By the time of Flodden they owned extensive lands, and an increasing number of Ardincaples were witnessing important documents. Aulay Ardincaple of that Ilk is on record in 1515 and 1529, and in 1518 and 1536 he appears as Aulay Macaulay of Ardincaple; the name seems to have been finally changed to its present form in the reign of James V, 'to humour a patronymical designation as being more agreeable to the head of a clan than the designation of Ardincaple of that Ilk'. In the roll of Highland landlords drawn up in 1587 appears 'the Laird M'Cawla of Ardincaple', and his clan is listed among those having some 'broken men'.

Feuds were common in this corner of the Lennox, and one with the Buchanans began through the killing of a Macaulay at Dumbarton fair in 1590. The chief allied himself with the MacGregors, using some tradition of kinship as a basis; in a bond of manrent signed at Ardincaple in 1591 with the outlawed Alasdair Macgregor of Glenstrae, Aulay acknowledged himself 'as brenche of his hous' although he is 'to haiff his awin libertie of the name of M'Cawlay as chyffe'. Before the year was out the Buchanans were complaining that a great number of Macgregor 'broken men and sorners' had been brought into Buchanan territory by Macaulay under pretence of avenging the slaughter of some of his men.

Friendship with the Macgregors became more dangerous as events moved towards their proscription after the massacre of the Colquhouns at Glenfruin in 1603. Lennox and Argyll had a contest over jurisdictions, and as bailie within the Lennox regality Macaulay was obnoxious to his Campbell neighbour. In 1602 Argyll was charged with 'lying at await for the Laird of Ardincapill upon set purpois to have slane him', and Glenstrae alleged that he had been enticed to do the deed. When Argyll accused him of dealings with the Clangregor, Macaulay was on his way to London with the Duke of Lennox as James travelled south to take over the English throne, and the king himself wrote from Berwick assuring Argyll of Macaulay's innocence, and ordering the proceedings to be stopped. The clan had some strange assignments in support of the royal authority, and Macaulay (who was later knighted) had twenty of his vassals with him when he and Macdonald of Sleat were sent to the Isles in 1614 to try to secure the surrender of the castle of Dunyveg.

With Sir Aulay the power of the lairds reached its peak, but there were some further additions to the estates before a 'system of extravagant living' compelled them to dispose piece by piece of every acre. Archibald, 'the bloody Ardincaple' to the Covenanters, disposed of the land on which Helensburgh was later built. Faslane and Blairnairne followed, and at Laggarie, sold to a cadet of the family in London, the last chief died landless about 1767. Ardincaple had a brief return to Macaulay ownership in the 1920s, but the clan are scattered throughout the world.

Of Norse extraction, and unconnected with Ardincaple, were the Macaulays of Uig in Lewis, of whom Donald *cam* figures prominently in island folklore; from this family came a notable line of ministers, and Thomas Babington, Lord Macaulay the politician and historian. A 'numerous sept' of Macaulays in Caithness and Sutherland, of whom Buchanan of Auchmar wrote in 1723, traced their descent from the Ardincaple family and accepted the laird as their chief.

MACBEAN

MACBEAN

AMONG the staunchest supporters of the Clan Chattan confederacy, with a tradition of descent from the ancient Clan Chattan in Lochaber, the Macbeans (or Macbains) had their territory at the north end of Loch Ness. The Kinchyle and Drummond families lived in the parish of Dores, in Strathnairn were the Macbeans of Faillie, and in Strathdearn those of Tomatin. Kinchyle, with a frontage to Loch Ness and an expanse of hill land by Loch Ashie, was the chief place associated with the name.

According to Mackintosh tradition, a father and four sons named Macbean came from Lochaber to the parish of Petty, near Inverness, in the 14th century, after slaying the Red Comyn's steward, and placed themselves and their posterity under Mackintosh's protection. Many of the 'Clanbean' fell at the battle of Harlaw in 1411, when Mackintosh supported Donald of the Isles in his effort to secure his rights to the earldom of Ross. It is not always easy to identify the Macbeans in early records, and the first appearance of the present surname is in a Kinchyle sasine of 1650 to 'John McBean *alias* McAngus vic Phaill lawful son and nearest heir of Angus McPhaill vic William vic Gillies' —a patronymical form simply meaning that John was son of Angus son of Paul son of William son of Gillies (another document takes the pedigree back to Gillies son of Paul, on record in 1492). In this succession it is not hard to recognise as Macbeans the William McGillies McFaill of the Clan Chattan bond of 1543, and Angus mac Phaill who signed the bond of union among the Clan Chattan in 1609 'for himself and taking the full burden in and upon him of his kin and race of Clan Vean'. But Paul Macbean of Kinchyle, who undertook to join Mackintosh against the Camerons in 1664, and five years later promised to follow him with all his men, tenants, family and followers, held back from the Lochaber expedition in 1667, and in 1680 actually acknowledged Cameron of Lochiel as his chief.

Æneas Macbean younger of Kinchyle was a captain in Mackintosh's regiment in 1715, and his brother, known as Gillies *mor* from his unusual height and strength, earned lasting fame for his bravery at Culloden. The next chief, finding his affairs hopelessly embarrassed, joined one of the earliest Highland regiments and saw service in North America. Four Macbeans and another relative who acted for him in his absence found it necessary to sell Kinchyle and other lands, and they passed from the name in 1760. Meanwhile the Macbeans of Tomatin were so successful as merchants (their business extending to London and the East Indies) that they managed to retain their property while others all over the Highlands were changing hands.

The succession to Faillie, which was sold to Macgillivray of Dunmaglass in 1771, gave rise to one of the few decisions in the law courts on the legal status of clanship in modern times. The first Macbean of Faillie was Donald mac Gilliphadrick, who in 1632 held his lands from the Earl of Moray on a succession strictly limited to 'heirs male and assignees of the clan of Clan Chattan allenarly' (only). This limitation, repeated in 1707, 1749, and again in 1771, also appears in a Macqueen charter of 1661. When the issue was raised in Macgillivray v. Souter (1860), Lord Ardmillan declared: 'Clans are not now corporations which law sustains nor societies which law recognises or acknowledges. . . .' His comments have been challenged by the former Lord Lyon, Sir Thomas Innes of Learney, who described them as 'disfigured by really glaring errors in elementary legal history'; and in fact the Court of Session merely held that membership of a clan was not a recognisable limitation to the destination of property.

Whatever the law may say, the Clan Macbean has shown its vitality and lived up to its traditions. An American business man, descended from the Kinchyle family and acknowledged as chief of the name and head of the clan in 1959 by the Lord Lyon, has taken his place as McBain of McBain among the chieftains of Clan Chattan, and established a 'memory park' near Kinchyle on the road from Dores to Loch Ashie with a magnificent view over the old clan country.

CLAN DONALD

MACDONALD

WHEN the Scandinavian hold on the Hebrides was weakening in the 13th century, the Clan Donald rose to power in the islands and western seaboard. Their name derives from Donald of Islay, son of Reginald and grandson of the mighty Somerled, King of the Isles. Donald's son Angus *mor,* who submitted to the King of Scots after Hakon's disastrous attempt to maintain Norse sovereignty in 1263, may be reckoned as the first 'MacDonald'; he appears as Angus, son of Donald, in the records of Parliament in 1284, and his successors were known simply as 'MacDonald' or 'the great MacDonald', although they used 'de Insulis' or 'de Yle' as a family designation in formal documents.

John of Islay, son of the Angus *og* who brought the islanders to the support of Bruce, and grandson of Angus *mor,* was the first of the family to assume and use the title *Dominus Insularum* (1354). By his first marriage with the heiress of another line, John became Lord of Garmoran, the Uists, Benbecula, the Small Isles, and half of Lochaber; by his second wife Margaret, daughter of the High Steward (later Robert II), he acquired further mainland territories as well as being allied to the family which reached the throne in 1371. He and his three successors—Donald, Alexander and John—ruled their cluster of mainland and island territories from a base at Finlaggan in Islay, where their council of sixteen included 'four great men of their royal blood of Clan Donald lineally descended', namely the chiefs of Clan Ian of Ardnamurchan[1], Clanranald, Clan Ian *mor* of Islay[1], and Clan Donald in Lochaber. The bond of blood between the island lords and their kinsmen, and the loyalty of the great clans which completed the confederacy (Macleans, MacLeods, Macneils, Mackinnons, Macquarries, Macfies) checked feuds between the clans and maintained a substantial degree of internal peace, in which the arts could flourish. 'In their time there was great peace and wealth in the Isles through the ministration of justice', wrote a nostalgic cleric who lived through the period of anarchy which followed the forfeiture of the lordship in 1493. A centre of disaffection, more than once allied with the English, it had become incompatible with the unity of the Scottish kingdom; but its fall had the effect of splitting the Clan Donald, with the right to the chiefship 'more effective in dividing than in uniting them', and armed attempts to resuscitate the lordship were continued for more than half a century under the last lord's nephew, grandson, and great-nephews, with widespread support but no lasting success.

When towards the end of the 16th century James VI tried to make the Highland and Border chiefs responsible for their clansmen, his ministers found it impossible to make one man answerable for the whole Clan Donald. Six were named in the legislation of 1587–94, and when a similar policy was pursued after the Restoration three of them—Sir James of Sleat, the captain of Clanranald, and Lord Macdonell (Glengarry)—were among those ordered to appear annually before the Privy Council to renew their bonds for keeping the peace in the Highlands; a few years later all three were lodged in Edinburgh castle until they found caution for the appearance of heads of families 'descended of their houses'. Some of the loyalty enjoyed by the old Lords of the Isles was shown to the Stewarts in the civil wars of the 17th century. Sir Donald of Sleat reported from Knoydart in 1638 that he had convened Clanranald and Glengarry 'with our whole name of the Clan Donald', and they swore to 'do and live' with him in the king's service. MacDonalds flocked to Montrose's standard in 1644, when Sir Alasdair was his right-hand man; many were 'out' under Dundee in 1689, and again in 1715 and (without Sleat) in 1745, when the strength of the chief branches were given as—Clanranald and Sleat, 700/1,000 each, Glengarry 500, Keppoch 300, and Glencoe 100/150.

The supreme chiefship remained unsettled. In 1911 the chiefs of Clanranald, Glengarry and Sleat agreed that when two or more of them met at any gathering the right of precedence for that occasion should be decided by drawing lots, and this method worked amicably. In 1947 the then Lord Lyon, Sir Thomas Innes of Learney, officially recognised the resumption by Lord Macdonald of the surname 'Macdonald of Macdonald' (used by his predecessor in 1727), and restored to him as inheritor of the estate and representer of the family the arms appropriate to the chief of the name of Macdonald.

[1]Ceased to exist as clans in early 17th century (W. R. Kermack, *The Scottish Highlands,* pp. 81, 83–5). For others see pp. 80, 88, 90, 92 and 94.

MACDONALD OF CLANRANALD

MACDONALD OF CLANRANALD

One of the most dramatic sights in the Western Highlands is the castle of Eilean Tioram, rising proudly from a rocky base on a tidal islet in Loch Moidart at the eastern neck of the Ardnamurchan peninsula. As striking, and at times as proud, is the story of the Macdonalds of Clanranald, whose stronghold it was for some 400 years.

As a separate house of Clan Donald, the Clanranald arose from a mid-14th century arrangement made by John, Lord of the Isles. Ranald, his son by his first wife Amy MacRuari, was to have her patrimony of Moidart, Arisaig, Morar, the Small Isles, Uist and Benbecula, while the eldest son by his second marriage (with the Steward's daughter) became Lord of the Isles. During the 15th century the family had to fight for the lands they occupied before acquiring a legal title, but they were a prolific line linked by marriage with almost everyone of note in the Isles and adjacent Highlands.

An unusual departure from the direct line of succession is often given as an example of 'deposing' a legal heir and 'electing' a successor, although the part played by the clan in the affair is obscure. Allan, the chief who died in 1509, was twice married, first to a daughter of Macian of Ardnamurchan and then to a daughter of Fraser of Lovat, and had children by both. His eldest son Ranald was followed as chief by his son Dugall, who for some reason (later accounts speak vaguely of his 'cruelties') was killed by his cousins. Instead of his sons succeeding him—one actually received lands which remained in his family for generations—the estates passed first to an uncle and then to his bastard son John, famous in Highland history as *Iain Muideartach;* he assumed the chiefship apparently with the consent if not the approval of the clan, secured a royal charter in favour of himself and his heirs, and was officially legitimated. When John was seized by James V along with other chiefs during his visit to the Hebrides in 1540, Lovat took the chance to push the claims of his nephew Ranald, and the king replaced the previous charter (said to have been granted *'ex sinistra informatione')* with one to Ranald Alanesoun as his father's heir. Put in possession of Castle Tioram, he was quickly thrown out when John gained his freedom, and his supporters defeated in a battle at Loch Lochy where both he and Lovat were killed.

John was one of the council which met to plan the restoration of the Lordship of the Isles in Donald Dubh's rebellion a year later, but he lived to enjoy his hard-won position for another forty years. His grandson Donald, who had a charter of the barony of Castletirrim as captain or chief in 1610, was one of the chiefs who assented to the Statutes of Iona in 1609, and the more detailed agreement with the Privy Council in 1616; this allowed him a 'civil and comelie' house at Eilean Tioram, limited his household to six gentlemen, and as there was no 'mains' or home farm at the castle he agreed to cultivate the lands of Howbeg in South Uist.

Strong and prosperous, the Clanranald took a leading position among the clans from the time of Charles I to Culloden. There were 700 of them at Killiecrankie, and the young chief, after going abroad rather than take the oath of allegiance to William, fell at the head of his clan at Sheriffmuir; his brother Ranald, also 'out' in 1715, died in the certainty that his successor 'and all his clan' would always be among the first to appear for the king 'as they ever had been when occasion offered'. But their cousin the laird of Benbecula, who succeeded, left a cautious brother to make his excuses when Prince Charles arrived off their islands; and the family reputation was only saved by the chief's son Ranald promptly raising 300 men, officered by Clanranald cadets, and standing firmly by the prince from Glenfinnan to the end. Being wrongly named 'Donald' in the Act, he escaped attainder, but assured Charles that if his estate was regained he would venture it again whenever H.R.H. required. Regained it was, and then lost by an extravagant grandson, despite a net income from his kelp shores of £10,000 during the 'boom' years.

The family's last territorial possession was Castle Tioram and a small piece of land round it.

MACDONALD OF KEPPOCH

MACDONALD OF KEPPOCH

ALTHOUGH the story of the Macdonalds of Keppoch may seem to be merely a record of continual strife with those in authority, it has other points of interest which illustrate the relations between government and chief and between chief and people, and the position of the bard in the life of the clan.

Alasdair Carrach, the youngest son of John Lord of the Isles by his marriage with a daughter of the Steward (later Robert II), was Lord of Lochaber. He supported his brother Donald at Harlaw in 1411, and is said also to have helped his nephew Donald Balloch to defeat the royal forces at Inverlochy twenty years later. For this his lands in Lochaber were forfeited and granted to the

Mackintoshes, who had fought on the king's side; but Alasdair's descendants, the Macdonalds of Keppoch, refused to acknowledge Mackintosh's superiority, claiming possession as well as tenancy of their lands by right of the sword and not of sheepskin. Every effort to dispossess them was unsuccessful until the ruin of Keppoch and his people after the Rising of 1745.

Not unnaturally, such unsettled conditions were sometimes reflected within the clan itself. About the end of the 15th century the chief, Iain Alainn, displeased his clansmen by giving up a local trouble-maker to Mackintosh for punishment, thereby appearing to recognise his authority in Lochaber; he was accordingly 'deposed from the chiefship by the elders of his tribe' (according to a local tradition accepted by the historian Donald Gregory), and the succession eventually settled on the family of his uncle. Most of the descendants both of the late chief and of another competitor accepted this arrangement, but some generations later, in 1663, the young chief Alasdair and his brother were murdered by some discontented followers. The crime may have been caused by attempts to bring order into the country, but no steps were taken to punish those responsible until the Keppoch bard, Iain Lom, horrified by his clansmen's indifference, pleaded first with Glengarry and then with Sir James Macdonald of Sleat to use their influence. Sir James obtained a commission of fire and sword against the murderers, and the crime and its avenging are commemorated by the 'well of the heads' near Invergarry —a striking example of the power of the poet in clan affairs.

The most remarkable chief of Keppoch was 'Coll of the Cows', who earned his soubriquet from Dundee himself (Graham of Claverhouse) because of the ease with which he found any cattle driven out of the way into the hills. He was a born rebel, even if conditions had not made him one, and it was typical that at the Revolution he was in trouble with the governments of both James and William. At Mulroy, near Keppoch where the rivers Roy and Spean meet, he defeated Mackintosh in 1688 in the last clan battle fought in the Highlands. Because an officer in the king's service was killed, a troop of dragoons and 200 foot guards were sent to 'destroy man, woman and child, pertaining to the Laird of Cappagh, and to burn his houses and corn'. Meantime Coll had an old score to settle with the burgh of Inverness, where as a boy the magistrates had allowed Mackintosh to imprison him without trial; so when he went to join Dundee at Inverness in 1689 he laid siege to the town and extorted the huge sum of 4,000 merks, for which he was rebuked by Dundee in 'very sharp terms'.

The Macdonalds of Keppoch were 'out' in 1715 and again in 1745 for the Jacobite cause. After the skirmish at High Bridge on the Spean which opened the second Rising, the chief personally received the surrender of the Government party, and he joined the prince with 300 of his clan at Glenfinnan soon after the standard was raised. They fought through the campaign, losing their chief at Culloden, and were still in arms more than a month later, when most of the clans had submitted.

There are still living those who claim descent from Keppoch, including several notable families in Canada, but Skene's epitaph on the family is worth recalling: 'They were the last of the Highlanders who retained the system of predatory warfare, in which at one time all were equally engaged; and . . . they preserved the warlike and high-spirited character of the ancient Highlander until it terminated with their own existence'.

MACDONALD OF SLEAT

MACDONALD OF SLEAT, DRESS

As the heirs of the last Earl of Ross and Lord of the Isles of the Macdonald line, and occupying lands granted to their ancestor by him and later confirmed by the crown, the chiefs of Sleat had a place of special importance in the Clan Donald. Their people were known as Clanhuistean or *Clann Uisdean,* from Hugh the brother of the last lord to whom Sleat was granted in the 15th century, or as Clan Donald North to distinguish them from the Islay Macdonalds, and six of the early chiefs in succession were named Donald—Donald Gallich, Donald Gruamach, Donald Gorm, Donald Gormson, Donald Gorm *mor,* and (Sir) Donald Gorm *oig*.

Donald Gruamach (the grim) tried to recover the forfeited Lordship of the Isles, but was killed by an arrow while laying siege to the Mackenzie stronghold of Eilean Donan in 1539. He left a child as heir, and it appears that some of the clan as well as their leader were held responsible, for along with the young chief's two uncles, twenty-seven others with various patronymics were granted remission for their part in the siege and in the 'herschip' (or plundering) of Kinlochewe and Trotternish during the same expedition. Donald Gormson took Queen Mary's side and gave his support in the 'Chase about Raid', and to settle a quarrel with Mackenzie of Kintail he accepted the mediation of the Regent Moray. But the greatest of these early chiefs was Donald Gorm *mor,* who after a turbulent career came to terms with James VI in 1596 and obtained a Great Seal charter of his lands, including part of the disputed Trotternish. He had led 500 warriors to help the Irish rebels against Elizabeth two years before; and having been warned not to do so again he is found offering the English queen his services as 'Lord of the Isles of Scotland and chief of the whole Clan Donald Irishmen wheresoever' in 1598, recalling their predecessors' friendship and mutual help, listing the island chiefs who would follow him on any enterprise, and blandly proposing to induce Macleod of Harris and Sir James Macdonald to stir up rebellion and trouble for King James in the West Highlands. Soon afterwards the Macdonalds of Sleat and the Macleods were pursuing a sharp quarrel between Donald and Sir Rory of Dunvegan, whose sister he had married and then repudiated, and only after some bloodshed was a reconciliation effected by some of their friends.

During his later years this great Donald is found supporting authority, and just before his death he acquiesced with other island chiefs in a limitation of their households. Duntulm in Trotternish was named as his residence, replacing Dunskaith on the north side of Sleat (which had been the family's first home), and it was not finally deserted until 1732. His son Donald Gorm *oig* (one of the first Baronets of Nova Scotia, and nominal owner of 16,000 acres in New Brunswick) was a man of means and importance at a time when the chief was still regarded as a leader of men in war and his hall as a centre of culture and social intercourse. The family bards and pipers were given lands in Trotternish and elsewhere, along with a victual and money payment, in return for their services on a hereditary basis.

There can be little doubt of the Jacobite sympathies of the Macdonalds of Sleat, but their record is confused by the illness and untimely death of a succession of chiefs—one Sir Donald in 1692, another in 1718, and Sir Alexander in 1746. The clan played its part under Dundee, for 500 or more joined his rising and five near relations of the chief fell at Killiecrankie; Sir Donald was 'out' again in 1715, but his two brothers led the clan. After an expensive appeal, the estates were forfeited, but later restored to the family; and in 1745 Sir Alexander, disappointed that the prince came without support and influenced by Duncan Forbes of Culloden, refused to raise his clan. His son was made an Irish peer as Lord Macdonald and married a Yorkshire heiress, but a runaway marriage in the next generation led to the division of the family's Scottish and English estates between two brothers, backed by a private Act of Parliament. Following a Court of Session judgment in 1910 the senior line resumed the baronetcy and chiefship of the Macdonalds of Sleat, while Lord Macdonald remained in possession of much of the territory inherited from their common ancestors.

MACDONELL OF GLENGARRY

MACDONELL OF GLENGARRY

In one of Macaulay's graphic phrases the Macdonells of Glengarry are pictured as coming from the great valley where a chain of lakes, unknown to fame and scarcely set down in maps, was later to become the daily highway between west and east. And with that process their history is largely bound up.

The Glengarry chiefs descend from Donald, son of the founder of Clanranald of Garmoran who was passed over in the succession to the Lordship of the Isles. He established a separate branch, whose first possession was North Morar, but shortly afterwards they had the lands of Glen Garry which formed part of the lordship of Lochaber. In the first half of the 16th century half the lands of Lochalsh, Lochcarron and Lochbroom, with the castle of Strome, came to the family by marriage with an heiress of the House of the Isles. This brought them into conflict with the expanding power of the Mackenzies, and the later part of the century was filled with incessant feuds. There was time, however, to carry on a timber trade with Inverness by taking wood down in boats through Loch Ness, until it was interrupted by Lovat (according to a complaint by Glengarry to the Privy Council in 1575) to the hurt of the burgh and the country in general. In the 17th century Glengarry and his people gave powerful support to Charles I and II, and the chief Æneas or Angus was created Lord Macdonell and Aros at the Restoration (when this spelling of the name was adopted).

Not content with a peerage and a pension, and being regarded by the king as the leading chief of Clan Donald, Lord Macdonell wanted to be made Earl of Ross. His excessive pride brought discord into the clan; living at court or on a small estate which he acquired near Inverness, he may well have lost touch with his clansmen and turned a blind eye to some of their activities. When two Macdonells were killed in a market day quarrel in Inverness in 1665, the chief proposed an 'offensive and defensive league' between his clan and the burgh, on condition that a heavy fine was paid, any citizen who had shed Macdonell blood given up, and 'wheresoever the people of Inverness or any person of them sees my Lord McDonald, his friends, followers or any one of them, that then and immediately they should lay down their arms on the ground in token of obedience and submission'. The council refused to listen to 'such despotic insolence' (as Macaulay called it), but on reference to the Privy Council the town was ordered to pay £4,800 Scots in name of damages with the fees of the surgeon who attended the wounded clansmen. Along with Sir James and Clanranald, Lord Macdonell was ordered in 1669 to appear annually before the Privy Council to renew a bond for keeping the peace in the Highlands, and he saw the inside of Edinburgh castle for four months in 1672 when (as 'cheiff of the name and clan of McDonald') he failed to produce Keppoch and others to become caution for their dependents.

On his death in 1680 the title expired and the chief reverted to the name Glengarry. When Dundee raised the clans for King James in 1689 it was Alasdair *dubh* who commanded the Glengarry men, and at Killiecrankie 300 of them fought under him and 100 under his brother. Invergarry castle was so strong that King William, in his order for the massacre of Glencoe, allowed discretion in the case of Glengarry who had also not taken the oath of allegiance, and Alasdair lived to fight at Sheriffmuir. In 1745, 600 of the clan under Lochgarry and the chief's son Angus joined the prince; after Culloden the treacherous Barrisdale made the excuse that he and others had been forced out, and Glengarry was arrested and not released until October 1749. The chief whom Scott knew and Raeburn painted 'retained in their full extent the whole feelings of clanship and chieftainship, elsewhere so long abandoned', but he carried to absurd lengths an argument with Clanranald over the chiefship, and as 'arch-enemy' of Government road and canal construction in the Great Glen he fought for his rights to privacy and compensation. In his successor's time, burdened with debt and saddened by evictions, the Glengarry property passed from the race, except for the site and ruin of Invergarry castle and the family burial ground.

MACDOUGALL

MACDOUGALL

DUGALD, one of the sons of Somerled amongst whom his kingdom was divided, was chosen King of the Isles in 1156. His descendants for several generations used the designation 'of Argyll' *(de Ergadia)*, later modified to 'of Lorn', and finally abandoned in favour of the patronymic name MacDougall. The family possessions included Lorn and Benderloch on the mainland, and Mull, Lismore, Coll and Tiree; their castles were Dunstaffnage and Dunollie, and great island fortresses like Cairnburg in the Treshnish group and Dunchonnel in the Garvellachs, all sea-based and calling for a sizeable fleet of 'birlings' or galleys to link them together and keep their garrisons supplied.

The family held their island territory from the King of Norway until it was ceded to Scotland in 1266, and for the forty years which followed they held the leading position there. As they were of the same stock as the Macdonalds, there was some rivalry between the two. The MacDougalls supported John Balliol as king, and later acted for Edward I in the Western Isles; Alexander of Argyll had married a Comyn, and after the murder of her nephew by Bruce at Dumfries in 1306 he and his son became the hunted king's bitterest foes. How nearly they came to capturing him was recalled by the traditional 'brooch of Lorn' which he is supposed to have left in their hands while making his escape; but in the later campaign in Argyll John of Lorn was defeated at the pass of Brander, Dunstaffnage was taken, and organised MacDougall opposition came to an end.

After King Robert's death some of their forfeited estates were restored to the MacDougalls. In 1354 another John of Lorn arranged with John of the Isles (his Macdonald cousin) to give up any claim to the islands of Mull, Tiree and part of Jura, receiving Coll and certain other lands with the right to build eight vessels of twelve and sixteen oars each. John had no sons, and his lands passed with heiresses to two Stewart brothers and then to the Earls of Argyll. But the MacDougalls came into some of their own territory again in 1451, when the Stewart lord of Lorn made a grant to 'John Macalan of Lorn called McCowle' of lands round Oban Bay, in Kerrera, and extending down the coast at least as far as Loch Melfort. Some events which followed, including the murder of the Stewart incomer, may be connected with intrigues by the Lord of the Isles with the King of England, or with discontent within the clan. By the 16th century MacDougall of Dunollie was acknowledging Argyll as his superior, and accepting office as Bailie of Lorn under him; and the family's old rights in the offshore islands of Seil, Luing, Torsay and Shuna were recognised.

Although they had largely dropped out of public affairs, the MacDougalls were not forgotten. In 1587 'McCoull of Lorne' and 'McCoull of Roray' were listed among the Highland landlords and chiefs, and the 'Clandowill of Lorne' among the clans; when the chief disclaimed responsibility for certain trouble-makers as not being his tenants, a full inquiry was ordered by the Privy Council. As late as 1712 the laird of Dunollie had to pay charges in the duke's court at Inveraray for having protected a Knapdale man (not a MacDougall) who had stolen a few horses, as 'his chiftain on whom he has dependence'. Besides the important Raray family, there were cadet branches of Gallanach and Soroba.

The MacDougalls were royalists, and suffered for it in the civil wars. In 1647 the chief and his young son took arms for King Charles with 500 of their kindred, friends and tenants; Dunollie was besieged, and Gylen castle on Kerrera sacked. Many MacDougalls died in the massacre after the capitulation of Dunaverty in Kintyre, but the young chief was spared and lived to recover his lands at the Restoration. In 1715 Dunollie held out under the laird's Macdonald wife, while he was 'out' with the Jacobite army at Sheriffmuir. The estate was forfeited to Argyll, and he went abroad for some time, but his infant son was brought up by a loyal clansman in Dumbarton. According to Sir Walter Scott, the young man planned to join Prince Charles in 1745, but was dissuaded just in time by Argyll and had his 'little estate' returned to him.

The story of the MacDougalls, wrote Sir Walter, 'affords a very rare if not a unique instance of a family of such unlimited power, and so distinguished during the middle ages, surviving the decay of their grandeur, and flourishing in a private station.'

MACFARLANE

MACFARLANE

One of the main routes from the Lowlands to the western and north-western Highlands passes over the narrow neck of land from Tarbet on Loch Lomond to Arrochar on Loch Long. This with the land to the north of it around Loch Sloy was the country of 'wild MacFarlane's plaided clan' (as Scott called them), and appears as a lovely land of lochs, waterfalls and glens, and a warlike people, or—according to the viewpoint—a 'land of savage hills, swept by savage rains, peopled by savage sheep, tended by savage people', as Robert Burns unkindly put it.

The keepers of this natural doorway were descended from the old Celtic Earls of Lennox, and the MacFarlane chiefs looked on themselves as 'the true representatives of that great and ancient family'. Proved by charter evidence, the descent dates from the first half of the 13th century, when the third earl gave the lands of Arrochar to his brother Gilchrist. The clan surname is derived from his great-grandson Bartholomew, in the abbreviated Gaelic form of Parlan or Parlane. Over the centuries the MacFarlane chiefs made their homes on an island in Loch Lomond, a castle at Inveruglas, and houses first at East Tarbet and then at Arrochar.

As kinsmen and followers of the Stewart Earls of Lennox who succeeded the old line as feudal superiors, the MacFarlanes found themselves involved in national quarrels. Lennox took the English side when Henry VIII stirred up trouble during Queen Mary's childhood, and when he landed at Dumbarton in an attempted invasion in 1544 he was joined by Walter MacFarlane of Tarbet with seven score men from the head of the Lennox—'light footmen, well armed in shirtes of mayle, with bows and two-handed swords', according to Holinshed, speaking Gaelic and English. Three years later the English under Somerset invaded Scotland on the east, and MacFarlane is said to have joined the national levies and fallen at Pinkie with at least one of his cadets (from Ardleish near the head of Loch Lomond). His son Andrew led the clan against the queen's supporters at Langside in 1568, and in Cromwell's day the chief was twice besieged in Inveruglas and had his castle burned down.

There was practice too for the art of war at home, where the moon was known as 'MacFarlane's lantern', and feuds and raids kept them and their neighbours busy. In 1592 MacFarlane and some of his people murdered Sir Humphrey Colquhoun, and some of 'Clanfarlane' were listed among the 'broken clans' two years later. In 1624 they had a blood feud on their hands from the slaughter of a MacFarlane by the Buchanans and of a Buchanan by the MacFarlanes. Both clans were represented at a special meeting with Highland landlords called by the Privy Council, when John MacFarlane of that Ilk and his eldest son agreed for themselves and 'taking the burden on them for the whole clan' to submit their quarrel to the council's judgment. No more is heard of it in the record.

The chief at the Revolution was appointed a colonel of local volunteers, and was one of the few Highlanders who subscribed to the Darien scheme. He was sanguine enough in 1697 to build a 'handsome house, beautiful with pleasure gardens' at New Tarbet, and there his son Walter, though a Jacobite at heart, stayed at home when Prince Charles swept southwards in the autumn of 1745. A branch of the family in Ireland trace their descent from a MacFarlane who had fought at Prestonpans, and had three uncles killed under Marlborough at Malplaquet; Walter preferred quieter pursuits, with a 'zest for a good pedigree, intense love of Scotland, and jackdaw-like acquisitiveness' which give permanent value to his antiquarian and genealogical collections.

Times were changing, and the building of a new road from Dumbarton to Inveraray, interrupted by the Rising, was resumed in 1746. Lowland sheep farmers, at first unpopular as 'neither lineal descendants nor collateral branches of the Macfarlane race' (as an alien minister sourly observed), came and gradually broke down the old attachment to the laird as chief. Walter's brother William, a physician in Edinburgh, had to sell the estate in 1784, although another brother had acquired a fortune in Jamaica. But the name lingered on in the district, and when Loch Sloy became a focal point in hydro-electric development after the Second World War a MacFarlane lady of ninety-six, brought up in the days of tallow candles, was found to switch on Arrochar's first electric light.

MACFIE

MACFIE

AMONG the familes associated with the Clan Donald, and perhaps descended from the same stock, were the Macfies or MacDuffies of Colonsay. Their title to the island is supposed to have been one of 'immemorial occupation', in the absence of any evidence of the tenure by which they held it from the Lord of the Isles. There were presumably also the usual conditions of military service, and the Macdonald annalist records a MacDuffie of Colonsay in the forces of Donald Balloch when he raised a rebellion on behalf of the Lord of the Isles and defeated a royal army at Inverlochy in 1431.

Although not named as a member of the council of the lordship, which met at Finlaggan in Islay, MacDuffie was hereditary keeper of the records of the Isles. 'Donald McDuffee' witnessed a charter of John, Earl of Ross and Lord of the Isles at Dingwall in 1463, and another by the earl's half-brother Celestine (whose mother was said to be a MacDuffie of Colonsay) at Inverlochy nine years later. From a tombstone in Iona, on which he is called 'Lord of Dunevin in Colonsay' (the name of a hill fort overlooking Scalasaig harbour), we know that Malcolm MacDuffie married a sister of John Macian of Ardnamurchan, one of the most powerful Clan Donald chieftains at the close of the 15th century.

When the Lord of the Isles was forfeited in 1493, the superiority of Colonsay passed to the Crown, but the MacDuffies' tenure does not seem to have been affected. Macian was active in helping to suppress attempts to revive the lordship, and one of the claimants, Celestine's son Sir Alexander of Lochalsh, was caught in Oransay, so it is likely that MacDuffie would be involved. The laird who was summoned to answer for treason in 1531 was presumably the 'Murchardus' whose finely decorated tombstone in Oransay records his death in 1539. It seems that a succession of MacDuffies were priors of Oransay, but one who was accused of having attacked and robbed a vessel off the entrance to Loch Foyle in 1583 would be a layman and not a cleric.

The Macfies took the Macdonald side in the great feud with the Macleans, and when James VI tried to bring about better order in the Highlands and Islands, 'McFee of Collowsay' was listed among the chiefs and landlords to be held responsible. His successor was one of the twelve leading islanders who accepted the 'statutes of Iona' in 1609. When Sir James Macdonald of Isla raised a new rebellion in 1615, however, Malcolm Macfie of Colonsay joined him with 'his haill name' (another report said he commanded forty men) and became one of his chief supporters. As a result Colonsay was 'violently wrested' from him by Coll *Keitach* (left-handed) Macdonald, who handed over Malcolm and eighteen others to Argyll; brought before the Privy Council in Edinburgh, they spent many weary months as prisoners in the Tolbooth. Malcolm managed to return to his island, but was hunted down and caught, after seeking refuge in Oransay; Coll and five others were charged in 1623 with the 'cruell slaughter' of Malcolm and four companions at the instance of his widow, son and three daughters.

The memory of the old 'lords of Colonsay' lived long on the island. Martin wrote about 1700 of the MacDuffie tombs on Oransay that their 'coats-of-arms and colour staff' was fixed in a stone, through which a hole was made to hold it; seventy years later the traveller Pennant was told that on this 'miraculously preserved' staff depended 'the fate of the *Macdufian* race'. It seems to have been renewed from time to time even as late as 1850, when a Macfie from Islay whose father had been a tenant in Colonsay came over to perform the ceremony. Over the years the island population fell and the clan dispersed, but even when only one Macfie family was left in Colonsay the dark complexions noticed in Martin's day persisted. A branch of the Colonsay clan settled in Lochaber, where they followed Lochiel, and they were once numerous in Glendessary and on Locharkaigside. A Macfie helped to support the staff when the royal standard was raised at Glenfinnan in 1745, and another, as senior resident magistrate, welcomed George IV when he landed at Leith in 1822. Landed families have included the Macfies of Langhouse in Renfrewshire, who hailed from Ayrshire, and their cadets of Airds in Argyll and of Dreghorn near Edinburgh.

MACGILLIVRAY

MACGILLIVRAY

THERE is a tradition that the MacGillivrays came from the west, and the name was once prominent in the Isle of Mull, but as a clan they were associated for some five centuries with the Clan Chattan. Neither sharing nor claiming to share any common descent, they appear to have been the first independent small clan to join the confederacy.

The MacGillivrays were settled in and around upper Strathnairn in Inverness-shire, where their earliest possession was Dunmaglass. Various writs in the Mackintosh collection carry their genealogy back to one Ian *ciar* (brown John), about the mid-15th century. Those were the days of Gaelic patronymics, before surnames were in general use, and in 1549 the scribes recorded Ian's grandson Farquhar as 'Farchar M'Conquhy M'Ankeir of

Dowmachglas' and other uncouth spellings. In 1609, when Clan Chattan met at Termit in Petty near Inverness to show their loyalty to Mackintosh as chief, the 'haill kin and race of the clan M'illivray' were represented by their leading men, Malcolm M'Bean in Dalcrombie, Ewen macEwen in Aberchalder, and Duncan macFarquhar in Dunmaglass. Malcolm, one of the Clan Chattan leaders called to answer before the Privy Council in 1607 for good rule during the Mackintosh chief's minority, was probably acting as tutor for his own young chief two years later. In 1626 Farquhar macAlister became the first MacGillivray to secure a heritable right to Dunmaglass from the Campbells of Cawdor, and in his time the MacGillivrays were probably at the height of their influence. There were three MacGillivray heritors in the parish of Daviot and Dunlichity in 1644, and Farquhar signed the Clan Chattan bond of 1664 along with his two sons, Donald (known from his later position as 'Tutor of Dunmaglass'), founder of the Dalcrombie line, and William of Lairgs, ancestor of another family.

The MacGillivrays were active in the Jacobite rising of 1715, when the chief's two sons were captain and lieutenant in the Clan Chattan regiment; a MacGillivray was executed at Wigan in 1716. In 1745 Alexander, the chief, was chosen to command the composite regiment raised by Lady Mackintosh, consisting of Mackintoshes, MacGillivrays, Farquharsons and Macbeans; at Culloden their charge penetrated the enemy front, and they lost a great many men and most of the officers, including their leader. The chief's brother William survived, and after army service in India he was able, with the help of another brother who had made a fortune in America, to increase the family estate.

His son's death was followed by lawsuits over the succession, and in 1858 Neil John of the Dalcrombie line, whose father was a member of the Legislative Council in Canada, came into possession. After his death Dunmaglass was sold, and by 1890 another of the old Clan Chattan families was landless in Strathnairn. The burial grounds at Dunlichity of the Shaws of Tordarroch and the MacGillivrays of Dunmaglass are now marked by armorial panels, the latter bearing the arms matriculated in 1967 in the name of Farquhar, who was chief when the Lyon Register was established in 1672.

The MacGillivrays are reckoned as an old family in Mull, and according to one account they sat on the council of the Lords of the Isles. After the fall of the lordship in 1493 they followed the Macleans of Duart, and 'Neil MacIlra' was one of a dozen or so principal vassals named by Hector of Duart in 1616. Two years later Donald MacGillivray of Pennyghael, near the head of Loch Scridain, appears on record, and his son and successor Martin was a churchman and a militant supporter of the king who suffered for his loyalty. Pennyghael seems to have passed from the MacGillivrays in the time of his great-nephew Alexander, who was served heir in 1731, but the name was still fairly common (particularly in the districts of Ross and Brolass) when it was bought back in 1819 by William McGillivray, the Canadian fur-trader and head of the North West Company. Born not far from Dunmaglass, like his uncle and patron Simon McTavish, he ended his days as the owner of another old MacGillivray property. This is appropriate in a clan which may have originated in the west, and so is the fact that the Macgillivray who arranged for the name to be commemorated at Dunlichity comes from Fort William, Ontario, itself named in honour of the head of the old fur trade empire of which it was once the centre.

MACGREGOR

MACGREGOR

CLAN Gregor are as notable for their 'unsubduable vitality' as for the savagery of the official attempts to exterminate them. For long landless and even nameless, they became the victims of king and privy council, the prey of more powerful neighbours, and an object of sympathy and admiration among many of their fellow-Highlanders.

With a firm belief in their royal descent, the MacGregors claimed some of the finest valleys of western Perthshire and Argyll as the possessions of their ancestors. As Campbell lairds grew in influence, the leading families were reduced to the role of tenants owing military service as well as rents to an alien proprietor. Their natural allegiance was to their own chief, MacGregor of Glenstrae, but while he was answerable by law for any offences they committed, he could hardly control a clan so widely scattered on other men's lands. It is not surprising that the clan became a byword for raiding, burning and killing; as early as Queen Mary's reign, in 1562 and 1564, neighbouring chiefs were set to pursue the Clan Gregor with fire and sword. They must have been glad to have official sanction for expelling the clan from their own bounds, and Campbell of Glenorchy in particular abused it to such an extent that his commission was rescinded.

James VI, who tried to bring order into the Highlands after he assumed control in 1587, resolved to make an example of 'the wicked and unhappie race of the clan Gregour', and gave orders 'to pursue and prosecute them with all rigour and extremetie'. Their insolence, and the king's vengeance, came to a head with the massacre of the Colquhouns at Glenfruin in February 1603. On the very day he set off from Edinburgh for his new throne in London, his 'parting thunderbolt' was an Act of Council proscribing and abolishing the name, because 'the bair and simple name of McGregoure maid that haill Clane to presume of thair power, force and strenthe, and did encourage thame, without reverence of the law or fear of punischement, to go forward in thair iniquities'. Within a year the chief and eleven of his clan were hanged at Edinburgh, and a price of £1,000 each was put on the heads of other leaders, 100 merks for lesser men, and any clansman could earn his own pardon by bringing in the head of another of equal rank. For years the pursuit continued with no lasting effect, although when 'ane McGregouris heid' was handed in to the Privy Council the reward was paid. In 1611 a new commission was given to Argyll to 'root out and extirpate' all of the race and their collaborators; women and children were to be moved to the Lowlands, the MacGregors' wives being branded 'with ane key upon the face'; in 1613 it was ordered that no MacGregor who had been concerned in Glenfruin and other incidents should carry any weapon 'except ane pointless knife to cut their meat', and that not more than four of the clan were to be seen together, even under changed names.

London influence did nothing to diminish the king's anger, and on his return to Scotland in 1617 he saw to it that the laws on name, knife and numbers were re-enacted. The only bright spot in the whole 'sickening story' was that the MacGregors found shelter, in spite of the heavy fines imposed on their protectors, even in distant parts like the Grant and Mackenzie countries. The campaign was continued by Charles I, but 'few or nane' appeared to renounce their names and the 'haill surname' was denounced afresh in 1635. Yet a MacGregor contingent joined Montrose, and they asked to be allowed to serve as a united clan in the campaign which ended at Worcester. This 'loyalty and affection' was rewarded at the Restoration, when the penal enactments were rescinded, but after a brief interval during which the name could be freely used the Revolution parliament of 1693 re-enacted the whole lot. Two companies of the clan from Balquhidder fought for the Stuarts in 1745–6, and in 1774, when people were already using the name again, the proscription was at last removed for ever. As if to make belated amends, when the 'Honours of Scotland' were carried before the Sovereign in Edinburgh in 1822 and 1953 the MacGregors were given a place of honour in the escort.

The fame of Rob Roy's exploits did something to even the score between authority and the clan that was for so long made 'nameless by day', but the survival of the Clan Gregor shows how impossible it is to eradicate the spirit of a Highland clan.

MACKAY

MACKAY

MACKAY's country was the great district of Strathnaver, which once stretched from the bounds of Caithness to Cape Wrath. There fertile valleys like Strathhalladale, Strathnaver and Strathmore contrasted with the great expanse of mountain and moorland in Durness and Eddrachillis in the west. This north-west corner, 'the outmaist boundis of Scotland', produced a hardy and independent race of men, who fought long to protect their possessions and maintain their patriarchal society when it was threatened from outside.

The Mackays were known as the 'Clan Morgan', a designation hard to explain unless they were connected with the Aberdeenshire Morgans, as they were with the Forbeses. Their chiefs first come into history as a clan in opposition to Donald of the Isles in his bid for the earldom of Ross, but within a few years Angus of Strathnaver, now married to Donald's sister, received from him a charter of Strathhalladale and other lands. When Angus answered James I's summons to Inverness in 1427 he was described as a leader of 4,000 men, which may represent the strength of the joint force which he had commanded in the north.

The whole clan were involved in their chief's struggle against the earldom of Sutherland, an outpost of feudal power which passed into Gordon hands soon after Flodden. In ten pitched battles fought between 1400 and 1550 Mackay manpower was seriously reduced (it was down to a mere 800 by 1745). Their possession of Strathnaver goes back beyond recorded history, but the chief held no lands by royal charter before 1499, when he received Strathy and others as reward for capturing a Sutherland outlaw. It was probably to secure his rights by legal documents that the chief Aodh (a popular Gaelic name, sometimes rendered Y or Iye) had the Lord of the Isles charter put on record in 1506, and in 1511 his two sons were formally legitimated. He even acknowledged the Gordon 'takeover' by bonds of friendship with Huntly's son, who had married the Sutherland heiress, and with their son and successor. The position might have been thought secure, especially when Donald Mackay received a royal charter in 1539 erecting his lands into the barony of Farr. But he lost favour with the ruling faction, and on the old pretext that his father was not legitimate (despite all the formalities) he became a vassal first of Huntly and then of Sutherland, from whom Mackay eventually agreed to hold his lands in 1589; a reconciliation and marriage alliance could not disguise the fact that the Mackay country had been annexed to the earldom of Sutherland.

This sad period of Mackay history was followed by events which raised the name to military distinction in Europe. Donald Mackay of Farr, knighted in 1616 and created a Baronet of Nova Scotia and Lord Reay (from a new part of the estate on the borders of Caithness) in 1628, arranged for a large body of his clansmen and neighbours to fight under the Protestant banner in support of Charles I's sister, Elizabeth, Queen of Bohemia. Mackay's Regiment learned the art of war under Christian IV of Denmark and perfected it with the 'invincible Gustavus', King of Sweden. Later Hugh Mackay of Scourie (who became King William's commander-in-chief in Scotland) raised a new regiment in the Netherlands which many clansmen joined. At the end of the 18th century Mackay of Bighouse commanded the Reay Fencibles (the 'brave and honest Reays'), and the 93rd Highlanders consisted largely of Sutherland men.

Ruined financially, the first Lord Reay sold some of his lands to pay his debts, and Strathnaver passed finally to the Sutherland family. Others followed, and before the last of the Mackay country in the chief's possession was sold in 1829 the old order was passing and the glens and straths were being cleared of their people to make way for sheep. The notorious 'Sutherland clearances' scattered the clan far and wide, as the people made new homes round the coast or overseas. Some clansmen in Glasgow banded together in 'Mackay's Society' and no doubt smoothed the path of city life for many from the Reay country; after being reconstituted in 1888 as the first modern clan society they led the way in historical research and other activities.

There have been other Mackays in Galloway and Kintyre since the days of Robert Bruce, and the only surviving Gaelic charter (1408) was granted by the Lord of the Isles to a Mackay in Islay.

MACKENZIE

MACKENZIE

ALTHOUGH the territory of the Mackenzies came to stretch from sea to sea, their first homeland was the Kintail country around Loch Duich in Wester Ross, among mountains pierced by the valleys of Glenshiel, Glen Lichd and Glen Elchaig, and its seaward entrance guarded by the castle of Eilean Donan. Gradually they pressed outward, establishing themselves in Lewis across the Minch, and in the fertile valley through which the River Conon flows to meet the Cromarty Firth. Leaving Eilean Donan as a western outpost, they lived in the 15th century at Kinellan, near Strathpeffer, before making their home at Brahan, near Dingwall, where they built themselves a castle.

The forfeiture of the earldom of Ross (1476) and Lordship of the Isles (1493) opened the way for the 'land-hungry' Mackenzies. Their chief Alexander, who had some contact with the court after meeting King James at Inverness in 1427, had already received lands in the earldom, and later he obtained forfeited Macdonald lands without antagonising any powerful neighbours. The Mackenzies resisted attempts to restore the earldom, and increased their influence by advantageous marriages. The chief was given feudal jurisdiction in 1509, when his estates were erected into the barony of Eileandonan; he was able to weather a storm raised by his uncle Hector (founder of the Gairloch line), who thought he had a better right to the chiefship.

The Mackenzies had an unusual number of landed cadet families, most of them founded before 1600; six men, all younger sons of a chief with their descendants founded twenty-five separate landed families, ten of them springing from Gairloch. After 1600 five main cadets appeared, and they founded another sixteen landed families within the clan. Kenneth was created Lord Mackenzie of Kintail in 1609, and his son raised to the earldom of Seaforth in 1623, but the family relationship remained as several incidents show. The chief took twenty-four of his ablest men in Kintail and Lochalsh along with some of his kinsmen when he tried to bargain with his cousin the laird of Grant over a claim against Glengarry; thinking the price excessive, he insisted on consulting his clansmen, who offered to take what their chief wanted by force—with the result that Grant promptly reduced his demand to one-third. At another time, when an Earl of Seaforth took it into his head to pull down Brahan castle, the 'brave Mackenzies' came to him in a body and said, 'Wiser men than you built this castle—you shall not demolish it'.

After some wavering during Montrose's early campaign, Seaforth took up the Stewart cause which was ultimately to ruin his family. Opposition to Cromwell's government brought down on Kintail an army under Monck himself, and a garrison was planted in Brahan 'uppon Seafort's nose'. In 1715 Earl William brought 3,000 men into the field for King James, and many of them fell at Sheriffmuir; forfeited, he escaped to France (where his tenants' rents were sent to him), but returned in 1719 and was wounded at Glenshiel. With a chief in exile, and the notable Cromartie cadet family in financial difficulties, Mackenzie influence waned in the North. It was reckoned in 1745 that Seaforth could raise 1,000 men, and the Mackenzie lairds 1,500 more; some of them were 'out', including the Earl of Cromartie, but the clan as a whole remained at home. When Seaforth himself tried to persuade some Kintail men to fight on the Government side, they are said to have 'twitted him to his teeth' and gone home saying 'they knew but one king, and if they were not at liberty to fight for him they would do it for no other'.

When infantry regiments were being raised by the chief towards the end of the 18th century, clansmen from all the Mackenzie estates enlisted, with most of the cadets contributing their quota on receiving commissions. An old Mackenzie prophecy was fulfilled when Lord Seaforth died in 1815, after losing his four sons; his lands passed to a daughter and her son sold all but Brahan and a small part of the ancestral estate. The line continued and another Seaforth peerage was created in 1921, but it too expired, and Brahan castle was demolished soon after the Second World War. The 14,000-acre estate of Kintail was acquired by the National Trust for Scotland, and today the mountaineer, the hill walker, and the naturalist enjoy the area where Mackenzie's warrior herdsmen once were bred.

MACKINNON

MACKINNON, DRESS

ALTHOUGH usually regarded as one of the lesser clans of the Hebrides, the Mackinnons must have been of considerable importance in the days of the Lordship of the Isles. A stipulation by the Lord of Lorn, when he surrendered Mull and other lands in 1354, that the keeping of the castle of 'Kerneburch' (Cairnburgh) in the Treshnish Isles should never be given to any of the race of 'clan Fynwyne', suggests that they were feared as well as respected. In an account of the Council of the Isles, which used to meet at Finlaggan in Islay, the Mackinnon chief is named as one of the four members of middle rank, after the chief barons and before the Clan Donald kinsmen. He figures in traditional accounts as 'master of the household' to the Lord of the Isles and later as 'marshal of his army', and in the records as a witness to charters at

Ardtornish in 1409 and at Dingwall in 1467. A humbler duty was to see weights and measures adjusted, and disputes over cards and dicing settled.

At first the Mackinnons seem to have had lands in the south of Mull, but these were exchanged for Mishnish in the north, which gave the chief his designation in 1467 and was held by the family for another 300 years. Their Skye lands were in the parish of Strath, known as Strathordill or *Srath Mhic Ionmhuinn* (Mackinnon's vale); after leaving the great castle of Dunakin, which commands the narrows at Kyleakin between Skye and the mainland, the chief's home was at Kilmorie in Strathaird. Now held direct from the Crown, their two properties were assessed at equal value, but Strathordill was the more important and by the 17th century it was a Mackinnon barony.

Along with the Macleans and other clans, the Mackinnons took part in attempts to revive the forfeited lordship. The rebel chiefs met at Dunakin in 1513, and Ewen Mackinnon of Strathordill was a member of the claimant Donald Dubh's 'council' in 1545. The 'Clankynnoun' were listed among the troublesome clans in 1587 and 1594, but the chief accepted the 'statutes of Iona' in 1609, bound himself to keep good order, and agreed to limit his household on the same scale as the Maclean lairds of Coll and Lochbuie.

There was trouble in Strath when the chief Lachlan *mor* died in 1696, leaving a boy of thirteen as heir. His stepfather and neighbour Sir Donald MacDonald and his kinsman Mackinnon of Corrichatachain (known as 'Corry') took over, identified the offenders and obtained authority to deal with them. It was feared that sending them for trial by the sheriff at Inverness might 'discover so many more as would go near to put the half of Mackinnon's lands out of tenantrie'. The chief, known as John *dubh*, was 'out' in the Rising of 1715 with 150 men, and had his estates forfeited (they were later restored); thirty years later he rose again, while MacDonald and MacLeod stayed at home or supported the Government, marched at the head of his own tenants to Edinburgh, and joined the Prince with 120 of 'the warriors of Mull and Strath'. When the Prince reached Skye during his wanderings after Culloden, he had to assume a disguise on entering Mackinnon's country, because 'he was liable to be discovered in every corner of it'. A cave in Strathaird was chosen as a hiding-place, and the chief later conducted him to the mainland.

A strange situation arose over the Mackinnon lands. Although the chief was attainted, and a prisoner for three and a half years, there was some doubt whether his estate could be forfeited as he was said to be only a liferenter. His only son had died in 1737, and his cousin John of Mishnish had been allowed to take possession as the next heir; but the old laird (who lived until 1756) married again and had another son Charles. Steps were taken to put Charles in possession and to recover what had been alienated because of Mackinnon's debts and Mishnish's 'impecuniosity'. A favourable decision in the Court of Sessions was reversed in the House of Lords, and all that fell to Charles was the Strathaird part of the Skye estate and Mishnish in Mull, both of which he sold—'and there is the end of a very ancient honourable family', wrote MacLeod of Talisker in 1789. The Strath tenants, about half of them Mackinnons, were at first much displeased with the decision 'from feelings of clanship and attachment to their chieftain'. After the death of Charles's son in 1808, the head of a branch of the family who had gone to Antigua found his way back to the Highlands, and round his descendants as chiefs the clan has recovered some of its old sense of kinship.

MACKINTOSH

MACKINTOSH

MACKINTOSH history ranges from Lochaber at the south end of the Great Glen to Petty on the shore of the Moray Firth, and eastwards into the valleys of the Nairn, Findhorn and Spey. The clan name means 'son of the *toiseach*' (or thane), and tradition traces them from a descendant of the Earls of Fife who received the lands of Petty and Strathdearn, with the office of keeper of the royal castle of Inverness, in the mid-12th century.

After one of the early chiefs had married Eva, 'heretrix' of Clan Chattan, the lands of Glenloy and Locharkaig in Lochaber were granted in the next generation, in 1336, by the Lord of the Isles. This led to some resentment among the Camerons, already living in the area, and a feud which broke out spasmodically and lasted for more than 300 years. Malcolm Mackintosh, who took over as chief from an easy-going nephew in 1409, added Glenroy and Glenspean to his Lochaber lands, and in doing so took on with the Macdonald of Keppoch inhabitants another fruitful cause of trouble.

The Clan Chattan confederacy, of which Mackintosh appears on record as captain in 1442 and thereafter frequently as captain or chief, gave him even wider interests and influence. He had a strong position in the North, where Moy was acquired as early as 1336 and he owned Dunachton from 1514, but his clansmen were put in a difficult position by the fact that the Lochaber situation was here reversed, as the Mackintosh lands lay partly within the old bishopric and earldom of Moray, and partly within Huntly's lordship of Badenoch. Such conflicting loyalties may have had something to do with the Mackintoshes' reputation for quick and fiery temper, and their being described in an old poem about the muster of the Lords of the Isles not only as lively and active, like several other clans, but also as numerous, powerful and arrogant. Even where he was not their feudal superior, the chief's role was important to his clansmen, and in the mid-16th century Bishop Leslie wrote of Mackintosh: 'He defends them against the invasion of their enemies, their neighbours, and he causes minister justice to them in the manner of the country, so that none should be suffered to make spoil or go in sorning, as they call it, or as vagabonds in the country'. The 1609 bond of loyalty to their chief provides that in the event of quarrels within the Clan Chattan he should name twelve principal clansmen to decide the issue with him and make the offender give satisfaction.

After the Restoration Mackintosh tried to settle the two major feuds which had troubled the clan. He secured a commission of fire and sword against the Camerons, but not unreasonably others were lukewarm in helping to put it into effect, and some of his own clansmen were prevented from joining him. A curious attempt at mediation was made at Inverness in 1664, with the Camerons on one bank of the River Ness and the Mackintoshes on the other, while the Bishop of Moray and Cumming of Altyre were rowed back and fore between them. But this and the Keppoch feud were not settled without some fighting, including the last clan battle at Mulroy, and until Lochiel acquired the superiority of Glenloy and Locharkaig and Mackintosh was confirmed in the superiority of Glenroy and Glenspean.

In 1715 and 1745 the Mackintoshes and Clan Chattan played their part on the Jacobite side. One of the most remarkable among the many Mackintosh cadets was William of Borlum, who led a division of the Jacobite army into the Lowlands in 1715, was captured and escaped, returned for the 1719 'attempt' and was again taken, and while in prison wrote an essay on agricultural improvement in which he insisted on tenants' rights to security of tenure. There was no comparable figure in 1745, when the chief held aloof and it was his wife who brought out the clan. There was a skirmish with Government troops in which the Prince narrowly escaped capture after spending a night at Moy, and at Culloden the brunt of the battle fell on Clan Chattan. Between 1704 and 1833 no Mackintosh chief left a son to succeed him—the so-called 'curse of Moy'—and as the senior lines died out one chief had to be sought in Jamaica and another in Canada. But in the 20th century Moy has seen a succession of public-spirited chiefs, and the old spirit of clanship has been linked with efforts to bring new life to the Highlands.

MACLACHLAN

MACLACHLAN

WITH Castle Lachlan as its centre, the territory of the Maclachlans stretched about ten miles along the east side of Loch Fyne, and about the same distance on the west where it extended across the isthmus north of Crinan to the ancient rock fortress of Dunadd.

Gillespie Maclachlan, already a prominent baron of Argyll by the end of the 13th century, attended Bruce's first Parliament at St Andrews in 1309, and received at some time in his reign a charter of 'Shirwachthyne' and other lands. He himself granted a charter in 1314, at his castle of 'Castellachlan' in Argyll, allowing an annuity to the Blackfriars of Glasgow from the lands of Kylbryd beside his castle (a grant confirmed by a descendant in 1456). The Maclachlan chiefs held some of their lands in Cowal from the Earl of Argyll, had links by marriage and common interest with their Lamont neighbours to the south (although this did not prevent an occasional quarrel), and also held lands from the crown in Bute. Lachlan Maclachlan of that Ilk witnessed an Argyll charter in 1533 (a comparatively early use of such a style by a Highland chief), and in 1574 his successor Archibald had his lands in Cowal and Glassary confirmed to him and his heirs male bearing the name and arms of 'Clanlachlane'. The chief figures simply as 'McLauchlane' in the list of Highland landlords who promised to keep good rule under the 'general band' of 1587.

Special measures were taken to exercise control in Maclachlan territory on the west side of Loch Fyne. In 1436 the chief appointed his cousin Allan, son of John *reoch* Maclachlan, to the office of 'seneschal and toiseachdeora' of his lands in Glassary, and seven successive generations are on record of this family, the Maclachlans of Dunadd. Even longer established (from 1525 at least) were the Maclachlans of Craiginterve, near the head of Loch Awe, who held their property for more than 300 years; three generations were physicians to the Argyll family, being sometimes known under the professional surname of Leech (1591); and because a cadet branch were captains of the great fortress of Inchconnel in Loch Awe from 1613 onwards (when it was still used as a prison), it has been surmised that they were of Campbell descent. The clan also spread north into Lorn, with a branch in Kilbride which had a grant of lands in the Garvellach islands including the castle of Dunconnel (1666); and round Loch Sunart, where Lachlan MacIain mhic Alasdair dhuibh alias MacLachlan was bailie to Campbell of Lochnell in Resipol (1655), and Dr John MacLachlan was known as the 'sweet singer of Rahoy'. In Lochaber the principal family of the name were dependents of Lochiel, at Coruanan on Loch Linnhe where a Cameron 'colour' saved from Culloden was long preserved, and where the Gaelic poet Ewen Maclachlan was born. In Menteith some of the name were accused of aiding the proscribed MacGregors, and a small laird's house at Auchintroig dating from 1702 is a reminder of their ownership of that estate.

Archibald Maclachlan of Maclachlan, who married a daughter of Lochnell, had his lands erected into a free barony named Strathlachlan in 1680, giving him legal right to try offences as well as the patriarchal influence he exercised as chief. Although Inveraray was not far away, the Maclachlans maintained their independence of action, and in 1745 the chief managed to slip out of Cowal and join the prince at Edinburgh with 180 men; Kenneth of Killinochonoch, near Dunadd, was adjutant and very active in raising men, and the clan unit may have increased to some 250; but Maclachlan himself fell at Culloden, with Lachlan of Inchconnel and no doubt many more. A grant of the family estate to his son Robert made in 1733 was produced for registration in Edinburgh five days after the battle; although it was surveyed for the Government it was eventually found not to have been forfeited, and the young heir's possession was confirmed by a crown charter in 1747. The old fortress by Loch Fyne was abandoned and a new Castle Lachlan built early in the 19th century, and the chief took his part in modern developments as secretary of the Highland and Agricultural Society from 1804 to 1813. His son and grandson, successively chiefs, were both trained lawyers and Writers to H.M. Signet, and on the death in 1942 of the last of the old male line his daughter Marjorie succeeded, being the first woman to enter on the inheritance.

MACLAINE OF LOCHBUIE &c.

MACLAINE OF LOCHBUIE

AMONG notable families of the Clan Maclean, besides Duart, were the Macleans of Lochbuie (who adopted the phonetic spelling 'Maclaine'), of Coll, and of Ardgour. They were all active within the Lordship of the Isles in the 15th century, and after its fall held their lands from the crown. During the 17th and 18th centuries, while the Duart family were dispossessed, they preserved their estates nearly entire, as vassals of Argyll.

The Lochbuie family are descended from Hector, brother of the Lachlan Maclean who received Duart from the Lord of the Isles in the 14th century; he too was given lands, probably in Mull, Tiree and Morvern. Lochbuie was a member of the Council of the Isles, along with Duart, and one of the last grants made before the forfeiture was of the office of bailliary of the south part of Tiree conferred on John of Lochbuie in 1492. The Macleans of Coll came from John, and those of Ardgour from Donald, both sons of the Duart chief who succeeded in 1411.

After the break-up of the lordship, the subordinate clans lost some of their own unity. Towards the end of James IV's reign a feud between the Macleans of Duart and Lochbuie over lands in Morvern and Tiree was carried on with much bitterness. Soon after Queen Mary began her personal rule there was a quarrel between Duart and Coll, who as a crown tenant refused to follow Duart as his chief; Duart invaded Coll and took over his kinsman's lands and castle until ordered by the Privy Council to relinquish them and make reparation for injuries to property and tenants. Yet between these two episodes, when Donald *dubh* made the final attempt to restore the lordship in 1545, more than one-third of his rebel council of seventeen were Macleans—Duart, Lochbuie, Torloisk, Coll, Ardgour and Kingairloch. Under the peace-keeping arrangements made in the later years of James VI's reign, Duart, Lochbuie and Coll each had to answer before the council for the good conduct of their tenants.

The Macleans were loyal supporters of the Stewart dynasty. Montrose was joined by 700 of the clan under Duart and Lochbuie, and a fierce charge by a detachment under Ewen of Treshnish marked the battle of Kilsyth. At Inverkeithing young Sir Hector of Duart fell, shielded to the end by his foster-father and seven foster-brothers, who died one after another crying 'Another for Hector!' Donald of Brolass was tutor to the infant who succeeded, and during the long struggle with Argyll his family resisted all moves to secure the chief's lands. Attempts to wean the tutor from his allegiance failed, and in the belief that the earl 'intended the extirpation of their name and family altogether' the Macleans resolved to defend themselves in arms. Argyll had the support of Government troops, and when Lochbuie, Ardgour, Kinlochaline and Torloisk rose on behalf of their chief, they were declared outlaws. But although they stood shoulder to shoulder, their resistance was in vain.

Several Maclean leaders distinguished themselves in Dundee's rising of 1689. Lochbuie won a brilliant skirmish with Mackay's cavalry on Speyside; Sir Alexander of Otter (one of his cadets) seized an enemy standard at Killiecrankie; Ardgour led the clansmen from Morvern, and Coll and Torloisk also had companies. The Macleans were 'out' again in 1715 under Sir John of Duart; in 1745, after the chief had been taken prisoner, Maclean of Drimnin led the clan, with Torloisk and Ardgour among his officers, and only thirty-eight men out of nine score are said to have returned home. Lochbuie wavered, and Brolass and Coll raised companies of militia for the Government, although few Macleans would join them.

Mull is still the land of the Macleans, but a gap was left while Duart was lost to the clan. Lochbuie, 'rough and haughty, and tenacious of his dignity', kept up appearances by trying to exercise the right of pit and gallows long after it was withdrawn. 'Young Coll' was Dr Johnson's intelligent guide in this part of the Hebrides, and Torloisk was a centre of Maclean hospitality until it fell to an heiress. Coll sold his lands about 1840, Lochbuie's passed from the family in the 1920s, but there is still a Maclean of Ardgour on the old lands beside Loch Linnhe as well as a Maclean of Duart across the Sound of Mull.

MACLAREN

MACLAREN

To Alan Breck in the novel *Kidnapped,* as a Stewart of Appin, Balquhidder in Perthshire was 'the country of my friends the Maclarens'. In particular the Braes of Balquhidder, lying in the valley of Loch Voil between the head of Loch Lomond and Loch Earn, is the recognised home of the clan. But in the early middle ages the name covered a wider territory, and the MacLarens were then at the cross-roads where four regions met—Dalriada or modern Argyll to the west, Atholl to the north, Strathearn to the east, and Lennox to the south.

Once, it is said, the MacLarens were so numerous and powerful that no-one else dared to enter Balquhidder church till they had taken their places. As kinsmen and vassals of the Celtic Earls of Strathearn they flourished until the mid-14th century, when the earldom failed. At that time, for some reason not clearly established, the MacLarens did not obtain a crown charter of their lands, and by the late 16th century the feudal superiority was divided between Murray of Tullibardine, Lord Drummond and Campbell of Glenorchy. They got on well with their Stewart and Fergusson neighbours, but there was trouble with the MacGregors, who in one raid slew eighteen MacLaren households and then settled on their holdings. This forced the clan to seek protection from Glenorchy, and an old bond of defence with Argyll was transferred to his expansionist clansman in 1559. An even more comprehensive agreement was entered into in 1573, in which 'the whole surname and clan of the Clanlawren' were declared to have elected (*i.e.,* chosen) Glenorchy and his heirs to be their chiefs in return for his protection. Eight individuals were named as the 'most able persons of the surname' before whom anyone failing with the promised payment of their best beast as 'death duty' would be tried; four of these have been identified from their patronymics as belonging to the chief's family, and descended from Patrick *mor* MacLaren.

The MacLarens were never entirely dispossessed of their lands, but they were unable to settle younger sons on land of their own within the clan country. This meant the departure of some in search of better opportunities for their families, but the clan showed resilience and recovered some of its former strength and independence. 'Clanlawren' was named in 1587 among the clans with chiefs on whom they depended, often against the will of their landlords, and it is significant that after each MacGregor outrage the MacLarens had appealed not to the Drummonds as their feudal superiors, but to Argyll with whom they had a bond of defence. They supported Montrose and Dundee in their royalist risings, fighting alongside the Stewarts of Appin, and in 1715 and 1745 they again rose as a clan, losing thirteen killed and fourteen wounded at Culloden. Their leader, Donald of Invernenty (who took his *Theophrastus* in Greek and Latin on the campaign) was captured and made a spectacular escape at the Devil's Beef Tub near Moffat while on his way to Carlisle for trial.

It was hard to believe that the Rising had failed, and six weeks after Culloden had been fought it was reported that 'the people of Balquhidder not only keep their arms but wear their white cockades'. Only a dozen years earlier a clan battle had been narrowly averted in the heart of Balquhidder. Feeling had run high with the MacGregors over the disposal of a farm, and the MacLarens called for support from Appin; when the two forces met below the Kirkton, the MacGregors saw themselves outnumbered and proposed to settle by single combat, as a result of which Stewart of Invernahyle fought and wounded the famous Rob Roy—whose son shot a MacLaren dead two years later in revenge. A young lawyer's clerk from Edinburgh named Walter Scott who went with a posse of soldiers in 1790 to serve a writ of removal on the MacLaren tenant found the house deserted, but he later made Invernenty and the region round it famous in the novel *Rob Roy*. It turned out that the householder and his family had gone to Canada—neither the first nor the last to leave Balquhidder.

The clan were rapidly dispersing—Duncan McLaren, Lord Provost and M.P. for Edinburgh, and father of a Lord of Session and the first Lord Aberconway, came from Lismore; Colin Maclaurin the mathematician and his son Lord Dreghorn from Inveraray. But Achleskine near the foot of Loch Voil remained in the chief's family until 1892, and sixty-five years later a new chief, by acquiring Creag an Tuirc and some other land in Balquhidder, regained after 600 years a legal title to part of their ancient patrimony.

MACLEAN OF DUART

MACLEAN OF DUART, DRESS

One of the great seafaring clans of the Hebrides, where they exercised an important influence from an early period, the Macleans became scattered through many islands from Rum to Islay, and split into a number of branches of which several maintained a separate existence.[1]

In the days of the Lords of the Isles the Macleans formed an active and lively part of the island host. They first come into prominence through the marriage of Lachlan, son of John called 'Maguilleon' (*Mac Gill' Eathain*, son of the servant of John), to a daughter of John Lord of the Isles, for which a papal dispensation was authorised in 1367 as they were nearly related. This Lachlan, nicknamed 'the wily', had a charter of Duart castle and neighbouring lands from his brother-in-law Donald of the Isles in 1390, with a share in the keeping of Cairnburgh, Dunchonnel and other royal castles off the coast of Mull, and the office of Steward of the household and bailie in Tiree. This gave the Duart family a leading place in the clan, and an importance even in national affairs. While James I was a prisoner in England, Lachlan's son Hector had a safe conduct from Henry IV to visit 'his liege lord the king of Scotland' just before direct negotiations were entered into with Donald of the Isles, and in 1411 Lachlan fell at Harlaw in supporting Donald's struggle for the earldom of Ross. In the next generation a twice-married chief founded the families of Coll and Ardgour, and a group in the Ross of Mull known as 'the race of the iron sword'. The clan was steadily growing in strength and influence, and both Duart and Lochbuie (descended from a brother of the wily Lachlan) were numbered among the island magnates who sat in council at Finlaggan in Islay.

After the lordship was forfeited in 1493 Hector of Duart had his family's earlier grants of 1390 confirmed by royal charter, and thus they came to hold lands and offices direct from the crown. As he had no lawful son of his own, Hector secured letters of legitimation for his natural son Lachlan, who displaced at least one legitimate heir when he had a charter of the barony of 'Dowarde' in 1496.

During the minority of Queen Mary and the years that followed, the Macleans reached the height of their power. A brother of Duart was one of the commissioners appointed to treat with Henry VIII during Donald *dubh*'s rebellion in 1545. Maclean infiltration into Islay and Jura menaced the trade-route between Scotland and Ireland, and a bitter feud with the Macdonalds had disastrous consequences for the Macleans. Lachlan *mor,* the astute chief who had tried to bargain with Queen Elizabeth over the use of Highland mercenaries to aid Irish rebels, fell in battle in Islay in 1598 with (according to tradition) fourscore 'chief men of his kin' and 200 'common soldiers'. The crown rents of Duart were unpaid, and in 1604 the chief had to agree to deliver the castle to the king's representative on demand; along with Lochbuie and Coll, he accepted the 'Statutes of Iona', and promised to appear before the Privy Council annually with a certain number of their kinsmen. Sir Lachlan, created a Baronet of Nova Scotia in 1633 with a nominal estate in Anticosti, borrowed money from Argyll, who secured a further hold over him by paying up what was due to the crown and other creditors.

The Macleans were the centre of the king's supporters in the Western Isles,[1] and their losses in men and money, together with a succession of five minorities (1648–1716), enabled Argyll to wage a 'private war' in the field and in his own courts for possession of the Maclean lands in Mull, Morvern and Tiree. After the Revolution Sir John Maclean formally conveyed Duart to Argyll, and the family remained landless until 1783, when Sir Allan (who had been host to Dr Johnson at Inchkenneth) made good his claim to the lands of Brolass in the Ross of Mull. Duart housed a garrison up to the end of the 18th century, after which it became a ruin, but it was bought back and restored by Sir Fitzroy Maclean of Duart. Since 1912 it has been the chief's permanent home, and the family are determined that the castle of their ancestors shall never again pass into other hands.

[1]See page 116 for Lochbuie, Coll and Ardgour families, and the clan's service in the Stewart cause.

MACLEOD OF HARRIS

MACLEOD OF HARRIS, HUNTING

DUNVEGAN in the Isle of Skye, in its early days 'ane stark strenth biggit (built) on ane craig', appeared to James Boswell 'as if it had been let down from heaven by the four corners to be the residence of a chief'. So it has been for 500 years of recorded history, and no doubt long before that; and so it is today, as the home of MacLeod of MacLeod and the centre of a clan scattered throughout the world.

The clan's traditional founder was Leod, thought to have flourished at the end of the 13th century and perhaps the son of a Norse king of Man. His sons, Norman and Torquil, founded the MacLeods of Harris and of Lewis, two powerful clans 'perfectly distinct and independent of each other' but usually living in amity. Norman's line, regarding themselves as the senior and adopting the style of MacLeod of MacLeod, owned Harris in the Outer Hebrides and Glenelg on the mainland, as well as two-thirds of Skye. They were essentially an island clan, using the sea as their high road, and Dunvegan had no landward entrance before 1748.

From David II, about 1343, Malcolm the son of Tormod MacLeod had a charter of two parts of Glenelg and the MacLeod lands in Skye from the crown. Under the Lords of the Isles the MacLeods of Harris and Lewis held high and equal rank; both were members of the council which met at Finlaggan in Islay, and as charter witnesses Harris was nearly always named first. The decline and breakup of the lordship found the Dunvegan chief resisting Macdonald claims to Uist, Sleat and Trotternish.

Alasdair *crotach* (hump-backed) was chief in 1493 (in securing royal charters for his lands he undertook to maintain one twenty-six-oar and two sixteen-oar galleys for the service of the crown). He is remembered as builder of the 'fairy tower' at Dunvegan, and St Clement's church at Rodil in Harris, where his finely-carved tomb can be seen; he also established the MacCrimmon college of pipers at Borreraig near Dunvegan. After the death of his son William in 1551, leaving a daughter Mary, the leadership of the clan was assumed by a cousin, and there was a struggle for power—in which some vital decisions are said to have been made at meetings of the clan in Skye and Harris—before an heiress (who married a Campbell) resigned her claims to the lands on receiving a dowry, and left her uncle Norman in possession.

One of Norman's sons was Sir Roderick MacLeod of Dunvegan, knight, the Rory *mor* of clan tradition, who lived in the old castle surrounded by a retinue of gentlemen and their retainers, with his own pipers, harpers, bards and jesters. In his younger days he led 600 islesmen to Ireland to help O'Donnell's rebellion, and his clan was one of considerable importance in Highland politics. The chief was supported by a number of branch families, cadets of his own, and younger sons of Sir Rory added those of Bernera, Talisker, Grishornish and Hamer. The clan took no part in Montrose's campaigns, but a detachment 1,000 strong was raised for the king's service before Worcester, when they suffered so heavily and had so little thanks that a MacLeod chief never again took the field for the Stuarts. Norman raised an 'independent company' for King George in 1745, and was the first of the family to 'mix in the pursuits and ambitions of the world', with the result that his trustees had to sell Harris, Bernera and St Kilda in 1779 (to a MacLeod) after which Glenelg (1811) and others followed; his grandson rose to high military rank abroad and entered politics, and impoverished his heirs without materially benefiting himself.

When Skye was struck by the famine in 1847–48, the chief ruined himself to help his people, and while he moved to London to find employment many tenants had to leave as their land was let to sheep farmers. As the clan lands shrank in size the clan became more and more dispersed, but the MacLeods found a new unity under the leadership of Dame Flora MacLeod of MacLeod, who inherited Dunvegan in 1935 and travelled constantly as an ambassador from the homeland to her clan overseas. Through 'MacLeod days' held since the first Skye Week in 1950, and the clan 'parliament' inaugurated in 1956, Dunvegan became more than ever before a world centre for the Clan MacLeod.

MACLEOD OF LEWIS

MACLEOD OF LEWIS AND RAASAY, DRESS

THERE is some truth, as well as some bias, in a 17th century assessment of the Lewis MacLeods: 'The clan Torkil in Lewis were the stoutest and prettiest men, but a wicked bloody crew whom neither law nor reason could guid or moddell'.

Descended from Torquil MacLeod, a brother of the founder of the Harris line, they held Lewis from at least David II's reign. About 1343 the chief had a royal grant of the lands of Assynt in Sutherland, with its isle and fortress; they also owned lands in the Trotternish district of Skye, the isles of Raasay and South Rona, and Gairloch and Coigach in Wester Ross. The family showed constant loyalty to the Lords of the Isles, and their chief Torquil was at Ardtornish in 1461 when preparations were being made for an alliance with Edward IV of England. The next chief made his submission to the Scottish king after the forfeiture of the Lord of the Isles in 1493 and married a daughter of Colin, Earl of Argyll, but the family joined in the various attempts to restore the lordship. Roderick (or Rory) MacLeod of Lewis was one of the rebel Council of the Isles which planned an abortive rising in 1545, and off and on for half a century was a thorn in the side of the authorities. In 1576, for example, when the king's subjects were being molested while fishing in the lochs of Lewis, he and his son had to bind themselves and their clan to keep the peace.

Towards the end of the 16th century the MacLeods of Lewis were weakened and their supremacy in the island ended by 'one of the most barbarous, sanguinary, and fratricidal conflicts recorded in clan history'. Rory was three times married, to a Mackenzie, a Stewart and a Maclean, and each wife had a son Torquil: the first, known as Conanach from his mother's people, he disowned; the second, Torquil the heir (because of his Stewart blood Queen Mary ordered him not to marry without her advice and consent), was lost in a storm while crossing the Minch; and the third, black Torquil, was murdered. The chief's private and public reputation gave King James some pretext for fixing on Lewis as the scene of a misguided attempt at 'development' with the double aim of swelling the royal revenues and rooting out disorderly elements. No title-deeds having been produced in compliance with an act of 1597, Lewis was forfeited and granted for a substantial rent and with despotic powers to a Lowland company known as the Fife Adventurers. The scheme failed through local opposition; in spite of internal dissension, the MacLeods offered a heroic resistance under Neil *mor,* one of Rory's natural sons, who was eventually taken and executed in 1613. In the meantime Mackenzie of Kintail, who had been absorbing MacLeod's mainland possessions, bought out the Fife Adventurers, and in putting down resistance to his ownership the Tutor of Kintail ruthlessly exterminated the immediate family of the chief.

To the MacLeods of Raasay fell the representation of the Lewis family. Malcolm, whose father was a cousin of the three Torquils, managed to escape another massacre during the conflict; he signed himself 'Gillecallum Mak Gillicallum of Rasay', but the name MacLeod was not abandoned, and after passing to two heiresses, the estate returned to the male line in 1688. Another Malcolm of Raasay was 'out' in 1745 with 100 fighting men, of whom all but about fourteen returned; and there was no forfeiture, because the chief had cautiously conveyed the estate to his son in advance. The old patriarchal life continued, and when Dr Johnson visited Raasay in 1773 he was pleased and told Boswell, 'This is what we came to find'. During a rage for emigration not a man left the estate, and the laird boasted that it 'had not gained or lost a single acre' in 400 years. Johnson understood that Raasay acknowledged MacLeod of Dunvegan as his chief, 'though his ancestors have formerly disputed the pre-eminence', and when his *Journey to the Western Isles* appeared Raasay protested that he had never made 'such an unmeaning cession'. A correction was published and Johnson wrote a charming letter of apology which (according to Boswell) 'he says you may read to your clan or publish it if you please'. Raasay was sold by his son in 1846, and the family emigrated to Australia, but the 'clan Torkil' is not forgotten in the Hebrides.

MACMILLAN

MACMILLAN, DRESS

WITH a name supposed to be of ecclesiastical origin, no single place or district can be claimed as that where the Macmillans first settled. From an early date there were Macmillans beside Loch Arkaig in Lochaber, where they were found in Murlaggan and Glenpean, and on the north side of Loch Tay in Perthshire, where they are said to have been given the barony of Lawers. Some of these Macmillans may have migrated to Knapdale in Mid Argyll and some to Galloway, but documentary evidence of such a move is lacking.

We are on firmer ground in relating the name to Knapdale, although here too tradition has to be called in. Part of Castle Sween is still known as 'Macmillan's tower', and in the ancient churchyard of Kilmory Knap stands a finely ornamented and well preserved Celtic cross inscribed '*Haec est crux Alexandri*

Macmulen'. The Macmillans are believed to have obtained their lands in Knapdale by marriage with the heiress of the Macneils who were constables of Castle Sween; according to a popular tradition their right to these lands was carved in Gaelic on a rock at the extremity of their estate—a tenure, it has been remarked, which 'proved but a feeble security against the rapacity of a barbarous age'. One Macdonald seneachie included 'Macillemhaoel' or Macmillan among the councillors of the Lords of the Isles who used to meet at Finlaggan in Islay, and it has been suggested that they lost most of their estate in Knapdale at or even before the forfeiture of the Lord of the Isles near the end of the 15th century. But a family of the name continued to hold the adjoining lands of Dunmore on West Loch Tarbert: Alexander of Dunmore died shortly after taking part in Argyll's rebellion in 1685 (when thirty-four Macmillans in Knapdale, Kilberry and parts of Kintyre were listed as rebels); Duncan was granted arms in 1742 as 'representative of the ancient family of Macmillan of Knapdale', and was father of Alexander, Deputy Keeper of the Signet; and in 1951 General Sir Gordon Macmillan, General Officer Commanding -in-Chief, Scottish Command, was acknowledged by the Lord Lyon as chief of the clan and granted the undifferenced arms of Macmillan of Knap.

Macmillans were among the most extensive occupiers of land in Kintyre from the 16th century, and the founders of the Macmillan publishing house had Arran and Ayrshire origins. In Galloway the name has been most prominent in the parish of Carsphairn, in the Glenkens district among the uplands of Kirkcudbright. Macmillans were notable among the Covenanters who suffered religious persecution, and among many of the name charged in 1684 with being 'disorderly' (refusing to conform to the current laws) was John Macmillan of Brackloch, whose home lay between Carsphairn and Loch Doon. Of this family, on record from 1584, an heiress married David Macmillan of Holm and so united the two principal local families of the name in 1741. In the Covenanting tradition was John Macmillan, minister of Balmaghie, a Cameronian 'apostle' and founder of the Reformed Presbyterian Church, whose followers were known as 'Macmillanites'.

The Macmillans have made their mark in various ways throughout the world, and the tower on Castle Sween and the Kilmory cross are not their only monuments. There is a town called Macmillan in the United States, between Lakes Superior and Michigan, and a Macmillan river rises in a high range of mountains in British Columbia and flows into the Bering Strait. In 1802 some 200 Macmillans from Lochaber emigrated to Canada and settled in Ontario; Angus Macmillan from Skye discovered the fertile region of Gippsland in the Australian state of Victoria; and, nearer home, a Dumfriesshire blacksmith named Kirkpatrick Macmillan invented the pedal bicycle.

From the Macmillans on Loch Tayside came a family which produced one of the clan's most distinguished men. The Rev. Dr Hugh Macmillan, first president of the Clan Macmillan Society, who put the aims of such a society and what he could glean of Macmillan history and tradition into prose, once said: 'We have never as a clan, I think, produced a real live lord or even a baronet'. He did not see his son Hugh, successively Lord Advocate, Lord of Appeal and Minister of the Crown, become Baron Macmillan of Aberfeldy in 1930, with a seat in the House of Lords, choosing a territorial designation in filial tribute to his father's birthplace.

MACNAB

MACNAB

MOST of what is known of Macnab history has to be pieced together from outside sources, as no connected chronicle or collection of papers of their own has survived. Sometimes holding their lands by charter from the crown, and sometimes from powerful neighbours, they were for a time entirely landless; but in recent years some of the old Macnab lands near the head of Loch Tay in Perthshire have been bought back by a clansman who was later recognised as chief.

The heart of the Macnab country has been called 'the most extraordinary collection of extraordinary scenery in Scotland . . . a perfect picture gallery in itself since you cannot move three yards without meeting a new landscape'. It stretched from where the village of Killin stands today up Glen Dochart towards Tyndrum, and the clan spread also along the south side of Loch Tay. Near the head of the loch, in a commanding position on the north bank of the River Lochay and frequently surrounded by water, stood the old Macnab castle of Eilean Ran. Known as the 'children of the abbot', the chiefs seem to come from a line of hereditary lay owners of the lordship of Glendochart. The clan suffered for opposing Bruce in his fight for the throne, supposedly from some connection with the Comyns and MacDougalls, but a charter to 'Gilbert Macnab' of which only scant details survive suggests that they had come to the king's peace by the next reign.

Finlay Macnab of Bovain is found holding property in Glen Dochart in the time of James IV, but another of the same name sold or at least mortgaged Bovain and other lands in 1552 to Campbell of Glenorchy. Even if that lost him some control over his clan, the Macnabs were able to join Montrose when he swept through Glen Dochart on his raid of vengeance into Argyll. Their wily chief, known as 'Smooth John', led 300 of the clan to Worcester in 1651, and is said to have been killed there, but two years later a Cromwellian officer reported the death of 'the Lord Mac-Knab, one of the greatest Montrossians' in a local shooting affray in which his whole clan had risen against a party of Government troops. The castle was burnt, the country ravaged, and the chief's estates passed into Campbell hands, but Monck himself intervened to protect his widow and children from being dispossessed. After the Restoration most of the estates were returned, but Eilean Ran was never recovered.

The Macnabs were in Dundee's rising in 1689, and many were 'out' again in 1715, although the chief held back. In 1745 his two sons were officers in the Government service, but some of the clan took the Jacobite side and are said to have joined the Breadalbane men under Glenlyon. But the days when a chief's strength lay in his fighting men were ending, and during the reign of the magnificent eccentric whom Raeburn's portrait immortalised as 'The Macnab' 100 of the clan emigrated to Canada, and another 300 left after his death in 1816. The next chief was Archibald, whose inheritance consisted mostly of his uncle's debts, but he secured a grant of 80,000 acres of undeveloped land in Ontario and tried to establish the old feudal authority in the extensive 'township' of Macnab above Ottawa. He arranged for twenty-one families to emigrate in 1825, but as the years went by his 'arbitrary bearing and persecuting spirit' brought increasing opposition and complaint, and after an official inquiry his 'wanton oppressions and outrages upon humanity' were ended.

Any idea that the Macnab lands in Scotland might be redeemed came to an end with their purchase by Lord Breadalbane in 1828. At Inchewen, however, was a Macnab family who had occupied the same farm for nearly four centuries, and at Barachastalain near Dalmally lived another who for generations had been smiths and armourers, and whose knowledge of Ossianic poetry had attracted the notice of travellers. Other cadet branches had established themselves beyond the old clan country, and Archibald (who died in France in 1860) left it in writing that Sir Allan Macnab, of the Dundurn family, who was Prime Minister of Upper and Lower Canada, was the representative of the branch nearest to his own. When Lord Breadalbane sold the last of his family estates in 1949, Kinnell House and 7,000 old Macnab acres were bought by the head of a cadet family from near Coupar Angus, and five years later he was granted arms as chief of the name and clan by the Lord Lyon King of Arms.

MACNACHTAN

MACNACHTAN

ALTHOUGH the name flourishes in Perthshire, Galloway and other parts of Scotland, once they settled in Argyll the Macnachtans seem to have maintained their strength and size almost unaltered for several centuries. Their lands between Loch Fyne and Loch Awe, in Glenaray, Glenshira and Glenfyne, lay not far from what became the heart of the Campbell country.

The earliest hint of their presence on Loch Awe is a charter said to have been granted in 1267 to Gillechrist Macnachdan, son of Malcolm, charging him with the keeping of the royal castle of 'Frechelan' (Fraoch Eilean) at the north end of the loch, in a strategic position near the entrance to the pass of Brander. The Macnachtans fought on the Balliol side with the MacDougalls of Lorne, but a reference by Barbour to the 'baroune Maknaughtan' suggests that he may have changed his allegiance during the war of independence.

The Loch Awe lands passed from the Macnachtans about the end of the 14th century, and thereafter the chiefs were nearly always identified with Dundarave, on Loch Fyne. In 1473 Gilbert Macnachtan obtained a charter of the lands of Dundarave and others on his own resignation from Colin, first Earl of Argyll (perhaps for political reasons preferring to hold of the great man whose influence was increasing rather than from the crown), and in 1513 'Gilbert Maknactane of Dundaraw sheriff in that part' is mentioned in the Treasurer's accounts. 'Beetling against the breakers, very cold, very arrogant upon its barren promontory', Dundarave figures in Neil Munro's *Doom Castle*, and above the entrance, with the date 1596, is the inscription: 'Behold the end. Be not wiser than the highest. I hope in God'.

In 1600 the chief and his two brothers were in trouble for raiding the Macaulay lands of Ardincaple. When James VI made landowners and chiefs answerable for the good behaviour of their tenants and clansmen, there were already some 'broken men' among the Macnachtans. Only one soldier in the company of 200 Highland bowmen raised by the laird in 1627 for service in the war with France was named Macnachtan, but the variety of patronymics may well include those of clansmen who did not use the surname, at any rate within the clan country.

By 1653 political differences had separated the Macnachtans from Argyll, and right up to the Revolution the chiefs continued to support the Stewart cause. They raided their former patron's lands, and when young Macnachtan, 'conspicuous in shining armour', joined in Dundee's rising he had with him kin, clan and retainers from Lochfyneside, 'nourished by the finny *(piscosa)* lake'. After Killiecrankie, when the loyal chiefs before dispersing pledged support for the future, Macnachtan promised fifty men for the king's service and mutual defence. He escaped forfeiture, in spite of a decree against him being passed, but lost his lands shortly before 1715, when they passed to the Campbells in settlement of an old debt. The Campbells cannot have been sorry at the chance to rid the neighbourhood of a troublesome Jacobite enclave so near the heart of their territory. Now indeed, with no chief at Dundarave, the Macnachtans were a broken clan, and they played no organised part in the later Jacobite risings. From various parts, however, clansmen came to fight for the Stewarts, and one who was taken prisoner is remembered as 'honest John': known to have been in rebellion, he was offered a pension of £30 if he would turn King's evidence, but refused and was hanged at Carlisle in October 1746.

The last chief to live at Dundarave died at Edinburgh in 1773, a retired Inspector-General of Customs. Nearly fifty years later, the head of a branch settled in Ireland since the reign of Queen Elizabeth, was persuaded to come forward. In 1818, 'on the attestation and at the desire of upwards of 400 of the clan', Edmund Alexander Macnaghten petitioned the Lyon Court and had the arms of the chief confirmed to him. An earlier society having failed to survive, a Clan Macnachtan Association was formed in 1952, deliberately choosing a compromise spelling of the name so as to embrace all variations. Dundarave was no longer in the hands of the clan, but it had been restored to something of its former glory under the guidance of Sir Robert Lorimer, and at one of the clan's early outings the chief's flag was flown there for the first time in some 250 years.

MACNEIL OF BARRA

MACNEIL OF BARRA

One of the few purely island clans, with no possessions on the mainland, the Macneils of Barra have a stirring history which has to be pieced together, in the absence of their own charters and with the disappearance of their Gaelic chronicle, from scattered references in the public records, the history of other families, and local tradition and archaeological evidence.

Claiming to derive their name and descent from Niall of the Nine Hostages, an early High King of Ireland, they first appear in the records of the Hebrides at the beginning of the 15th century. From a later royal confirmation, we know that Gilleonan, son of Roderick son of Murdo son of Neil had a charter of Barra from Alexander, Lord of the Isles in 1427. Macneil was one of the lesser barons or 'thanes' who sat on the Council of the Isles, and whether or not he was one of the 'oldest surnames' in that company of magnates, the clan boast of their chief's sea-girt castle of Kisimul as 'our ancient glory'. After the fall of the lordship in 1493 Macneil made his submission to James IV and had his lands confirmed to him. In the disordered period which ensued he followed Maclean of Duart; they may have shared a hankering after the old ways, for they were both members of the rebel council which supported Donald Dubh's attempt to restore the lordship in 1545.

In James VI's reign, Macneil of Barra was made responsible for the good behaviour of 'Clanneil' by order of parliament, but while it could be troublesome to the authorities the clan was not large in numbers (a later estimate put its military strength at 120). When Rory the turbulent, whose raids extended as far as the Irish coast, was brought to account and accused of harassing Queen Elizabeth's subjects, the chief craftily replied that he thought to do his Majesty a service by annoying the woman who had killed his mother. Going well with this chief's reputation is the story that a herald used to be sent each evening to the battlements of Kisimul, with a trumpeter, to proclaim at each point of the compass: 'Hear, oh ye people, and listen, oh ye nations! The great Macneil of Barra having finished his meal, the princes of the earth may dine'. Once when a Spanish ship went ashore on Barra, and there was some talk of the consequences if she were plundered, a clansman is said to have reassured his fellows with the remark that 'Macneil and the king of Spain will adjust that between themselves'. Martin tells us that Macneil used to find wives for widowers and husbands for widows among his tenants, take into his own household those who became too old to support themselves, and replace milk-cows which any of his tenants lost by misfortune. As Buchanan of Auchmar says, of all the Highland chiefs of clans, Macneil must have retained 'most of the magnificence and customs of the ancient Phylarchae'.

Such self-assurance must have received a sharp blow in 1612, when a quarrel broke out among Rory's sons and he found himself a prisoner in his own castle. Two of his sons were trying to seize control of the chief and his rightful heir, and Rory complained to the Privy Council; but he seems to have died before the affair was settled. It was perhaps an echo of this dispute which made a visiting priest remark of Kisimul: 'Whatever member of the family is in possession of it, even though not the eldest, is regarded as the chief of the whole island'.

Macneil was 'out' in Dundee's rising, when we catch a glimpse of him helmeted and panting under the weight of a huge battle-axe, and leading 'a great company of the youth of his name'. The clan were less prominent in 1715 and 1745, but in the last rising a Spanish ship landed arms and money on Barra for the Prince's army, and Macneil came near to forfeiting his estate. His son was killed at the taking of Quebec in 1759; the next chief, Colonel Roderick, moved from Kisimul to a house on the Barra 'mainland'; and his son, a Peninsula and Waterloo officer who became a full general, sold the island in 1838 after a brief heyday of prosperity based on the kelp industry. Kisimul was left to the mercy of the elements 'after 700 years of usefulness', until the estate was bought back and the castle restored by Robert Lister Macneil of Barra, whose fulfilment of a youthful dream by making a home in the castle of his ancestors is one of the romances of clan history in the 20th century.

McNEILL OF GIGHA &c.

McNEILL OF COLONSAY

No record survives to tell when the McNeills first held land in the Isle of Gigha, off the west coast of Kintyre, but the earliest contemporary reference to them carries the connection back to the first half of the 15th century. The head of the family was then keeper or constable for the Lord of the Isles of the great castle on Loch Sween, one of the most remarkable fortresses on the western seaboard. Both the Gigha and Barra chiefs had a place on the Council of the Isles which used to meet at Finlaggan in Islay (the Macleans and Macleods also had two representatives), but they operated independently of each other at least after the fall of the lordship in 1493.

A charter by which John, Earl of Ross and Lord of the Isles confirmed certain lands in Gigha to Neill M'Torquell M'Neill, his constable of Castle

Sween, in 1455, says they had been granted to Neill's father by his own father, Earl Alexander, before his death about six years before. Kintyre and Knapdale were attached to the crown when the earldom of Ross was forfeited in 1475, and three years later (when Malcolm of Gigha was chief) Neil McNeill was accused with others of 'stuffing' Castle Sween with men, victuals and arms, making war on the king's lieges and destroying his lands, with the support of the Lord of the Isles. Colin, Earl of Argyll became keeper of the castle in 1481 (it is also said to have passed with an heiress to Macmillan of Knap), and there is a haunting lament for the last of the McNeills of Castle Sween by an early Gaelic poetess which recalls the many guests who came from as far away as Ireland, and how his death had left the castle still and silent, 'just like the winds when it is calm, so without music is Dun Sween'.

With the supremacy of the Lords of the Isles at an end, and no single authority to replace them, the McNeills of Gigha followed their Clan Donald neighbours in Islay and Kintyre, while the Barra Macneils sided with their enemies the Macleans of Duart. Duart's brother, the piratical rover known in island tradition as Allan na Sop, is said to have been the leader of some rebellious islesmen who in James V's time slew Neil McNeill of Gigha and 'the greater part of his clan'. There was no legitimate son to succeed, but Torquil, as 'cheif and principale of the clan and surname of Maknelis', was granted the profits and dues of the estate during his good service and the king's pleasure; later Annabella, Neil's daughter and heiress, resigned the lands of Gigha and others to her natural brother Neil, to whom they were granted in heritage by the king in 1542, along with the office of 'Toschachdoir' or coroner of all Kintyre. Some hold over Gigha seems to have been retained by the Macleans since Allan's raid, and in the minority which followed the king's death Neil joined the English expedition which ended ignominiously at Ancrum Moor in 1545, perhaps as some kind of emissary from the island clans. Pardoned for his rebellion, Neil sold Gigha to Macdonald of Dunyveg, but the Macleans disputed his possession and ravaged Gigha with fire and sword, killing some of the people and taking others prisoner.

With the failure of the direct line of Gigha, the McNeills of Taynish became chiefs of the southern 'Clanneil', and they acquired Gigha in 1590. They held their lands from the Earl of Argyll, and during Sir James Macdonald's rebellion in 1615 Hector of Taynish sent news of rebel activities to the Privy Council in Edinburgh. In the arrangements subsequently made for keeping order in the earldom, he was appointed to support Campbell of Kilberry in Knapdale along with Hector of Carskey, who was keeper of the king's new castle where Campbeltown now stands. Donald of Gallachallie in Gigha was prominent in Dundee's rising in 1689, and found refuge from pursuit in the island after its failure. Taynish appears to have enjoyed undisputed control of Gigha under Argyll, and it remained in the family until the reign of George III. Thereafter it was acquired by a cadet branch who already owned Colonsay and Oronsay, which included Duncan, Lord Colonsay, who was head of the Scottish judiciary and created a peer; Sir John McNeill, who was envoy to Persia and later conducted an official inquiry into conditions in the Highlands and Islands in 1851; and Sir John Carstairs McNeill, V.C., in whose day Gigha again passed from the clan.

The Carskey family held their estate in the male line from 1505 to about 1824, and the McNeills of Tirfergus and Lossit acquired Ugadale in Kintyre by marriage with a Mackay heiress.

MACPHERSON

MACPHERSON

As their name means literally 'son of the parson', Macphersons in different parts of the country may have a different origin; but the clan as it became established in and around Badenoch, as part of the wider confederacy of Clan Chattan, claim descent from a specific individual whose name and the precise nature of his office are matters of controversy.

The clan falls into three main divisions, which retained their separate identities until the end of the 18th century. As they are descended from Kenneth, John and Gilles, sons of a Ewen who flourished in the mid-14th century, the clan is sometimes known as the race or descendants of the three brothers. The *Sliochd Choinnich,* consisting of many Badenoch families, and others in Strathdearn and Strathnairn, was always represented in clan affairs by Macpherson of Cluny; the *Sliochd Iain,* generally by Macpherson of Pitmain, but at times by Invertromie or Strathmashie; and the smaller *Sliochd Ghilliosa,* by Macpherson of Invereshie or his principal cadets Phoness and Dalraddy.

Andrew Macpherson, living in Cluny at the close of the 16th century, gave unity to the clan, and helped to maintain its independence in the face of Mackintosh's leadership of Clan Chattan and Huntly's feudal superiority in Badenoch. But the three divisions remained, and when Andrew signed the Clan Chattan bond in 1609 for himself and the Brin and Breackachy families, Pitmain, Phoness and Invereshie still signed for their own branches. The 'Clan Fersane' was named in 1611 in a complaint to the Privy Council about the sheltering of Clan Gregor outlaws in Badenoch. Ewen of Cluny joined Montrose's royalist rising in 1645 with a strong force, and the clan voluntarily joined Mackintosh when he marched into Lochaber to pursue his old dispute with the Camerons.

Cluny disputed the chiefship of Clan Chattan with Mackintosh on several occasions. When Duncan Macpherson was given the arms appropriate to the 'only true representer' in 1672, Mackintosh protested and the decision was reversed. The Privy Council confined Cluny's responsibility to 'those of his name of Macpherson, descendit of his family, his men, tenants and servants'. At the same time leading members of the other families objected to Duncan's attempt to get them to sign letters of security for their good behaviour, even alleging that he was not their chief and that his predecessors had never claimed to be. But they showed a different spirit, and the importance they attached to the chiefship, when in 1689 Cluny married his only child Anne to a son of Campbell of Cawdor. Believing that if 'the representation of us and all others our kinsmen' were to pass to a stranger 'our ruin is thereby threatened', his nearest male relative Macpherson of Nuide and others (including Pitmain and Invereshie) drew up a protest declaring that they would only 'own and countenance' Nuide and his heirs male. Their opposition was successful, and when Duncan died Nuide's son duly succeeded.

A bond of friendship between the Frasers, Camerons and Macphersons signed in 1742, and the bitter memory of two Macphersons shot in the Black Watch mutiny (when they feared being sent overseas in breach of previous promises), helped to sway the clan to the Jacobite side in 1745. Cluny, although he held King George's commission at the outset, brought over about 300 fighting men after some slighting treatment when he met Cope at Dalwhinnie. They fought through the campaign, but the finest part of the story is the sequel, when for nine years Cluny was able to elude a large body of troops stationed in Badenoch for the express purpose of finding him, although many of his clansmen might have claimed the £1,000 reward offered for information. One of his refuges was 'Cluny's cage' on Ben Alder, where he received the Prince and other wanderers, and he eventually escaped and died an exile in France. The estates were restored to his son in 1784, and Cluny remained the home of the chiefs until 1932, finally passing from the clan during the Second World War. But the Macphersons retain some property in Badenoch, and in 1952 they opened at Newtonmore the first purely clan museum ever established.

MACQUARRIE

MACQUARRIE

PERHAPS the smallest of the Highland clans, and the one with the most circumscribed territory, the MacQuarries have spread far from their ancient home in the Isle of Ulva and the adjacent part of Mull. Within this limited compass are to be found many of the characteristics of the greater clans; in later years the clan can boast its great man, Lachlan Macquarie, the 'Father of Australia'; overseas branches became more numerous, as in Nova Scotia, and more clan-conscious, as in the United States, than at home; and, while the chiefship has been undetermined for over a century, claims are cherished in more than one family living far from the shores of Ulva.

When the Lord of the Isles held sway in the Hebrides, the 'fierce undaunted' MacQuarries formed part of his forces, and the chief had a place of honour as an 'ancient thane' in his councils. Two charters, granted by the lord as Earl of Ross in 1463 at Dingwall and Tain, are witnessed by John MacQuarrie of Ulva. After the lordship was forfeited in 1493 the clan followed the Macleans, and John's son Dunslaff (once a popular name in the Highlands as well as in Ireland) began a trail of troubles by supporting the Macdonald claimants to the lordship which led the clan into raids on the islands and mainland.

Small as their territory was, like many larger estates it was divided to give a home and livelihood to younger sons and their families. Allan MacQuarrie of Ulva, who was killed at Inverkeithing in 1651 along with Sir Hector Maclean and most of their followers, had three younger brothers (or half-brothers) who founded the cadet branches of Ormaig, Laggan and Balligartan. The Isle of Staffa, later to become famous, was part of the eldest brother's share of the estate. The MacQuarries were drawn into the war waged by the Earl of Argyll against the Macleans in Mull; John of Laggan took a leading part in refusing the king's messengers admittance to Duart castle in 1674, and helped to garrison Cairnburgh in the Treshnish Isles in 1680, and his nephew the chief was held responsible for clansmen raiding as far as the head of Loch Long. Eventually the Macleans had to submit, and the Ulva estate came to be held, like their wider possessions, of the Argyll family as superiors. Ormaig was 'out' with Dundee at Killiecrankie, and a few of the clan seem to have taken part in the later Jacobite risings, but Buchanan of Auchmar described the chief as living 'peaceable in his own island, not much concerned with any affairs that occur in any other part of this kingdom'.

Lachlan, the last of the MacQuarries of Ulva to own the ancestral estate, was a minor when his father died in 1735, and an uncle Allan of Culinish was his tutor. When Johnson and Boswell visited Ulva during their tour to the Hebrides in 1773, they found the laird 'intelligent, polite, and much a man of the world'. MacQuarrie had to part with his estate owing to financial difficulties four years later, and though then well past middle age he joined the army as a lieutenant in the Argyll Highlanders and saw active service in North America. Retiring on half-pay (which he drew for thirty-three years), he lived for some time on Little Colonsay, and then moved to Gribun and later to a clansman's house at Pennygown, on the other side of Mull, where he died in 1818, reputedly a centenarian. By two marriages he had at least seven sons and nine daughters, of whom the eldest, Marie, Mrs Maclaine of Scallastle, was known as 'mother of heroes' because of the distinction of her four sons in the Napoleonic wars. The senior cadets were the Ormaig line, who took their designation from a township on the south shore of Ulva; they intermarried with the Balligartan family, and descendants were still living on the island up to about the 1840s.

The most famous member of the clan was Major-General Lachlan Macquarie (as he spelled the name), who was rescued from obscurity by an Army career and became Governor of New South Wales from 1810–21. He brought the clan prominently into the *Army List* by securing commissions for innumerable cousins and nephews, as well as writing it large on the map of Australia. His brother Charles, also a soldier, was for several years laird of Ulva, though not chief, but the island's population was later drastically reduced and the clan became scattered.

MACRAE

MACRAE, DRESS

One of those names which come into existence quite independently in different places and at different times, Macrae has been variously interpreted as 'son of grace' or 'son of luck'. It must have been given to individuals who were not necessarily connected by blood or any other tie, and it appears in many parts of Scotland.

But it was especially in Wester Ross, around Loch Duich and in Glenshiel, that those of the name formed a community of their own. It is no accident that the six 'MacRa' signatories of a contract of friendship made in 1702 with another clan (the Campbells of Craignish)—on behalf of themselves and 'the hail remnant gentlemen and others of the name of Ra in Kintail and elsewhere lineally descended of their forebearers and predecessors'—all lived in Kintail.

The Macraes who settled there in the late 14th or early 15th century are said to have come from Clunes, a little west of Inverness in the lordship of Lovat, where they had a tradition of long-standing friendship with the Frasers. The loyalty of the Macraes to the chiefs of Kintail led to their becoming known as 'Mackenzie's shirt of mail', and they helped the family to expand their influence in the Highlands. They proved useful both in peace and war, and we find three Macraes as constables of Eilean Donan Castle, two in the 'desirable lucrative trust' of principal officer of Kintail, and others as Seaforth's factor or chamberlain, as well as several parish ministers.

Guarding the entrance to Loch Duich, Eilean Donan was of prime importance to the Mackenzies, as well as being one of the two castles considered 'rycht necessar for the danting of the Ilis'. It was garrisoned by the chief, but his possessions stretched right across Scotland, and even when he was not himself in the west it could be used to lodge important prisoners. To avoid jealousy, its keeping was not confined to any one family. A Matheson was constable when Donald Gruamach of Sleat laid siege to the castle in 1539, but the arrow which mortally wounded the Clan Donald chief came from the bow of Duncan Macrae, son of the previous constable. More than a century later, a Macrae slew one of the Commonwealth soldiers from Eilean Donan with one stroke of his sword after the garrison had demanded that the people of Kintail should provide them with fuel for the winter.

A pioneer in driving cattle to the markets in the South was Christopher Macrae, who became rich in that trade in the second half of the 16th century. His wife was a Murchison, whose brother was both minister of Kintail and constable of Eilean Donan, and their son Farquhar was given both offices in 1618 by Colin, first Earl of Seaforth. Among Farquhar's descendants were the Macraes of Inverinate and of Conchra, of whose position in the clan much has been said and written.

Many Macraes served in the Kintail and Lochalsh companies of the Jacobite army at Sheriffmuir, where they fell almost to a man. In the 'attempt' of 1719 Eilean Donan was held by a small company of Spaniards, battered from the sea and then blown up, and at least one Macrae fell in the brush with Government troops in Glenshiel. If the sorry picture of the Macraes who surrounded Dr Johnson and Boswell in 1773 is anything to go by, it is small wonder that they enlisted in the Highland regiment raised a few years later by Lord Seaforth; when another was raised in 1804 a Macrae ensign brought eighteen of his own name as part of his quota of twenty recruits. That they did not leave their pride and independence at home is shown by the 'affair of the wild Macraes' who in 1778 encamped on Arthur's Seat in Edinburgh and refused to return to duty until their grievances were redressed.

The barony of Kintail passed from the Seaforth family in 1869, and when sheep farming and sporting rights became paramount the 'pet lamb of Kintail' belonging to a Macrae shoemaker at the head of Loch Duich became a symbol of individual freedom. A case of a different sort was debated before the Lyon Court in 1909, when the representative of Inverinate unsuccessfully petitioned for arms suitable to the chief of Clan Macrae. A few years later one of the Conchra line, Lieut.-Colonel John Macrae-Gilstrap, acquired the ruins of Eilean Donan castle and completed its restoration as a residence in 1932.

MACTAVISH

MACTAVISH

SOME curious patronymic forms like McCaus and McCawis in early records hide the identity of the 'sons of Thomas' who since about the mid-18th century became fixed in the surname MacTavish. Those in Argyll are probably of the same race as the Campbells, although unlike other septs none of them ever seems to have used that name; but a considerable group of MacTavishes in Stratherrick, on the Lovat estate in Inverness-shire, are regarded as a sept of the Frasers.

Ten generations from father to son owned the estate of Dunardary, near the western end of the Crinan canal in Argyll, for just over 250 years. In 1533 John McAllister VcEwin VcCaus and his son Dugall McAne had a feu charter from the Earl of Argyll of the lands of Tonardare, Dunnavis, Bardarroch, Barinloskin and Barindaif. Dugall's son Patrick is on record between 1547 and 1580 (perhaps even longer) under the designations Patrick McDoule VcAne VcAllexander or more simply as Patrick Makcause of Tonardary.

By the time of Argyll's rebellion (in association with Monmouth) in 1685, the name MacTavish was spread throughout Knapdale, Kilmichael Glassary and Kilberry, with a few scattered individuals in neighbouring parishes; in the three parishes alone twenty-five MacTavish rebels and forty fencible men of the name were listed. One of the Dunardary family (some say the chief himself or his heir) was hanged by the besiegers of Carnasserie castle, which was held for Argyll by Campbell of Auchinbreck. Archibald of Dunardary, who succeeded as a minor, was thought to be sympathetic to the Jacobites in 1715, and in 1745 some 'treasonable' correspondence by his son Dugald with Sir James of Auchinbreck led to their arrest (the duke hoped this would 'put an end to plotting' in Argyll), and it was not until a general amnesty in 1747 that young Dunardary was released; but he seems to have won the duke's confidence, for by 1757 he was made one of his factors and chamberlains, with the office of baron bailie. At the judicial sale of Auchinbreck in 1767 Dugald bought the estate of Inverlussa, to the south of his own; but his successor Lachlan had to put his affairs into the hands of trustees, and Dunardary was sold in 1785.

Relief came to the distressed chief from an unexpected quarter. 'A kinsman of mine who has lately made his appearance in England with an immense fortune, acquired in the wilds of North America, has put upon me to take out arms', he wrote. Simon McTavish, known in Montreal as 'the marquis', was the most powerful man in the fur trade; he persuaded his chief to have himself 'traced to the roots', and following the record of his arms in Lyon Register in 1793 are those of his clansman 'of Gartbeg', suitably differenced according to the law of arms in Scotland. The chief died in 1796, and Simon, learning of the 'embarrassed situation of his affairs and family', gave his widow generous financial help, took his second son (John George) into his firm as a clerk—and in 1800 bought Dunardary so as to keep it 'in the family'. The new laird was one of the Stratherrick MacTavishes (he himself used the form 'Mc'), who are known to have been settled on the Lovat estates as far back as the 16th century.

In the hills above Loch Ness, round the smaller lochs which are now joined to form a storage reservoir for hydro-electricity, lived the Frasers, MacTavishes and MacGillivrays whose homes became a nursery for the Canadian fur trade. There was an Alester McTaves in Little Garth whose testament was recorded in 1632, and a Taus oig McEane VcConnochie of Garth in 1639, and a century later their descendants were still there. Emigration began after the 'Forty-Five (when of forty-four Stratherrick men in Lovat's regiment there had been thirteen MacTavishes from Aberchalder); Simon, who was born in 1750 and sailed for the New World at thirteen, was son of John MacTavish of Fraser's Highlanders, but as little is known of his further ancestry as of any relationship that existed between Inverness-shire and Argyll. He died in 1804, leaving Dunardary to his son William and his heirs bearing the name McTavish; but after William's death in 1816 it had to be sold again, and the last of Simon's four children died in 1828. Meantime the chief's eldest son had a good start in life as a lawyer, and his son (another William) ended a career in the Hudson's Bay Company as governor of Assiniboia and Rupert's Land.

MATHESON

MATHESON

THOUGH the Clan Matheson in the 14th century rivalled the neighbouring Mackenzies in position and power, they were reduced in the following century to the status of a 'minor clan' while their rivals prospered and expanded. But in the 19th century two individuals of the old stock, by their own enterprise and success in commerce, won a position of wealth which enabled them to purchase estates and command a following which far exceeded those of their ancestors.

The Mathesons in the north, known in Gaelic as *MacMathain* and collectively as *Mathanach,* can be traced as a family or community through many centuries, unlike the unrelated 'sons of Matthew' who are found in different parts of Scotland. They owned Lochalsh in Wester Ross, and the first historical reference to them is in operations under the Earl of Ross in 1262 and 1263, when King Hakon Hakonsson was trying to hold the Hebrides for Norway. According to the Sagas, Kjarnak son of Makamal was the earl's henchman in attacking the Norsemen in Skye, and the Exchequer Rolls show that he (as Kermac Macmaghan) was compensated for his services.

No connected story of his successors is possible, but in 1427 one of the chiefs arrested at Inverness by James I was 'MacMakan', who was said to be able to muster 2,000 men. Recording a rebellion in the north fostered by Alexander, Earl of Ross and Lord of the Isles in that year, an annalist says that with him were his 'gray hondes', namely Alexander Macmurkine and four others, whom the king caused to be hanged 'to terrify others'. Ross was spared, and he gave Lochalsh to one of his sons, thereby reducing the Mathesons to the status of tenants. Their position was also much weakened by feuds with and among the families who inherited or acquired various parts of Lochalsh in the 16th century, including the Macdonalds of Glengarry and the Mackenzies of Kintail. John *dubh* Matheson was Mackenzie's constable of Eilean Donan castle at the entrance to Loch Duich in 1539, when he was killed in defending it against the chief of Sleat. All the extant chronicles centre on his grandson, Murchadh *buidhe* of Fernaig and Balmacarra, from whom many of the families who survive today are descended. From his elder son Roderick came the Mathesons of Bennetsfield in the Black Isle, and the younger son Dugald, chamberlain of Lochalsh in 1631, was ancestor of the Mathesons of Ardross and Lochalsh.

The Mathesons in Sutherland are believed to be an offshoot of the Lochalsh clan. They were fairly strong by about 1500, and associated with a branch of the Mackenzies until, in 1616, Sir Robert Gordon contrived to separate the two by persuading the Mathesons (whom he calls the 'Seilwohan' or *Siol Mhathain)* to choose 'a heid of ther owne race and familie, who wold be, from tyme to tyme, ansuerable for the rest of his tryb to the Earle of Southerland, or to any haveing his place'. He argued that they would be held in greater account by him and more respected by other people; and the choice fell on John, son of John son of Donald *ban* in Shinness near Lairg, from whom the Mathesons of Shinness were descended, and those of Achany and the Lews.

The last of the old Matheson possessions went with the sale of Attadale in 1825 by the descendant of Malcolm's son Dugald. The seller had married a daughter of Matheson of Shinness, and this reunited family brought about the revival of the name in the Highlands. With their fortunes made by trade in the East, James Matheson, a son of Captain Donald of Shinness, bought the estates of Achany and Gruids, near Lairg, and his nephew Alexander Matheson bought Ardintoul and Letterfearn on Loch Duich and began the purchase of Ardross near Invergordon. These were the first of a succession of Highland properties acquired by the two men as a means of investing capital in developing local resources, without disturbing the traditional occupations of the inhabitants. Both sat in Parliament, both were made baronets: Sir James added Lewis in 1844 and Ullapool in 1847, and Sir Alexander followed with the old Matheson estates of Lochalsh in 1851 and Attadale in 1861, as well as Inverinate, Strathbran and Strathcarron. Within about twenty-five years of their purchases starting, Sir James owned over 800,000 acres in Ross-shire and his nephew over 200,000; but it was a short-lived 'empire', and if people of their own name numbered only a small portion of the inhabitants this was probably not much different from the position 450 years before.

MAXWELL

MAXWELL

On the north shore of the Solway Firth, facing towards England, the Maxwells were the most wealthy and powerful family group in Dumfries-shire and its vicinity. As well as their splendid baronial castle of Caerlaverock, whose tall gatehouse and triangular plan make it one of the most impressive ruins in Scotland, the castles of Lochmaben, Dumfries and Threave were at various times in Maxwell hands. They were for many years wardens of the west march, and also held the hereditary offices of steward of Annandale and of Kirkcudbright.

Caerlaverock was probably Maxwell property from the early 13th century, when John de Maccuswell, sheriff of Teviotdale, turned his attention to the western Border. In 1312 the castle was in the keeping of Sir Eustace Maxwell, a man who lived 'between the hammer and the anvil' of two warring nations, which led to Caerlaverock being besieged and changing sides more than once. After the defeat of the Black Douglases in the mid-15th century, the crown looked largely to the Maxwells for the defence of the Border against the English. In the period after Flodden the west wardenry of Scotland came to be almost exclusively a Maxwell perquisite, especially from 1515 until 1553, when John Maxwell of Terregles (who became Lord Herries in right of his wife) resigned because he could no longer effectively exercise the wardenship on account of feuds; he was succeeded by his uncle Douglas of Drumlanrig and later alternated with him in the office.

The power of the great Border leaders was based on the possession of lands held from the crown, which were leased to kinsmen and followers for feudal services. It seems that more 'bonds of manrent' for mutual support were obtained by the Maxwell chiefs than by any other Border family, not even the Douglases excepted. The Maxwells were also prolific in cadet houses, which spread their name and influence far beyond the early bounds; a dozen or so were descended from the oldest branch, the Maxwells of Pollok in Renfrewshire. The need for such family backing and alliances in exercising the wardenship is illustrated by the feud between the Maxwells and the Johnstones which lasted throughout the second half of the 16th century. Arising out of the killing of an Armstrong in 1527, and Maxwell encouragement of his kinsmen's retaliation, it led to a succession of disturbances; an attempt at arbitration through the Privy Council in 1574 did not prevent it from breaking out again when a Johnstone was appointed warden in 1580. At Dryfe sands near Lockerbie in 1593 Lord Maxwell was killed while on a punitive expedition as warden against the Johnstones. The last of the Maxwell wardens, William Lord Herries, was defeated in 1595, and later agreed to submit his difference with the laird of Johnstone to the arbitration of the king and others, reserving his duty of blood and friendship to Lord Maxwell. Just before the union of 1603 brought the prospect of permanent peace on the Border, twelve Maxwell lairds subscribed with the king and other leading men a 'general band' against thieves, murderers and oppressors, and by 1607 Caerlaverock had become merely 'a weak house of the barons of Maxwell'.

But the family's troubles were not over. Lord Maxwell himself killed the laird of Johnstone in an affray in 1608, fled to France, but returned and was beheaded in 1613. His brother Robert of Caerlaverock was deep in debt, and with the approval of eight Maxwell gentlemen the next brother (the Master of Maxwell) proposed in 1616 to relieve his own 'miserie' and the 'distressit hous of Maxwell' by persuading Sir John Maxwell of Pollok to advance the money needed to save the Maxwell estates, on a promise of being acknowledged as chief of the family on the failure of the main line. Pollok declined, and the plan fell through, but a fortunate marriage rehabilitated the family, and Robert not only received the earldom of Nithsdale but had heirs of his own to carry it on. Caerlaverock, after a 13-week siege and bombardment in 1640, was partially destroyed; its ruins passed by inheritance through the Herries family to the Duke of Norfolk, who placed it under Government guardianship. Meanwhile the Nithsdale title was forfeited when the fifth earl joined the Jacobites in 1715 (he escaped from the Tower of London in women's clothes through the cleverness of Lady Nithsdale), but the name has been carried on by a host of branch families, of which the Maxwells of Pollok have been the most eminent as well as the oldest.

MENZIES

MENZIES, DRESS

One of the oldest feudal lines in Scotland, the family of Menzies at various times possessed the baronies of Weem and Rannoch in Perthshire, Durisdeer and Enoch in Dumfries-shire, Vogrie in Midlothian, Culter in Lanark, and a number of estates in the north-east. For 100 years before 1590 the office of provost of Aberdeen was held by one of the name of Menzies, including members of the Pitfodels family.

When Alexander III succeeded to the throne in 1249, his Great Chamberlain was Sir Robert de Meygners (the earliest form of the name). His son, Sir Alexander, obtained a charter of the lands of Weem and Aberfeldy from the Earl of Athol about 1296, and was one of the earliest supporters of Robert Bruce, who later rewarded him with the baronies of Glendochart in Perthshire and Durisdeer in Nithsdale. The family long took their territorial designation from Weem, but it was not without difficulty that Menzies held his own in the midst of clan rivalries and powerful neighbours. In 1488 the chief obtained a bond of manrent from Duncan Campbell of Glenorchy, but despite this and several Campbell marriages the families were at constant feud during the greater part of the following century. A quarrel with the Stewarts of Fortingall relating to lands which had once belonged to Menzies broke out in 1503 when his lands were raided and the 'place of Weem' burnt. The name was changed to Castle Menzies by a charter of 1510, but it was not until 1571–77 that the present fine 'Z-plan' building arose, with its decorative wall-head contrasting with the gun-ports at ground level. Queen Mary showed an interest in the local problem of peace-keeping while on a visit to the district, and she asked the laird of Weem to allow his old MacGregor tenants in Rannoch to occupy their former lands on reasonable terms, without his having to find caution for their good behaviour.

It must have been inconvenient for one family to hold lands in both Strathtay and Nithsdale, although the establishment of cadet branches would make it easier. It seems likely that, at least in the later generations, the eldest son of Weem had Enoch as inheritance during his father's lifetime, but about 1605 they finally parted with this property. The lands were granted to another Perthshire Menzies, Adam of Baltoquhane, whose family lived there until it was sold to the Duke of Queensberry in 1703–4.

In the civil wars of the 17th and 18th centuries there were Menzies supporters on both sides, and it can be assumed that each laird whose part is remembered had some of the clan at his back. Weem was an ally of Argyll, but Pitfodels was killed carrying the royal standard at Carbisdale in Montrose's last campaign. James Menzies of Culdares commanded one of the earliest Highland companies raised in 1678, and in 1689 Robert, younger of that Ilk, was captain of another raised by himself for King William's service. Major Duncan Menzies was one of two emissaries sent to sound James VII in France about the oath of allegiance, but the authority to his loyal subjects to do what might be best for their safety did not arrive in time to avert the massacre of Glencoe. In 1715 Culdares was 'out', but he was reprieved and remained at home in 1745. Pitfodels too was 'out' in 1715, and in 1745 was active in raising men and forcing out tenants, and all his six sons fought for Charles. Menzies of Shian sent out the 'fiery cross' round Loch Tay in the later Rising, in which he commanded the clan detachment, but there were murmurings after Culloden from the widows of those 'who would have staid at home if they durst'. The Prince was at Castle Menzies on his way north, but it was later occupied by a garrison of Government troops.

But of course life was not all feud and warfare, in this or in any other clan. Culdares brought some of the earliest larches from the Tyrol to Perthshire, and in the very week of Culloden was placidly discussing with a Campbell neighbour his right to fish for salmon in the Lyon. There were musters of the clan in happier days, such as Queen Victoria's first visit to the Highlands in 1842, when they paraded under Sir Neil Menzies at Taymouth. The direct line of the chief's family died out in the male line in 1910, but a successor from the Culdares line has been recognised, and in 1958 the clan society bought Castle Menzies with a view to restoring it where possible as a clan centre.

MONTGOMERIE

MONTGOMERIE

ONE distinction 'the like whereof cannot be truly said of any other sirname in the world' was claimed for the Montgomeries in the 17th century—that it gave the title of count or earl in four kingdoms (Count Montgomery, Earl of Montgomery, Earl of Eglinton, and Earl of Mount Alexander, in France, England, Scotland and Ireland respectively); and it may be added that Montgomeryshire in Wales is the only British county which bears the name of a Norman lordship.

The first of the name in Scotland appears to have been Robert de Mundegumri, who is frequently on record between 1165 and 1177. He was granted the manor of Eaglesham in Renfrewshire, which was for two centuries the family's chief possession in Scotland, and remained their property undiminished for 700 years. His descendant, Sir John of Eaglesham, fought hand-to-hand at Otterburn with Percy (Harry 'hotspur') and took him prisoner; marriage with the heiress of Sir Hugh de Eglinton is believed to have brought him the baronies of Eglinton and Ardrossan. The head of the family was made a Lord of Parliament as Lord Montgomerie in 1445 and Earl of Eglinton in 1507. As Ayrshire magnates, the Montgomeries became involved in a long feud with the Cunninghams over the office of bailie of Cunningham; averted for a time by a declaration in favour of Eglinton in 1509, it broke out again with increased bitterness, and the manor-house of Eglinton was burned.

Feuds between powerful families were only too prevalent at the time. One means of trying to heal them is illustrated in an arbitration of 1530 between Earl Hugh and Robert Boyd (whose chief had been killed) and Mungo Mure of Rowallan, and their respective kin, friends, servants and tenants. Robert, Bishop of Argyll (who was Eglinton's son), and five others proposed, and it was agreed, that bygones would be bygones, there was to be a marriage alliance, Eglinton was to pay 2,000 merks, and the parties were to stand in 'unite, concord and hartly kyndnes' to each other, with penalties for any future discord. Whatever came of these conditions, the Cunningham feud continued, with the murder of Eglinton himself in 1586, until by 1607 it had the distinction of being rated as the last prolonged feud in the kingdom. In 1609 by royal decree the two principals shook hands with mutual forgiveness, and the king rejoiced that it had been 'taken up by the roote'.

Owing to failure of the direct male line, Sir Alexander Seton of Foulstruther became chief of the Montgomeries in 1612. A younger son of the Earl of Winton and Lady Margaret Montgomerie (his predecessor's aunt), and nephew of Chancellor Seton, he took the name and arms of Montgomerie and, in spite of some objection by King James, secured the Eglinton title with its original precedence as well as the estates. An unusual document of 1630 suggests that the ex-Seton—known as 'Grey-steel' on account of his courage in fighting for the Covenant—was anxious to secure himself in his adopted name. His kinsman Hugh, Viscount Montgomerie of the Great Ardes in Ireland (descended from an uncle of the first Lord Eglinton), signed an indenture promising that the duty which they owed to the honour of the house of the Earl of Eglinton would be acknowledged and respected by him and his heirs, and each would deliver on his succession 'one fair horse' to the earl and his successors 'being of the surname of Montgomery'. This last proviso was repeated thrice in the twenty-three lines of the document, which was engrossed on vellum with two coloured portraits at the top, and witnessed by four Montgomeries.

The ninth earl acquired the estates of Dundonald, Kilmaurs, Glassford and Southennan, additions nearly as valuable as the old Eglinton estate. The last two of the line were his sons, Alexander and Archibald, tenth and eleventh earls, who did much to improve their estates, and agriculture in general, by encouraging planned management. The earldom passed to the Montgomeries of Coilsfield—'a martial race, bold, soldier-featur'd, undismay'd' (according to Burns)—including the earl who was twice Lord Lieutenant of Ireland and organised the costly and splendid 'Eglinton Tournament' in 1839. To this the whole of the Montgomerie family, including the Irish branch, were invited, as well as nobles and princes of many lands; the event is still remembered as a romantic revival of the age of chivalry in which the Montgomeries were so deeply rooted in many lands.

MORRISON

MORRISON

WRITING in the late 17th century, Johne Morisone, 'indweller in Lewis', was bold enough to claim that all the Morrisons in Scotland could 'challenge' descent from a common progenitor. Such a statement would not now be generally accepted, and various explanations are put forward for the appearance of the name in one form or another in different parts of the country. The phrase 'the manly Morrisons'—however widely applicable it may be today—seems to have had special reference to a family group for long settled at Woodend in the parish of Kirkmichael, in Dumfries-shire; Morison of Dairsie in Fife was the first of the name to record arms with three Saracens' heads conjoined on one neck and facing in three directions; and one of the Morisons of Prestongrange sat as a lord of session in Edinburgh.

As a clan or community the Morrisons of the Outer Hebrides have a place of their own in Highland history and tradition. Alexander Carmichael, Celtic enthusiast and author of *Carmina Gadelica,* wrote this of them: 'The Morrisons have been celebrated throughout the ages for their wit, poetry, music, philosophy, medicine and science, for their independence of mind and sobriety of judgment and for their benevolence of heart and unfailing hospitality'. In Lewis a family of Morrisons held land in the district of Ness, where their home was at Habost, for acting as the island's judges or 'brieves' during the period of MacLeod possession, until the beginning of the 17th century. According to tradition they held this office for ten generations, and from it they were sometimes known as *Clann na Breitheamh.* 'The brieve', wrote Sir Robert Gordon, 'is a kynd of judge among the ilanders, who hath ane absolute judicatorie, unto whose authoritie and censure they willinglie submitt themselves, when he determineth any debatable question betuein partie and partie'.

No written judgments seem to have been found, and none may in fact ever have been recorded, but the existence of the office does not rest wholly on tradition. Hucheon Morrison, brieve, was summoned to Inverness in 1551 along with Rory MacLeod of Lewis for harbouring rebels; John Morrison, brieve, son of Hugh, was a chief supporter of Torquil Cononach during the troubles caused by the attempt to establish the 'Fife Adventurers' in Lewis; and Hucheon Breiff and Allane Breiff were among MacLeod of Lewis's 'household men' in 1600. It is said that a 'poke' containing the heads of a dozen Morrisons captured as 'special withstanders of the enterprise' was sent to Edinburgh where they were fixed to the city gates. The last notice of the office is the listing of 'Donald MacIndowie, Brieff' in 1616 among the rebels who resisted the settlers from Fife and later the Tutor of Kintail when the Mackenzies took over Lewis. Times had changed, and their legal authority, whatever its exact nature and extent, had come to an end.

In neighbouring Harris the Morrisons are found in the 17th century occupying farms in Pabbay, the island in the Sound of Harris where the MacLeods had a stronghold, and in Bernera, Taransay, Scarista and Borves. The hereditary smiths and armourers of the MacLeods of Harris were Morrisons, and from them descended John Morison *(Iain Gobha),* blacksmith, preacher and poet, whose 'spiritual songs' had a profound influence on the religious life of Lewis and Harris in the 19th century. From North Uist came the forebears of Viscount Dunrossil (W. S. Morrison), who was Speaker of the House of Commons from 1951–59 and died Governor-General of Australia, and whose elder brother was granted arms as chief of the Morrisons in 1967. The name is also prominent on the north-west mainland, where there was a tradition that a Morrison from Lewis settled in Durness on land given him by a bishop of Caithness, and brought over a colony of sixty families mostly of his own name.

Among the acknowledged varieties of the name are Morrison, Morison, Murison and Gilmour. To indicate the reawakening of kinship among those bearing these names a Clan Morrison Society was set up in 1909. They registered arms including the three Saracens' heads, and later acquired Dun Eistein, the rock fortress near the Butt of Lewis where the Morrisons had found refuge in times of stress.

MUNRO

BLACK WATCH (MUNRO, HUNTING)

ALTHOUGH their origin has been called 'one of the problems of clan history', the Munros can trace their story back for more than 600 years in Ross-shire through written evidence, and traditionally it goes back even further. Their territory, dominated by Ben Wyvis and coinciding roughly with the modern parishes of Alness and Kiltearn, stretched from Altnalait *(Allt na Lathaid)* on the outskirts of Dingwall to the Averon or Alness water. It was called Ferindonald, from the clan's supposed founder, and the home of the chiefs was and still is at Foulis.

Robert Munro appears on record in the early 14th century, and innumerable cadet branches sprang from the main stem, chiefly through two younger sons in the 15th century. From the fertile strip of land alongside the Cromarty

Firth the clan spread into the hills behind, and across the watershed into Sutherland. At first they held their lands from the Earls of Ross, in whose service a laird of Foulis was killed in 1369. They were 'bailies' in Ferindonald for the Macdonald earls who were also Lords of the Isles, and shortly after the earldom was forfeited in 1476 the chief became the king's chamberlain for the earldom. His successor Sir William had some arduous commissions from James IV, in carrying out one of which he was killed in 1505. When the kingdom itself was threatened the clan joined the muster in the south, and George Munro of Foulis fell at Pinkie in 1547.

First of a line of Protestant chiefs was Robert *mor*, who voted in the Reformation Parliament of 1560, and supported Queen Mary when she came north two years later. He was a man of influence in the north, being chamberlain of Ross, keeper of Dingwall castle for the crown, and 'customar' of Inverness-shire. By exchanging some lands in Dingwall for part of the old earldom in Strathoykell, where his family already owned lands, Robert added to the clan's influence on the borders of Sutherland, where many Munros settled and the barony of Culrain was later created for a cadet of Foulis.

The chief and many of his clan served in Mackay's Regiment under Christian IV of Denmark and Gustavus Adolphus of Sweden, the 17th century defenders of Protestantism. In that war there were three generals, eight colonels, five lieutenant colonels, eleven majors, and above thirty captains, all of the name of Munro. Robert *dubh* of Foulis went as a volunteer, and his namesake later appears as a major-general in the army of the Covenant, and was sent to suppress a Catholic rising in Ireland. The civil wars coincided with a long minority in the chiefship, following the death of Robert *dubh* and his brother Sir Hector on service in Germany; the clan's loyalties were probably divided, with their leading men favouring 'different principles'—Robert of Obsdale, who became chief in 1651, was sheriff of Ross under the Commonwealth, while his brother Sir George was a leading royalist and commander-in-chief in Scotland from 1674–77. Hostile clans took the opportunity to inflict loss and damage on the chief, his kinsmen, tenants and servants. Sir John, the next chief, known as the 'Presbyterian mortarpiece', suffered fines and imprisonment, and the ministers of Alness and Kiltearn were staunch Covenanters who both had a spell on the Bass Rock.

The Munros welcomed the Revolution settlement, and consistently supported the Government through the Jacobite risings of 1715, 1719 and 1745. In the last, Sir Robert of Foulis, who had commanded the Black Watch at Fontenoy, was killed (along with his brother Dr. Duncan) at Falkirk in command of the 37th Regiment; his son Harry, a captain in Lord Loudon's Regiment then being formed, met General Cope outside Inverness with the first loyal contingent he had seen, but was captured at Prestonpans; three more companies were raised under Sir Robert's brother George of Culcairn (later killed in Lochaber), Hugh of Teaninich and William of Achany, and they marched 200 strong as Cope's advance guard to Aberdeen.

There was a considerable group of Munros in and around Inveraray, where the Munros of Stuckghoy in Glenshira are on record from 1664 to 1794 and later at Barnaline on Lochaweside. There is also an Irish branch of the clan, descended from the Munros of Kiltearn; two British Commonwealth premiers have been Munros, a Speaker of the New Zealand House of Representatives, a President of the U.S.A., and a president of the General Assembly of the United Nations.

MURRAY

MURRAY OF ATHOLL

One of the oldest surnames in Scotland is derived from lands in the North whose owners first emerge into history under the Latinised form *de Moravia*. Many bearers of the name in one or other of its usual forms are probably descended from the powerful Murrays or Morays of Bothwell in Lanarkshire, whose castle is magnificent even in ruin, but the actual connecting links of descent are lost.

Three generations of Andrew Morays of Bothwell won fame and extended their influence in the 13th and 14th century wars of independence—Sir Andrew of Petty, justiciar north of the Forth; the Andrew who was joint commander with Wallace, and with him defeated the English at Stirling Bridge; and Andrew of Bothwell, made Guardian of Scotland after the defeat at Dupplin in 1332. A son of the last of this trio died in 1361.

The lands of Tullibardine near Auchterarder in Perthshire, which formed the 'divide' between Strathearn and Strathallan, came to the Murray family in the first half of the 14th century; they became a barony in 1444, and their owner was made a peer of parliament in 1604 and Earl of Tullibardine in 1606. Cadets of this family, whose head after marriage with a Stewart heiress became Earl of Atholl in 1629, marquess in 1676, and duke in 1703, include the Earls of Dysart (1643), Dunmore (1686) and Mansfield (1776), and the Murrays of Glendoick, Ayton, Pitcaithly, Lintrose, Dollary, Arbenie, Pitcullen, Woodend, Strowan and Tippermore. The Morays of Abercairney, one of the few whose descendants still use that form of the name, have claims of their own to an independent status; and important families in the south include the Murrays of Cockpool, who rose to be Earls of Annandale (1624), with their cadets; Touchadam and Polmaise, in Stirlingshire; and Falahill, hereditary sheriffs of Selkirk, with a host of cadets including the 'stirring race' of Blackbarony, created Lords Elibank (1643).

Both north and south, it makes a formidable array, and two important documents show that the Murrays had a sense of unity among themselves. In 1586 and 1598 'bonds of association' were executed by some of the leading men of the name, in each case headed by Sir John of Tullibardine (later the first earl), a childhood friend of James VI who evidently shared the king's dislike of family feuds. Under the first, signed at Tullibardine for mutual defence 'sua that one's cause shall be all, and all shall be one', any quarrels or debates were to be settled by Sir John with eight named 'friends' (or any four of them), and in difficult cases with 'the haill rest of the name and frinds'; all decisions were to be as effectual as if pronounced by a judge, and anyone contravening them would be 'accounted from thencefurth enemy to them all'. At Edinburgh in 1598, being 'far dispersed in sundry parts of this realm' and so less able to serve the king as they wished, it was agreed that 'any action or cause either criminal or civil' arising between Murrays should be submitted to 'eight of the most wise, well affectioned, and most efficient of the said surname', four nominated by each party with Sir John as 'oversman' in case of disagreement. Signing the first document were the heads of families in the north, such as Arngask, Tippermore and Ochtertyre, and in the second great southern lairds such as Cockpool, Blackbarony and Touchadam; Abercairney as well as Tullibardine signed both.

The next Earl of Tullibardine married the Earl of Atholl's daughter, and was entrusted with the administration of the district. The title itself was allowed to his son and the Tullibardine honours were passed on to a cousin, but they soon returned to the main line and are now merged with the dukedom of Atholl. The presence of a Whig duke in a district teeming with Jacobites (something like 1,000 Stewarts were among his vassals) had some strange effects in 1715 and 1745, but the titles and estates survived although his elder brother raised the standard for the prince and the youngest was his lieutenant-general. Lord George Murray led the Atholl brigade against Blair castle, and the family seat had the distinction of being the last castle in Britain to be besieged. In the more peaceful times that followed, Blair was remodelled, and it is now a treasure-house of family heirlooms in which the Murray background plays a part. The duke's ceremonial bodyguard, the Atholl Highlanders, which received a pair of colours from Queen Victoria, are the only 'private army' in the kingdom.

OGILVY

OGILVY, DRESS

In the glens and braes of Angus, where Glenisla, Glenprosen and Glenclova run up into the hills towards Deeside from the fertile lowlands of Strathmore, lies the land of the Ogilvys. It used to extend into the Sidlaw Hills on the south, where a valley above Glamis is still named Glenogilvie; and in fact the surname is derived from lands which became a barony possessed by the Ogilvys, based on Easter Powrie on the north side of Dundee.

In the reign of William the Lion, sometime between 1172 and 1177, Gilbert the son of the Earl of Angus had a charter of the lands of 'Purin, Ogguluin and Kynmethan'. These lands of Ogilvy and Easter Powrie passed in unbroken male descent for nearly 500 years in the family of Ogilvy of that Ilk. More influential, however, were those descended from Sir Walter Ogilvy of Auchterhouse, sheriff of Angus, who was killed near Blairgowrie in 1392 while repelling an inroad of Highlanders from the north. Sir Walter's eldest son, who fell at the battle of Harlaw, was ancestor of the Inchmartine line and the later Earls of Findlater; from another son, Sir Walter of Lintrathen, Lord High Treasurer of Scotland, came the house of Airlie and the Ogilvys of Deskford; and a third founded the Ogilvys of Inverquharity.

The Airlie line take their designation from the lands known as 'Eroly' in 1432, when they had a licence from James I to make a castle of their home on the edge of a ravine above the Isla. Their lands lay to the east of Kirriemuir, but on the failure of the Inverquharity line they spread westwards to the estate of Cortachy on the South Esk, including the glens of Clova and Prosen which had for long been in Ogilvy hands. The head of the family was raised to the peerage in 1491 as Lord Ogilvy of Airlie (the earldom did not follow until 1639), and the name spread through Angus and the south-east highlands of Perthshire. Three important Ogilvy lairds appear on the roll of Highland landlords drawn up for Parliament in 1587—Patrick of Inchmartine, James Lord Ogilvy, and Alexander of Clova.

The Ogilvys had some powerful neighbours, and they sometimes needed to draw together for mutual support. There was a battle with the Lindsays at Arbroath in 1446, when 500 Ogilvys were killed; and a long feud with the more distant Campbells began when in 1591 their lands in Glenisla were spoiled by Argyll's Highlanders and some of his men slaughtered. In the civil wars of the 17th century the Ogilvys were deeply involved, chiefs, lairds and people, for 'no Ogilvy was ever anything but a king's man' (as John Buchan wrote). Disturbed times offered a chance to pay off old scores: in 1640 Argyll with 5,000 men destroyed Airlie castle and 'left him not in all his lands a cock to crow day' (this gave rise to the song 'The Bonny House of Airlie'), but five years later the Ogilvys had their revenge by setting fire to Castle Campbell near Dollar. Airlie joined Montrose, and had a command at Kilsyth; many others were prominent on the royalist side; and we get a final glimpse of the older line when Thomas Ogilvy of Powrie (who had already lost the barony) fell in Montrose's last battle at Carbisdale in 1650.

The name of Ogilvy was also one of importance in the north-east, where it was borne by the Earls of Findlater (1638) and Seafield (1701) and the Lords Banff (1642). The estates of Deskford and Findlater came to the family through marriage, and their owner, after the lands in the counties of Banff, Aberdeen and Angus had been united into the barony of Ogilvy in 1517, was usually styled Ogilvy of that Ilk. In 1613 their cadets, the Ogilvys of Banff, acknowledged Findlater as their chief, but in 1641 the Earl of Findlater arranged that the succession should pass through his daughter to her husband Ogilvy of Inchmartine. As this was an older line, Airlie feared that this family would now claim precedence in the peerage, but in 1643 Charles I, being 'ripely advised', issued a royal mandate to the effect that this was not his intention, and that Airlie besides being an ancient nobleman was 'the chief of the family and surname of Ogilvy'.

The Airlie honours, lost through the family's service to the Stewart cause in 1715 and 1745, were eventually restored, and the name continues prominent in Angus. Although it is no longer confined to the traditional land of the Ogilvys, there was a sense of family pride when in 1963 Princess Alexandra of Kent became the first royal bride of a son of the house of Airlie.

ROBERTSON

ROBERTSON, DRESS

In a resounding phrase, the lands of Clan Donnachaidh have been described as stretching from the Moor of Rannoch to the gates of Perth. With a little pardonable exaggeration, this is no bad picture of a varied territory of mountain and moor, glen and strath, dominated by the fine cone of Schiehallion, which is the homeland of the scattered 'children of Duncan' most of whom are now called Robertson.

Descended from the Celtic Earls of Atholl, the stout Duncan *(Donnachadh reamhair)* from whom they take their Gaelic patronymic is said to have led his men to fight for King Robert at Bannockburn. Duncans alternated with Roberts for the first few generations, with '*de Atholia*' or 'of Atholl' as a territorial designation, and from them the two forms of the surname have arisen. The oldest cadet branch, the Robertsons of Lude, were at first *MacThearlaich,* sons of Charles, and another usage is shown by deeds addressed to them 'and sundry persons of the surname of Clandonoquhy'; some younger branches called themselves Duncanson or MacConachie, or just Duncan or Donachie, and the descriptive name Reid (red) was also used.

The barony of Struan, which gave a landed title to the chiefs, was created by a charter of 1451. It was granted to Robert Duncanson by James II in gratitude for his zeal in apprehending one of his father's murderers, Sir Robert Graham, at a spot in the hills behind Struan still known as Graham's Burn. The chiefs lived at a succession of dwellings, from an island stronghold in Loch Tummel, the castle of Invervack near Struan, a house in Kinloch Rannoch, Carie on the Loch Rannoch side, Mount Alexander or Dunalastair, and finally the Barracks at the western end of Loch Rannoch. The surname had become fairly general throughout the clan by 1545, when 'Robert Robertsone de Strowane' was acknowledged as heir to his father William. The 'laird of Strowane-Robertsone' was named among the Highland landlords in 1587, and the roll of dependent clans presented to Parliament included 'Clandonoquhy in Athoill and pairtis adiacent'. This period, when James VI was trying to enforce order throughout his realm, was one of chaos in Atholl, the earl himself being charged with misrule. The leading Robertsons rallied to support the authority of Struan, and in 1612 a deed was drawn up at Perth in the names of Faskally, Straloch, Lude, Dalcaber and three other cadets (although only five actually signed). Anxious to defend their chief and his house 'quhairof we ar descendit' and to maintain his estate, they entered into a bond with the Earl of Erroll (a neighbour to the south) in which they undertook by his advice to 'concur and assist the said Laird of Struan . . . so far as possibly we can be able'. To consolidate his position still further, with the support of his cadets, a later chief had himself formally acknowledged as heir, in 1657 and again in 1681, to Robert of the 1451 charter and even back another generation to his father Duncan.

In this troubled 17th century the clan needed to be firmly established. A solid phalanx of cadets is named in a roll of arms held in five Perthshire parishes in 1638, and when Montrose raised the royal standard at the back of Lude in 1644 the Robertsons joined the Atholl-men under their young chief's uncle, the Tutor of Struan, and took a full part in the fighting then and in later campaigns. With a few exceptions, they were passionately Jacobite, and their poet chief Alexander had the distinction of being 'out' in 1689, 1715 and 1745, and rode home to Rannoch after Prestonpans in General Cope's captured carriage, while Robertson of Woodsheal took command of the clan. But Struan and many of his followers never recovered from the Jacobite defeat, estates were gradually sold, and emigration though not eviction scattered the clan. The chief's lands were forfeited but later restored to a relative, but the remnant that remained to later generations was sold in 1926. A younger son had settled in Jamaica as a planter, and his descendants succeeded to the chiefship, taking a keen interest in the activities of the clan society. A Clan Donnachaidh museum was opened at Bruar Falls near the heart of the old homeland in 1969, where objects, pictures, and documents tell the story of the clan, the country and the society, and the life and achievements of individual clansmen and clanswomen. Central to the display is the *Clach na Brataich,* a charm stone traditionally linked with the fortunes of the clan since the days of Bannockburn.

ROSE

ROSE, HUNTING

FEW families can equal the record of the Roses of Kilravock in Nairnshire for direct succession and continued residence in the same spot. There has been a 'baron of Kilravock' for more than 600 years, son (or occasionally daughter) succeeding father in the family estates with the intervention of hardly a single collateral heir, and almost all of them bearing the Christian name Hugh. Perhaps the reason lies in their character, as described by an 18th century Rose minister who knew the family well: 'They were of a singular ingenuitie and integritie, plaine and honest in their deallings, lovers of peace, kindly and affectionat, given to hospitalitie, temperat, sober'.

The story of 'the long race', as it has been quaintly called, begins with Hugh of Geddes, who seems to have added Kilravock further up the river Nairn to his possessions through marriage with an heiress in the time of King John Balliol. Further lands in Strathnairn came with a later marriage, and in 1460 Hugh VII had permission to build a castle at Kilravock (probably not the first) from his superior John, Earl of Ross and Lord of the Isles, after the forfeiture fifteen years later he held direct from the king but his son joined in an attempt to restore the lordship. More typical of the family was the 'black baron', Hugh X, who lived peaceably through Queen Mary's troubled reign, attending to his own affairs and settling his neighbours' disputes ('ane honest man, ill-guided betwixt them both', he signed himself in the midst of a hot debate). The queen visited him at Kilravock in 1562, and when years later King James asked how he could live amongst such turbulent neighbours he said they were the best friends he could have 'for they made him thrice a day go to God upon his knees, when perhaps otherways he would not have gone once'. When some quarrelsome Rose kinsmen were at loggerheads with the powerful Dunbars, the next laird and his son were lodged in Edinburgh castle for failing to bring them to justice, and it was found necessary to make the Mackintosh chief accountable for 'broken men' of the name of Rose.

The two Jacobite risings inevitably brought some disturbance to the family's peaceful round. Hugh XV, an opponent of the Union and a member of the last Scots Parliament and the first of Great Britain, had in his early years some sympathy for the Stewarts, and he had friends and relations on both sides. When Inverness was seized by the Jacobites in 1715 he rallied 200 of his clan and helped to turn them out, and thereafter kept his men in arms, garrisoned Kilravock, and secured the peace of the country around. Rose of Clava was 'out' and just saved his estate from forfeiture, and a Rose minister was deposed for reading the Chevalier's proclamation from his Aberdeenshire pulpit. In 1745 the next laird took no active part, but he had to receive both Prince Charles and Duke William at Kilravock just before Culloden, of which the Roses were 'in a manner eye and ear witnesses'.

More domestic concerns filled the years that followed, with the first break in the long male succession. Hugh XVIII died in 1782 with no surviving family, and a change in the destination of the estate to 'heirs whatsoever' made by his father for electioneering purposes led to prolonged litigation between his sister Elizabeth, who had married a Rose cousin, and a stepson who claimed as heir male. First the Court of Session and then the House of Lords held that the barony of Kilravock went to the heir of line (thus including females), while the lands of Geddes and Flemington passed according to the old investitures to the heir male. Elizabeth, now XIX of Kilravock, kept a journal from 1771 until her death in 1815, a letter-book and 'book of meditations', and much improved her part of the family estates by fencing, draining and planting.

Her only son lived until 1827, but as three of his sons succeeded one another the homely picture fades—Hugh XXI served twenty years with the East India Company, John fell at the Alma, and James's twenty-four years in India included the Mutiny. Among the cadet branches, Holme Rose went to Colonel Hugh of the Indian Cavalry and General Sir John Rose of Holme, while Sir Hugh of the Earlsmill line virtually reconquered India and became Field-Marshal Lord Strathnairn. In the Second World War Hugh Rose, son of Hugh XXIV, was killed in the Western Desert, with the result that another Elizabeth Rose of Kilravock became chief of the name. In 1951 she held a gathering attended by Roses from all over the world.

ROSS

ROSS, HUNTING

UNLIKE many other Highland clans, the Rosses were fortunate enough to occupy a mainly flat and fertile piece of country which gave them room to expand without encroaching on the territory of others. Its base was the peninsula projecting between the Cromarty and Dornoch firths in Easter Ross, and it spread inland to the broad valleys at the head of the Kyle of Sutherland. The chief families and many of their supporters were descended from the old Earls of Ross, and they were also joined by others who had settled in the area, such as the MacCullochs, Denoons and Vasses.

On the death of Earl William in 1372, the earldom passed to his daughter, who carried it to the Leslie family from whom it was later inherited by the Macdonald dynasty of the Isles. Hugh Ross, second son of the previous earl by a daughter of the High Steward of Scotland, although deprived of the succession, had a charter of the lands of Balnagown in 1374 from his brother-in-law Robert II, and continued the old family in the male line. Not much is known of the clan built up under their leadership in its formative years; two of the chiefs met violent deaths, one falling with seventeen other landed gentlemen of the province and a great many 'common soldiers' in a fight with the Mackays in Strathcarron in 1486, and his grandson being killed in Tain forty years later. But after the Reformation the picture becomes clearer, when the chief was Alexander of Balnagown, who feared neither God, king nor government, and whose kinsman Nicholas Ross sat in the parliament of 1560 as abbot of Fearn and voted with the Reformers.

Over the previous century the younger sons of all but one of the chiefs had founded cadet houses (Shandwick being the earliest), and the clan now included influential leaders who could if necessary challenge the chief's authority. Fearing that Alexander's folly would bring about the ruin of his house and the loss of his lands, and that his replacement by a stranger would be to his and their 'uter wrak', fourteen of the principal gentry of the clan signed a petition in 1577 exhorting him to serve God, obey the Regent Morton, and seek a remedy for the troubles which threatened. With his son and heir apparent, and the Rosses of Tollie, Shandwick, Balmuchie and others among them, they asked him to confer with them, lest he 'perish his hous kyn and freinds and tyne the riggis (lands) that his fathers wan'. Neither this nor a spell in Tantallon as a state prisoner seems to have had any effect, and letters of fire and sword were issued against the chief in 1583, and his son George was one of those charged to 'convocat the lieges' to pursue him.

One of the clan's few appearances in the civil commotions of the 17th century was in 1651. Dressed in 'doublets and breeches of striped redd hieland stuff with blew French bonnets on their heads', the Rosses joined the national army raised for the invasion of England. Balnagown was taken prisoner at Worcester, and died in London two years later. After the Restoration there were difficulties with the Mackenzies, who showed 'implacable malice' under Seaforth as sheriff of Ross; David of Balnagown, last of the old line of chiefs, was ordered to Edinburgh as a prisoner after gathering at Tain with 200 or 300 followers in a 'bellical and military posture'; and when he cut open a kinsman's head with his 'whinger' in 1676, a dozen Ross arbitrators warned him that if he injured or wronged any of his kinsmen they would invoke the law against him, and 'withdraw from following or serveing him as kinsmen' if he rejected their advice.

The estate was heavily in debt when David died in 1711; one of the principal creditors was Lord Ross of Hawkhead, an 'old west country laird' from Ayrshire connected by no traceable relationship, who managed to contrive the succession of his family at Balnagown in spite of strong opposition from the heir male, Ross of Pitcalnie. The Rosses were mainly anti-Jacobite, but in 1745 they were lukewarm and divided, and young Pitcalnie threw up a government commission, joined the prince, and was attainted. Balnagown was later to the fore in agricultural 'improvements', including the introduction of sheep on the higher ground and the removal of tenants. Little now remains in Ross hands of the forty-eight properties of which Balnagown consisted in 1688; but many of the clan still live in the old territory, and the chiefship has passed through the Pitcalnie line to the representatives of Shandwick.

RUTHVEN

RUTHVEN

For forty years the name of Ruthven was proscribed by law in Scotland, and it has been well said that its history in two generations comprised 'more romance and mystery than have fallen to the lot of any other name in the Scottish peerage'. The first of the family to be called Ruthven seems to have flourished in the first half of the 13th century and married a daughter of the Earl of Strathearn. About 1298 William of Ruthven confirmed a charter by his father Walter son of Alan of the lands of Scone, in which his sons Walter and Gilbert were named as witnesses. William's successor had charters of the lands of Ruthven and the sheriffdom of St Johnston or Perth from Robert III, and Sir William of that Ilk was created Lord Ruthven in 1488. His grandson, who added to his broad domain in central Scotland by marrying the heiress of the Haliburtons of Dirleton in East Lothian, was chosen Provost of Perth by royal command in 1528, and the Ruthvens were provosts for sixty out of the next seventy years, until disaster overtook the family.

A shadow was first cast over the name in 1566, when Patrick Ruthven the third lord—one of the leading Protestant nobles of the day—played the chief part in the murder of Rizzio in the queen's palace at Edinburgh; his son forced Queen Mary to sign her abdication while a prisoner at Lochleven. For services to King James he was rewarded with an earldom, choosing the title of Gowrie; in the 'Raid of Ruthven' a year later he secured a change of ministry by kidnapping the king and keeping him for some ten months in Ruthven castle near Perth; but the king escaped, and after a second plot had failed Gowrie was executed in 1584. His widow and family found asylum in the Atholl country with one of her sons-in-law, until by a sudden twist of fortune's wheel the estates and honours were restored in 1586.

In the next generation the eldest son died young, and John Ruthven, who became Earl of Gowrie at eleven years old in 1588, went on from Edinburgh University to study law at Padua. In August 1600, less than three months after returning to Scotland, he was killed in his own house in Perth with his brother for an alleged attempt on the life of King James known as the 'Gowrie conspiracy'. Whether there was a crime at all, and if so what was the motive, remains a mystery. The king had been hunting near Falkland when Alexander Master of Ruthven persuaded him to ride to Gowrie house to meet a man who had been seized with a pot full of gold coins. After a hurried meal, Alexander led the king through various rooms, locking the door of each behind them, until in a small turret room he found himself confronted by a man in armour. A struggle ensued, James managed to reach a window and cry 'Treason!', his attendants rushed to the rescue, and the death of the brothers followed. The king convinced his subjects that his life had been in danger, and the dreadful crime of treason was fastened on the dead men, and on several of their household including two Ruthven cousins. When Parliament met in November, their corpses were produced along with a mass of evidence, and in pronouncing the doom of forfeiture it was also enacted that 'the surname of Ruthven shall now and in all time coming be extinguished and abolished for ever', and that those of the name innocent of treason should take and use any other 'honest and undefamed surname' on all occasions under pain of banishment. It was even directed that the name of the barony of Ruthven and the old family mansion above the Almond should be changed to Huntingtower, as it is called to this day.

The king's wrath against the Ruthvens never subsided, and it burst out even after he went to England. On his death King Gustavus Adolphus of Sweden interceded with Charles I on behalf of a Ruthven of the Ballindean branch in his service, asking that the family name and honour should be restored. The king allowed its use to this family alone in 1639, and in ratifying his letters patent two years later the Scots Parliament rescinded the Act of 1600 relating to the whole name and surname of Ruthven. Many Ruthvens have since been honoured for their public services: Gustavus's protégé was made Earl of Forth in 1642, and another (whose uncle had been outlawed at the time of the 'conspiracy') created Lord Ruthven of Freeland in 1651. Sir Alexander Hore-Ruthven of the Freeland family, Governor-General of Australia from 1936–44, was raised to a new earldom of Gowrie in 1945.

SCOTT

SCOTT

COMING into the Border country from upper Tweeddale and Clydesdale, and perhaps before that from Galloway, the Scotts settled on Teviot and Ettrick at the end of the 13th century. They emerge into Border history with the by-name of the 'rough clan', and were also known as the 'saucy Scotts' long before the chiefs were ennobled and took their place among the magnates of the land.

The original home of the Scotts, more or less at the centre of the territory later acquired, was a small area round Bellenden, a high plateau near the head of the Ale water in Roxburghshire, which became the rallying-ground and battle-cry of the clan. It was acquired in 1415, and by mid-century the Scotts owned Branxholme near Hawick, from which they took their designation before finally adopting the name Buccleuch from a remoter spot on the Rankle

Burn in the Ettrick valley. Originally heavily wooded, it is fine riding country, with ready access into England down Liddesdale and Redesdale; although puzzling to a stranger, it was easily ranged by those with local knowledge of hill and river crossings.

The Scotts were at their greatest as a clan between 1455 and 1603—from the fall of the Douglases to the union of the crowns. They had their reward out of Douglas lands, and expanded their influence at a time when the Border was constantly threatened and life was lived on a military basis. The Scotts of Buccleuch produced relatively few cadet branches, but those that were established multiplied quickly, and formed a band of supporters loyal to their chief. In 1526 sixty Scott gentry with their followers took Buccleuch's part in a raid, and he turned out 600 men in a battle. Support was needed, for three large-scale English expeditions passed through the Scott country, and Branxholme was burned more than once, during the 16th century. At this period, too, the Scotts were almost constantly at loggerheads with the Kerrs on the 'Middle March', which comprised the whole shires of Roxburgh, Selkirk and Peebles. Later the march was divided between them, with Scott as warden of the western part 'betwix Mynto Crags and Craycorse, in quhilk boundis his freindis, servandis and tenentis duellis'; but the rivalry continued, and when Sir Walter of Buccleuch was made warden over the entire march the Kerrs promptly had him murdered in the High Street of Edinburgh. Sir Walter's grandson, in a marriage contract between the two families, 'took burden upon him for all his surname'; and it is a tribute to the clan's solidarity that, although every inheritor of Buccleuch between 1470 and 1611 was a minor, neither those who wielded power nor other leading Scotts tried to take advantage of the situation.

With Scotland and England under one king, the need or excuse for fighting on the Border gradually ended. Old habits gave way to peaceful pursuits, and the 'bold Buccleuch' who stormed the castle of Carlisle in 1596 to rescue an Armstrong riever became Lord Scott of Buccleuch in 1606 and took 200 of his name to fight in Holland with the Scots Brigade. Twenty years later a further 100 followed under his son, made Earl of Buccleuch in 1619. There being no sons to succeed, the eldest daughter became countess at the age of five, with her mother and nine Scott cadets (and two Eliotts) as her tutors. Married early to a Scott of the Harden line, she died young; her sister Anna—at ten the greatest heiress in Scotland—was through her mother's influence married in 1664 to Charles II's son James Duke of Monmouth, who took the name of Scott. The couple were made Duke and Duchess of Buccleuch, both in their own right, so her title and estates were not affected by Monmouth's rebellion.

With changed conditions, and estates in England as well as Scotland, family ties were loosened. Marriage brought the vast Douglas of Queensberry estates to the Scotts, and also large English properties. The fourth duke was a great Borderer himself, and friend of the most 'clannish' Borderer of them all, Sir Walter Scott of Abbotsford (whose ancestors were Scotts of Raeburn, cadets of Harden). Besides Scottish estates, which reached a total of 400,000 acres, in Dumfries-shire, Roxburgh and Selkirk, the family still own a parcel of land in Peebles-shire which has been handed down for at least seven centuries in direct succession.

SETON

SETON

THERE is something doubly apt about the old description of the Setons as 'tall and proud', because it applies not only to the personal characteristics of some of the family, but also to the brilliant architectural heritage which they have left to future generations.

A century after building the collegiate church of Seton in East Lothian, completed after the founder's death at Flodden, the Setons commissioned some of the finest private houses of the day in Scotland. Any family which could boast of inspiring the princely Seton Palace, where kings and queens were entertained, Winton House and the stately Pinkie, all in the vicinity of Edinburgh, and the noble tower-house of Fyvie and Pitmedden garden in Aberdeenshire, could hold their heads high among the nation's benefactors.

If we include the Huntly and Eglinton families—Setons on the father's side, though taking the surnames of Gordon and Montgomerie—the circle of architectural patronage is widened further still.

After East Lothian, the counties where the Seton influence was strongest are West Lothian, Stirling, Fife and Aberdeen, in all of which (as well as in the north of England) the family at one time held extensive possessions. Philip de Seton had a charter from William the Lion in 1169 of the lands of Seton, Winton and Winchburgh, previously held by his father, and most of these lands remained with his descendants for some five and a half centuries. Sir Christopher Seton, a Yorkshire knight with land in Annandale, was the brother-in-law and ally of Robert Bruce; and Sir Alexander, who joined the king on the eve of Bannockburn and became his close friend and supporter, was rewarded with further lands in East Lothian. Styled Sir Alexander de Setoun, Lord of that Ilk, he had a charter of the free barony of Seton and was succeeded by an heiress who was married to Alan de Wyntoun, possibly a cousin.

In later reigns, loyalty to the Stewarts became a ruling passion with the Setons. Lord Seton was the 'truest friend' of Mary, and his daughter was one of the 'Queen's Maries'; King James created one of Seton's sons Earl of Winton, and another Earl of Dunfermline. Within three generations after James VI and Charles I had been received at Seton Palace, these and other honours had been willingly sacrificed. James, fourth and last Earl of Dunfermline, whose grandfather had been for eighteen years Chancellor of Scotland, brought out some of the Gordon clan (he was brother-in-law of the duke) to join Dundee's rising, commanded a troop of horse at Killiecrankie, and was outlawed and forfeited in 1690; George Seton, fifth Earl of Winton, called up his vassals and tenants in 1715 and joined the insurgents, opposed the march into England and was captured at Preston, was forfeited and attainted, but escaped from the tower of London before the death sentence was carried out; his cousins James third Viscount of Kingston, whose father had gallantly defended Tantallon castle against Cromwell's forces, and the baronet Sir George Seton of Garleton, were also attainted and their titles forfeited for their part in the rising. Sir George, who died in exile in France, was commonly known as the Earl of Winton, and would have been but for the earl's and his own loyalty to the Stewarts.

It is a remarkable record of solidarity, and yet there is little sign that the Setons acted together. Perhaps one reason was that their cadet families were comparatively few, if those who abandoned their paternal name are excluded. The first Lord Dunfermline, who was Chancellor during the fiercest persecution of the Clan Gregor, was certainly no friend to the clan system; and while some of the Seton tenants and vassals were 'out' with their lairds, they were probably more often concerned with working their farm lands, coal mines and salt pans than in such ploys. Individual Setons have earned glory for the name, one of the Mounie branch of the house of Pitmedden having commanded the troops on the *Birkenhead* when she was wrecked off the Cape of Good Hope in 1852. George Seton, family annalist, lawyer and heraldic writer, was head of the Cariston branch, descended from a half-brother of Mary Seton, and because of three Seton inter-marriages in five generations of his family a kinsman pronounced him '*Setonissimus Setonorum*'—the most Seton of the Setons.

SINCLAIR

SINCLAIR, DRESS

FIRST of the 'lordly line of high St Clair' from whom direct descent can be proved was Sir William Sinclair, who had a charter of the lands and barony of Roslin in Midlothian in 1280. He had been sheriff in various parts of the country, guardian of Alexander III's son the prince of Scotland, and a member of the parliament which settled the succession on Margaret maid of Norway after the prince's death in 1284. His son Henry, who had a grant of the king's lands on the Muir of Pentland, fought at Bannockburn and signed the 1320 letter to the Pope asserting Scottish independence; and his grandson was one of the band of Scottish knights who fell in Spain while carrying Bruce's heart against the infidel.

Nearly the whole length of Scotland separates the Pentland hills near

Edinburgh from the Pentland firth in the northern seas; but the marriage of Sir William Sinclair of Roslin (son of the knight killed in Spain) to a daughter of Malise, Earl of Strathearn, Orkney and Caithness brought the family into the line of succession to the islands then ruled from Norway. In 1379 their son Henry was formally invested by King Haakon as Earl of Orkney and Lord of Zetland. They still kept a semi-regal state at Roslin, where William the third earl founded the church which (although only the choir was completed) is widely famous for the 'astonishing exuberance' of its ornamental stonework. The founder of Rosslyn chapel, who gave up the earldom of Orkney, received the earldom of Caithness in 1455, and was also made Lord Sinclair, is a key figure in the family; by his marriages with a Douglas and a Sutherland he founded first the Sinclairs of Dysart and Ravenscraig in Fife, and second the lines which continued the Sinclairs of Roslin and also, through many ramifications, carried the earldom of Caithness down to the present day.

The senior line was that by the Douglas marriage, and Henry, third Lord Sinclair had a 'special and singular' Act of Parliament in 1489 declaring him 'cheiffe of that blude', to be called Lord Sinclair in time to come. With a lease of Orkney and Shetland for the rest of his life, he was also Master of Artillery and captain of the *Great Michael* (James IV's battleship for which all the woods of Fife had been laid low), but died with the king at Flodden. The royalist ninth lord was last in the male line, from whom the title passed eventually (though not by blood) to the Sinclairs of Herdmanston, landowners in East Lothian since the 12th century.

Meantime the barony and castle of Roslin, the lands of Pentland and Morton, and other property had gone to Sir Oliver Sinclair, one of the sons by the Sutherland marriage. All the barons of Roslin down to Sir William, who died in 1650, were buried in the chapel in their armour; and when the next was coffined like other men the widow acted against the sentiments of those 'well versed in antiquity'. William Sinclair of Roslin, who died in 1778 after his three sons, was remembered as the 'last Rosslyn', whose feats of strength and skill at golf and archery were the wonder of Edinburgh schoolboys; he had long since sold the lands of Roslin to General James St Clair, heir of line of the senior branch, from whom they passed to an Erskine great-nephew who also inherited the earldom of Rosslyn conferred on Alexander Wedderburn, Lord Chancellor Loughborough.

Both the other branches having failed in the male line, the Earls of Caithness, descendants of Sir Oliver's brother William, came to represent the family. The name Sinclair does not seem to have been known in Caithness before 1455, but the lands of the earldom were greatly extended by the family and included at one time the larger portion of the county. Its prosperity reached a climax under George fourth earl; decline set in with his grandson George fifth earl; under his great-grandson George, sixth earl (there were only three holders of the title in nearly 150 years), the estates were so burdened with debt that they were sold in 1672 to the earl's principal creditor Lord Glenorchy; he took over by force, much to the disgust of the Sinclair gentry, but the estates were later parcelled out among different proprietors. The empty title, limited to heirs male, passed from one cadet to the next—Keiss, Murkle, Rattar, Mey and Durran—as each line died out or ended with daughters, but substantial houses like the Sinclairs of Ulbster kept the name to the fore in the far north as well as in the Lowlands.

SKENE

SKENE

EVEN if the best authorities agree that the name Skene is 'plainly territorial', there is a strong temptation to relate it to the Gaelic *sgian*, or knife. An ancient dirk preserved in the Skene charter chest is thought to have been used as a symbol of investiture from the time when the lands were made into a barony by King Robert in 1317. There are three daggers on the seal of one of the earliest Skene documents (1296), and 400 years later an armorial stone carved for Skene House showed what the heralds called 'a highlandman in his proper garb holding a *skene* in his right hand in a guarding posture'.

The lands of Skene lie on the north side of the loch of that name, between the rivers Dee and Don, and roughly coincide with the modern parish of Skene. The old tower of Skene, built of three arches or stories and entered by a ladder on the second storey, was about eight miles west of Aberdeen; it was in the main portion of the barony, while the Kirk of Skene lay in the smaller or eastern part. This is a lowland area, but a sharp reminder of its nearness to the Highlands came in 1411 when Donald, Lord of the Isles swept across Scotland and was only prevented from giving Aberdeen the same rough treatment meted out to Inverness by the army which met him at Harlaw. The battle was fought only a few miles from Skene, and the laird is said to have been among the casualties. In the next few decades others of the same name besides his immediate family begin to appear on record, and the clan seems to have been spreading. When a force was being gathered in the south to meet the English invaders at the end of 1546, Alexander Skene of that Ilk was excused from joining it on account of 'infirmities and sickness' so long as he sent 'ane habill (able) furnished man with his household and servants'—an arrangement that sent his uncle James in Bandodle to his death at Pinkie, along with some unnamed followers; but the sick laird survived until 1604, and lived to see his great-grandchildren.

In the troubled 17th century Skenes did not always take the same side. The laird was said to have been a companion of Montrose, while his second son was executed as a Covenanter in Edinburgh. An Aberdeen magistrate named Skene and his family became Quakers, but there must have been many of the name in the city as two others who were enemies of the sect had to be distinguished as 'white James' and 'black James'. A professor of medicine who became King James VI's physician, and a lawyer and diplomat whose work on Scotland's legal antiquities and constitutional history is still studied, were the sons of an obscure notary on Deeside. Farther afield, a Skene became 'conservator of Scotch privileges' at Campvere in the Netherlands, and another settled at Venloo and founded a family which came to hold an influential position in Austria; while the younger son of a Belhelvie farmer acquired a fortune in Poland and returning home founded a county family.

After more than 500 years of nearly uninterrupted succession from father to son, Alexander Skene of Skene died in 1827, the last direct male descendant of his line. He was deaf and dumb, and already his elder brother George, having outlived every other relative of the name, had entailed the property so that it would go to their sister's son, the Earl of Fife; thus (in the words of a kinsman) 'notwithstanding his pride in the antiquity of his name and family, and the strong interest he was in use to express in the duration of the clan of which he was the chief', almost extinguishing the name of Skene of Skene. One of the Skenes of Halyards, in Fife, who carried on the representation of the family, had established Skeneborough on Lake Champlain while serving in North America, and was governor of the forts of Crown Point and Ticonderoga.

Two Skenes of Rubislaw, owners of the famous Aberdeen granite quarry, helped in the 19th century to preserve the history and traditions of the name —George, lawyer and litterateur, friend of Sir Walter Scott, and collector of material on the clan, and his son Dr William Forbes Skene, whose *Memorials of the Family of Skene of Skene* were published by the New Spalding Club in 1887, and whose *Celtic Scotland* and other works helped to secure recognition of the Celtic element in medieval Scottish history.

ROYAL STEWART

STEWART, ROYAL

EVEN before Stewart became a surname, the family which gave Scotland her royal line of kings was among the first in the realm for opulence and power. Walter FitzAlan, whose father was a man of note at the English court, entered the service of David I and was appointed Steward (or High Steward) of Scotland by him, with extensive estates in the west where he founded the abbey of Paisley. His grandson Walter, who was justiciar of Scotland in 1230 as well as Steward, is believed to have been the first of the family who adopted the name of its chief office as his surname.

James the Steward was one of the six Guardians of the kingdom appointed to rule in the name of Alexander III's infant granddaughter Margaret, the maid of Norway. A modern historian sees a recognisably Stewart 'canniness' in James's actions during the war of independence, but though not a consistent supporter of Bruce he ended his days in his rightful place as the senior officer of the royal household. In 1315 King Robert went further and gave his only legitimate child, Marjorie, in marriage to the Steward's son Walter, who also received the barony of Bathgate and other lands.

Robert, the next High Steward, born in 1316, was acknowledged as heir-presumptive to the throne from 1318 until the birth in 1324 of the king's son David. When he died after an inglorious reign in 1371 without direct heirs, Robert became the first Stewart king of Scotland and the succession was fixed on his eldest son (by Elizabeth Mure) and his heirs male. The royal Stewarts were an unlucky dynasty, for of fourteen crowned monarchs between 1371 and 1714 four were murdered or executed, two died in battle and one in exile, while seven in succession came to the throne as minors and between 1406 and 1587 there were nearly 100 years of rule by regents. To the more powerful among their subjects these Stewarts were at first merely a noble house raised to kingship by a 'lucky' marriage. James I had to overthrow a powerful group of kinsmen, the house of Albany; James II destroyed the power of the Douglases; James III was deep in trouble with sections of his nobility; James IV tried to keep order by exploiting private rivalries and enmities; and by sweeping forfeitures James V regained for the crown what the warring nobles had filched from it. But these early Stewarts were monarchs who knew, lived and moved amongst their own people.

Owing to the complete failure of male heirs, James V's daughter Mary became Queen of Scots in 1542, and her marriage to Henry, Lord Darnley united the two main Stewart lines. Stewart 'clannishness' is illustrated by her warning in 1563 to a MacLeod of Lewis whose mother was a Stewart (descended from the Regent Murdoch of Albany) that 'becaus ye hav that honor to be of the Stewartis bluid, we thocht expedient to gif you advertisment that it is our will and pleshour that ye allyat your self to na pairty in mareage without our avys and quhill (until) we declair our opinioun and mynd to your self theiranent'.

James VI was well aware of the importance of family relationships in establishing peace and order in his kingdom. One of his first acts on beginning his personal rule in 1587 was to settle the differences between some of his nobles at a convention in Edinburgh, and then lead them in public procession—'tua and tua tak uthers be the hands'—up the High Street from his palace. More significant, a few months later he had all landowners renew the 'general band' of earlier reigns, making them answerable for the good conduct of their followers, with the important addition that chiefs and chieftains became responsible also for their clansmen, whether or not they were their feudal vassals.

With the removal of the court to London the rule of the Stewart kings became more remote, but the succession continued through Charles I and II and James VII, Queen Mary and Queen Anne; after four unsuccessful attempts to restore the Stewarts, the direct male line came to an end in 1807 with the death of James VII's grandson Henry cardinal Duke of York. But James VI's daughter Elizabeth was ancestress of the house of Hanover and of their successors on the British throne, and the heir-apparent still bears the ancient title 'Prince and Steward of Scotland'.

Note: Stewart is the old Scots version of the name, but during Mary Queen of Scots' time, when there was much intercourse with France (and no letter W in the French alphabet), the spellings Stuart and Steuart came into use.

STEWART (ANCIENT)

STEWART, OLD

ALL Stewarts, says the old proverb, are not 'sib' (related) to the king. There are no legitimate descendants in the male line of the Stewart kings, but a number of families trace their descent from the ancestors of the royal house, and so can claim kinship with them. Walter, a younger son of the Steward who was the first to adopt the surname, and great-uncle of Marjorie Bruce's husband, founded the first cadet branch of the Stewarts; but the earldom of Menteith which he acquired by marriage was ultimately merged with the royal dukedom of Albany.

The largest group of legitimate but pre-royal branches of the house of Stewart was founded by Sir John, brother of James the Steward and uncle of Marjorie's husband, who was the companion of Wallace and fell while marshalling the Scots archers at Falkirk in 1298. He acquired the Berwickshire estate of Bonkyl (or Buncle) by marrying the heiress, and three of his sons founded noble families—Sir Alexander of Bonkyl, Sir Alan of Dreghorn in Ayrshire, and Sir James of Pearston in Ayrshire. By the end of Bruce's reign the senior line held the earldom of Angus, but before the century was out this had been transmitted through an heiress to the Douglases.

From Sir John's second son Alan (killed at Halidonhill in 1333) came the Stewarts of Darnley, later Earls of Lennox. The head of this family was killed in 1439 by Sir Thomas Boyd of Kilmarnock 'for old feud that was betwixt thame', and his brother 'manfullie sett upoun' and killed Sir Thomas in revenge. In the next generation, having acquired half the earldom of Lennox by marriage, Sir John Stewart assumed the title in 1473. The fourth Stewart earl was father of Henry Lord Darnley, who married Mary Queen of Scots, was given the title of king, and was father of James VI. While James remained childless a dynastic quarrel arose with the Hamiltons, whose descent from a sister of James III made them the nearest heirs to the throne until the birth of Prince Henry in 1594. The title, raised to a dukedom for Esmé Stuart, seigneur d'Aubigny, returned at the sixth duke's death in 1672 to Charles II, who conferred it on his son by Louise de Keroualle.

The male line of Lennox, though not the title, was extinguished with the death in 1807 of Henry cardinal Duke of York, brother of Prince Charles Edward, and since then the Earls of Galloway have been considered the senior legitimate representatives in the male line of the ancient High Stewards of Scotland. They are derived from the first offshoot from the house of Darnley, Sir William of Jedworth, sheriff of Teviotdale, who figures in the national records from 1385 to 1402. His son acquired Garlies near Newton Stewart by marriage with a Stewart cousin, and on several occasions the Lennox family acknowledged their kinship. When the laird of Garlies was made a peer in 1607 by James VI (who was head of the house of Lennox, through his father as well as king) it was in recognition of many years of good service and 'because of his uninterrupted descent from the ancient and most noble family of Lennox'. Lord Garlies was made Earl of Galloway in 1623, and a cadet branch who were for many years hereditary provosts of Glasgow held the title of Lords Blantyre.

From Sir James Stewart of Pearston, who fell at Halidonhill with his brother Alan, through his son Sir Robert of Innermeath, descended the Stewart Earls of Atholl, Buchan and Traquair, the Lords of Lorn, the Stewarts of Appin and of Grandtully, and some of the other Highland families of the name. *(See page 180)*.

The Stewart Society, of which the Earl of Galloway is honorary president, was founded in 1899 with patriotic, genealogical, historical and philanthropic objects. It has erected memorial gates at Bathgate to Walter the High Steward, immediate progenitor of the royal house, a statue near Fortingall to General David Stewart of Garth, historian of the Highland regiments and writer on the Highlands generally, and other memorials. It owns the island of Inchmahome in the Lake of Menteith, where some of the oldest Stewart effigies lie in the priory ruins among the great Spanish chestnut trees, recalling the branches which from earliest times have spread from the main Stewart stem.

STEWART OF APPIN &c.

STEWART OF APPIN

ALTHOUGH the Stewarts are not a clan in the ordinary sense, a 'clannish' feeling developed particularly among the descendants and following of an important branch which was established in Lorn as a result of Stewart marriages with heiresses descended from the mighty Somerled. In 1388 Sir John Stewart, son of Sir Robert of Innermeath *(see page 179)*, had a charter from Robert II of the lands of Lorn, Benderloch, Appin and Lismore, which he had exchanged for the lands of Durisdeer in Dumfries-shire with his younger brother Robert—both having married daughters of John (MacDougall) Lord of Lorn. Sir John died in 1421, and was the father of Robert, who succeeded him; Sir James, called 'the black knight of Lorn', ancestor of the Earls of Atholl, Buchan and Traquair; and Alexander, ancestor of the Steuarts of Grandtully. Among the descendants of these three brothers many Highland Stewarts are found, including the Appin line.

Taking the two junior lines first, the 'black knight' married Queen Joanna, widow of James I, and James II conferred the earldom of Atholl on his eldest half-brother Sir John of Balvenie, from whose Stewart descendants it passed after a brief interval to the Murray Earls of Tullibardine in 1627. A younger son of Sir James and Queen Joanna was 'hearty James', created Earl of Buchan in 1469, from whom came also the Earls of Traquair. The Steuarts of Grandtully had a 'handsome estate' in Strathbran and Strathtay (all holding of the crown) which could raise 300 men in 1745.

Returning to the main line, the Stewart lordship of Lorn lasted for only about eighty years. Robert's eldest son John was murdered at Dunstaffnage by one of the MacDougall family, leaving three daughters and a son Dugald (whose legitimacy has been doubted). Parliament took a serious view of the killing of 'the king's cusing', but some years later the victim's brother Walter resigned the lordship of Lorn to Colin Earl of Argyll (who had married the eldest of the heiresses) and became the first of seven Lords Innermeath who were latterly for a brief space Earls of Atholl.

Young Dugald, whose MacLaren mother is said to have married John Stewart of Lorn on his deathbed, tried to secure the lordship by force, but had to be content with the lands of Appin, which were preserved entire in the family for four centuries. Many Stewarts are supposed to have followed Dugald to Appin, and a writer in 1577 called them 'the best sorte of Stewartes, whereof be now but few, yet very valiant'. When the roll of clans was drawn up ten years later John Stewart of Appin was named among the Highland landlords, and Stewarts there and in Atholl and Balquhidder were listed among those who depended on their chiefs against their landlords' will; in 1601 his son, called 'Duncan of Lorne', was held responsible by the Privy Council for a theft committed by his men and was imprisoned until he made restitution.

The men of Appin ardently supported their kinsmen of the royal house, as well as fighting to preserve their lands and freedom. The clan was growing in strength, with the cadet families of Achnacone, Fasnacloich, Invernahyle and later Ardsheal springing from the chief's line in the 16th century. In 1645 the Stewarts of Appin, Atholl and Balquhidder showed their solidarity by a 'bond of association' signed by all the leading men of each branch; they were with Montrose at Inverlochy, Auldearn and Kilsyth, and the Appin estate was forfeited (but returned at the Restoration). The Appin men joined Dundee's rising for King James in 1689 under Ardsheal as tutor, and the young chief put off his submission to King William as long as possible; he was attainted after 1715, but they were 'out' again in 1745 under Charles of Ardsheal, and nearly 100 of the Appin regiment fell in the Jacobite charge on the right wing at Culloden. The pale blue silk colour with a yellow saltire under which they fought is preserved, but the estates were again forfeited, and when a Campbell factor for Ardsheal was shot dead in 1752 an innocent Stewart was hanged for the murder. Appin was sold in 1765, shortly before the main line of chiefs died out, but Ardsheal took over. His estate too passed from the clan in the 19th century, and Stewart of Achnacone is the last of the old landowning representatives still retaining possession of their lands in Appin.

STUART OF BUTE &c.

STUART OF BUTE

MANY families throughout the country are entitled to echo the proud boast of Alan Breck Stewart (in R. L. Stevenson's *Kidnapped)*—'I am come of kings; I bear a king's name'.

The biggest group of all are those descended from Robert Duke of Albany, third son of the first Stewart king (Robert II), who was regent to his father, brother and nephew, and was succeeded by his son Murdoch in both dukedom and regency. When James I, after returning from prison in England, had the duke and his two sons Walter and Alexander tried and executed for treason, he did not wipe out the family completely. A third son James, on hearing of his father's arrest, descended on Dumbarton with a party of followers, killed the Stewart governor and burnt the town; he fled to England and later to

Ireland, and from his natural son James *beag* the Stewarts of Ardvorlich and others in Balquhidder are descended. Walter, it appears, left two sons (later legitimated) from whom an even greater number of families are derived; one of his descendants was Andrew Stewart Lord Avandale, who fell at Flodden leaving three sons—Andrew, first of a series of Lords Ochiltree whose family included an Earl of Arran who was Chancellor of Scotland (from him came the Earls of Castle Stewart in Ireland); Henry Lord Methven, who married James IV's widowed queen, Margaret Tudor, and had two successors; and Sir James of Beith, whose son Lord Doune was father of the 'bonnie earl' of Moray whose murder caused such indignation in 1592 (his title, inherited from his father-in-law the Regent, still continues).

Robert II's fourth son, Alexander Earl of Buchan, earned the name 'the wolf of Badenoch' by burning Elgin Cathedral and other crimes, and from his illegitimate sons came most of the Stewarts in Atholl and many of the families of the name in Aberdeenshire, Banffshire and Moray. In Atholl alone, it was estimated in the early 19th century, there were no fewer than 1,500 male descendants of a son who inherited certain lands including Garth from his father.

Another son of Robert II named John was ancestor of the Stuart Earls (1703) and Marquesses (1796) of Bute, the Earls of Wharncliffe (1876), and their cadets. Sir John received a 'fair estate' from his royal father and half-brothers, and was given charge of the new sheriffdom comprising the isles of Bute, Arran and the Cumbraes in the Firth of Clyde. James IV made the head of the family also hereditary captain and keeper of Rothesay castle. In 1535 the sheriff Ninian and his eight sons, on their own behalf and for their kin, friends and servants, entered into a bond of manrent to James Earl of Arran; but during Arran's regency fourteen years later the eldest son lost some of his lands in Arran while trying to escape from accusations of treason. Sir James, a Baronet of Nova Scotia, was dispossessed of Rothesay castle by Cromwell, and at the Restoration prayed the king to order the survey and repair of 'so noble and ancient a possession of the crown', without much success; his grandson the third baronet was made earl, the third earl was George III's prime minister, and the fourth was made marquess (his son's marriage to the Earl of Dumfries's daughter brought that title also into the family, and the name of Crichton was added before that of Stuart). The third marquess was only six months old when his father died, and his guardianship led to prolonged litigation and an appeal to the House of Lords; he became a scholar and antiquary, being concerned to protect Rothesay castle, Falkland palace and other buildings, and for several generations the family have taken a lead in preserving the nation's architectural and cultural heritage.

From a natural son of Robert III comes a family which has played a notable part in affairs in Renfrewshire, early home of the Stewarts; the lands of Ardgowan, Blackhall and Auchingowan have passed in uninterrupted male succession from that day to this in the family now named Shaw-Stewart. In Perthshire the Steuarts of Ballechin, descended from Sir John of Sticks, in Glenquaich, a natural son of James II, were prominent supporters of the Jacobite cause. Queen Mary's half-brother the Regent Moray has already been mentioned; perhaps the less said the better about the earldom of Orkney conferred on another son of James V, except that the oppressions carried out in these islands were so flagrant that James VI did nothing to reprieve the second earl and his son from execution, although they were the king's own cousins.

SUTHERLAND

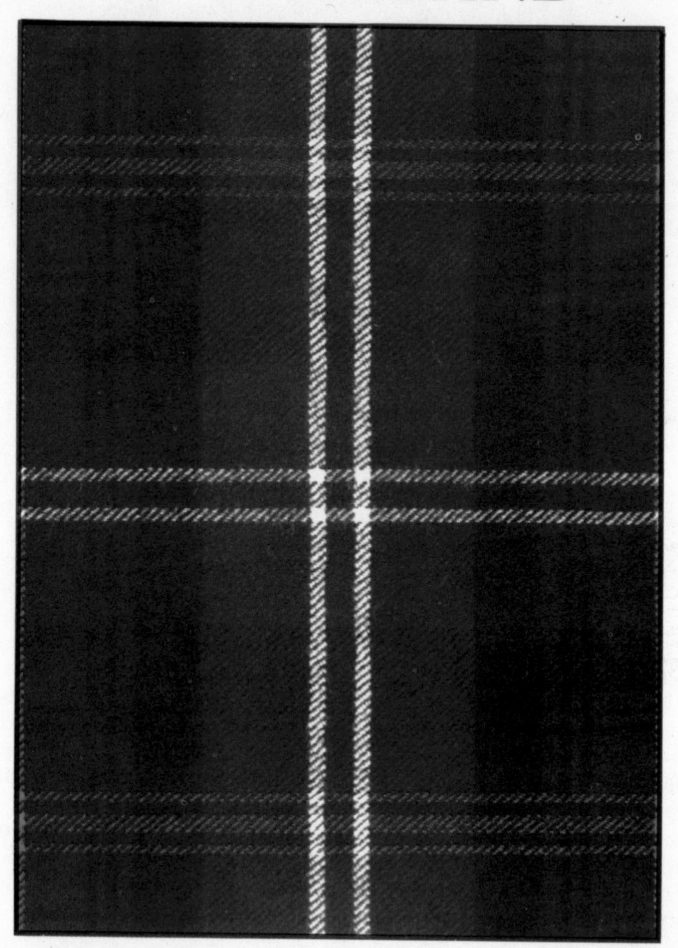

SUTHERLAND

SUTHERLAND was the name given to what the Norsemen regarded as the 'southland', the south-east portion of the modern county lying (as seen from their northern viewpoint) beyond the Ord of Caithness. Some time before 1211 a large tract of land there was acquired by Hugh, son of William son of Freskin, one of the powerful *de Moravia* family from the other side of the Moray Firth. William of Sutherland is on record in 1232, and the rulers of the region 'for divers succeeding ages' used the surname of Sutherland, until they exchanged it for that of Gordon.

There seems to have been an Earl of Sutherland since at least 1245 and probably earlier. In the wars of independence, after supporting the English crown, the earl had made his peace with King Robert by 1309. His powerful neighbour the Earl of Ross had married one of the king's sisters, and Sutherland had his daughter Princess Margaret as his wife, although it was not this marriage that carried on the line of the family. Nicholas, brother of the same earl, founded the Sutherlands of Duffus in Moray, who later sat in parliament as the Lords Duffus.

Dunrobin has for long been the seat of the Earls of Sutherland, and there in 1401 Earl Robert granted a charter to his brother Kenneth, ancestor of the Sutherlands of Forse. The earldom became a Gordon inheritance under curious circumstances. Two earls had been declared incapable of managing their own affairs, one in 1494 and the other in 1514; when the latter died within a month, the succession opened to his sister Elizabeth, who had married Adam Gordon of Aboyne, brother of the Earl of Huntly. They were styled Earl and Countess of Sutherland, and the sudden death in a skirmish of a half-brother who had objected and twice taken possession of Dunrobin removed the last obstacle to the Gordon takeover. When their son entered on his inheritance the two northern counties were in a state of turmoil, but he managed to curb some of the feuds and his countess (former wife of Queen Mary's Bothwell) began a saltworks at Brora and a coalmine which is still working.

Unlike the pattern set by other clans, comparatively few of the Sutherland followers used that surname. Many were Gordons, related to the earls, while others were Murrays whose allegiance may have stemmed from a common descent. The old rallying place of this mixed clan was at the head of a little bridge at the north end of Golspie village, where an obelisk marks the spot. Many Gordons occupied key posts, but it was a maxim laid down by the tutor Sir Robert (who administered the estates for his nephew from 1615–30) that the earl's representative 'sould be an equall judge to all the inhabitants of Southerland, without respect of persones or surnames'. The future chief's education was of such general concern that 'everie gentleman according to his meanes' subscribed a yearly sum to maintain the young Earl John and two younger brother at college; this earl was one of the first to sign the National Covenant at Greyfriars kirk in Edinburgh in 1638.

After some attempts to revert to the old family name of Sutherland, an obligation was entered into in 1682 by John, Lord Strathnaver as heir apparent that he and his successors would 'carry and use the surname of Gordon allenarly' (only), under a penalty of £20,000 Scots payable to the Huntly family. They remained cadets of Huntly for another two generations, but the surname of Sutherland was eventually adopted, in spite of Huntly's threats.

The Earls of Sutherland were early supporters of the Revolution, and in 1715 and 1745 they helped to lead opposition to the Jacobites in the North. The death of Earl William in 1766 left an only child Lady Elizabeth, one year old; after a celebrated lawsuit, in which her claim to the title and estates was opposed by Sutherland of Forse as heir male and a Gordon claimant, the House of Lords found in her favour, and she became countess in her own right in 1771. Along with her husband, a 'leviathan of wealth' who was successively Lord Gower, Marquess of Stafford and Duke of Sutherland, she brought the greater part of the county into the Sutherland estate, but their planned 'improvements' were carried out harshly and against the wishes of many of the tenantry. On the death of the fifth duke in 1962, that title passed to the Earls of Ellesmere, while the Scottish earldom went to his niece, another Countess Elizabeth, a direct descendant of the earls who ruled in the North before the days of Bruce.

URQUHART

URQUHART

Any notice of the Urquharts is almost bound to be overshadowed by the eccentric genius of Sir Thomas Urquhart of Cromarty, who took a fancy to draw up his pedigree from the Creation and had it printed under the title *Pantochronocanon* in 1652. In this remarkable fantasy he named a sovereign Prince of Achaia in ancient Greece in 2139 B.C. as 'father of all that carry the name of Urquhart', whereas in sober fact the 143rd in descent in Sir Thomas's list was the earliest ancestor of whom we have reliable knowledge.

Urquhart was originally a place-name, and the early members of the family were often called 'de Urquhart'. As nothing but a shadowy tradition links the Cromarty line with the great castle of Urquhart on Loch Ness, it seems likely that it was from Urquhart in Ross-shire's Black Isle that they took their name.

The family emerge into written history in the latter half of the 14th century as followers of the Earl of Ross and hereditary sheriffs of Cromarty—an office which was granted to Adam de Urquhart by the earl apparently with the concurrence of its previous holder, one Richard Mowat, and confirmed by David II in 1358. During the next three centuries the Urquharts became firmly established in Cromarty, and sent out offshoots into Moray and Aberdeenshire as well.

The family eccentricity showed itself early. Of Thomas Urquhart of Cromarty, who died in 1557, it is recorded that every evening about sunset in his old age he was brought out of his castle in his couch and solemnly hoisted by pulleys to the battlements, a ceremony from which he derived much comfort as 'emblematical of the resurrection'. He is credited with having thirty-eight legitimate children, including seven who fell at the battle of Pinkie. One was Walter Urquhart, sheriff of Cromarty, who was commissioned with others in 1577 and 1578 to seek out and apprehend a number of men and women suspected of witchcraft. Among the predictions of the famous seer, *Coinneach Odhar,* was one relating that the 'landgrasping' Urquharts of Cromarty would before long not own twenty acres in the Black Isle. As they then owned Kinbeachie, Braelangwell, Newhall and Mounteagle as well as Cromarty, this must have seemed nonsense at the time, but it is less surprising now.

The great Sir Thomas's father and namesake succeeded as a minor, and the family's close connection with kinsmen in Aberdeenshire is shown by the appointment as Tutor of Cromarty of Urquhart of Craigfintry, a great-uncle, who both improved the estate and also made a fortune for himself. The family cohesion, but not the prudence, was shown by the new laird, who involved himself in a Sunday rumpus in the kirk of Forres along with nine other Urquharts (two of them his own servants) in 1623, for which the sheriff of Cromarty was lodged in Edinburgh castle and had to pay costs and damages. It was probably to prevent him from further burdening the estate that in 1636 his two eldest sons confined him for nearly a week in an upper chamber of his own house, and the family differences were only settled by resort to arbitration.

Sir Thomas Urquhart, genealogist, patriot, and translator of Rabelais, was a man both of action and intelligence. He joined Mackenzie of Pluscardine's royalist rising in 1649, and two years later set off to join Charles I with three large trunks full of manuscripts; when captured and imprisoned after Worcester battle he lamented the reading public's loss of the books he might have written. As well as more abstruse topics, that 'eccentric overcrowded brain' (as Dame Veronica Wedgwood called it) had schemes to revolutionise the economy of the Highlands and to improve his estate and the harbour of Cromarty. On his brother's death Cromarty passed to the Tutor's descendants, who sold it to Lord Tarbat (later first Earl of Cromartie) in 1684. It was bought back by a junior branch in 1741, but only remained in the family for another twenty-five years before being bought by the Rosses.

The rest of the Brahan Seer's prophecy came only too true. Newhall's last Urquhart laird was M.P. from 1715 to 1727, when the estate was sold; Kinbeachie remained an Urquhart property into the 19th century; and a morsel was kept of Braelangwell, held by a cadet of Newhall, of whom David Urquhart was a propagandist in the true Urquhart tradition. His *Pillars of Hercules* introduced the Turkish bath into Europe, and called down a rebuke that he wrote to prove that 'the Highland clans, with clan Urquhart at their head' had come from Greece via Canaan and Egypt.

WALLACE

WALLACE

'At Wallace' name what Scottish blood
But boils up in a spring-tide flood!'

Robert Burns

ALTHOUGH the name of Wallace is illustrious in the annals of Scotland on account of one man's character and achievements, it has been known since the 12th century on the lands of the Stewards of Scotland in the south-west.

Richard Wallensis was a vassal in 1174 of Walter FitzAlan, who was appointed Steward by David I. The family was first established in Ayrshire, from which a branch settled in Renfrewshire early in the 13th century. Richard was grandfather of Adam whose younger son Malcolm was father of the patriot, and the family had held land under the Stewards for at least a century before William's birth about 1274. Though theirs was a small estate, they were of good blood, carrying with it a tradition of authority and leadership, a long attachment to Scottish soil, and hereditary service to one of the royal household.

As younger son of Sir Malcolm Wallace of Elderslie, who owned land in Ayrshire as well as the Renfrewshire estate from which he took his designation, William belonged to a cadet branch of this family, at the very centre of Steward influence. Probably he had already performed some feats of daring and laid the foundations of his popular reputation before his killing of the sheriff of Lanark in 1297 gave the signal for a general revolt against Edward I of England and his forces; but at the outset he must have owed much to the fact that the Steward was his patron and friend. As a modern historian has written, he fought for seven years with a constancy and singleness of purpose remarkable in any age, and for a man of his time and class altogether extraordinary. Alone among the Scottish leaders of his day he defeated a full-scale English army in the field, and roused a nation to a new sense of its unity and freedom.

Wallace was knighted and made Guardian of Scotland after his victory at Stirling Bridge, but in 1305 he was captured, and taken to London to stand his trial for treason. He declared that he was no traitor, that he had never taken the oath of allegiance to an alien monarch, and so could never have broken it. But he was found guilty and hanged at Tyburn. No wonder his memory is cherished as the greatest of Scottish patriots. There are monuments to him in many places, including Elderslie, Ayr, Dryburgh, Lanark, Stirling and Aberdeen, in Edinburgh and Glasgow, and what has been called the 'fantastic nightmare' on the Abbey Craig above Stirling at least testifies to his countrymen's pride in the man whom it commemorates.

The descendants of Wallace of Riccarton, already mentioned as the earliest of the name on record, took the designation of Craigie on acquiring that Ayrshire estate by marriage. Hugh Wallace of Craigie was created a Baronet of Nova Scotia in 1669, and the family came to an end in the male line about 1760. The last baronet's daughter became the wife of John Dunlop of Dunlop, and is remembered as the friend of Robert Burns. Elderslie had reverted to the Riccarton line on the death of the patriot's elder brother Malcolm, and was granted to a younger son of Sir John of Riccarton and the Craigie heiress in the reign of Robert III. A descendant had a charter of Elderslie from William Wallace of Craigie in 1554, but it was sold in 1678 to Sir Thomas of Craigie, whose son conveyed it back to the Elderslie family.

John Wallace of Cessnock, in Ayrshire, a cadet of Riccarton, a West India merchant in Glasgow, in 1792 purchased the estate of Kelly in Renfrewshire. His son Robert of Kelly, M.P. for Greenock from 1833–45, urged post office and other reforms which led to the penny post; another son was a Waterloo officer who rose to the rank of lieut.-general in the army.

There have been some forty or fifty territorial branches of the Wallace family, by far the greater number of which have long ceased to exist. After several generations in Jamaica, one family emerged as owners by inheritance of the estates of Busbie and Cloncaird, in Ayrshire. The head of this family has been recognised as representative in the direct male line of the Wallaces of Riccarton, Craigie and Elderslie, and head of the house of Wallace.

WEMYSS

WEMYSS

A group of caverns on a rocky seashore, however remarkable in themselves, may not seem to offer a promising origin for the naming of a family; but the name of Wemyss is said to be derived from just such a feature on the north coast of the Firth of Forth. It took so firm a hold that it now has a claim to be the longest-established name in Fife.

These particular caves (Scots 'weem', Gaelic *uaimh)* are believed to have provided shelter for early Christian missionaries, by whom the walls were covered with curious sculpturings. They gave a name to the estate belonging to this family, whose earliest proved ancestor was Michael of Methil and Wemyss, a man of note in the reign of William the Lion. In the mid-14th century the Wemyss estate was divided between three co-heiresses, who carried it out of the family—the first of a series of setbacks which it overcame successfully. The next heir-male, Sir John, as well as inheriting large possessions, reacquired part of the early Wemyss lands; he was constable of the castle and town of St Andrews, and the real founder of his house. In 1511 Sir David Wemyss of that Ilk had his estates erected into the barony of Wemyss, including not only the Fife properties but also lands in Perthshire (among them Elcho on the river Tay) and Angus.

As befitted men whose castle crowns a low cliff overlooking the waters of the firth, the lairds of Wemyss have been acquainted with the sea. In some accounts of the wars with England after James V died, the next Sir John Wemyss appears as one of the leaders who mustered the men of Fife and repulsed an attack made by an English fleet on St Monance in 1548 (a later laird was commissioned as Admiral of the Forth from Dysart to the water of Leven, and another was Lord High Admiral of Scotland). Sir John was an adherent of Mary Queen of Scots, whose first meeting at Wemyss with her future husband Henry Darnley had such dire consequences. From this laird's brother sprang the family of Caskiberran, notable for a mechanical genius who became Master Gunner of England and Master of War Ordnance in Scotland (and having served both Commonwealth and king signed himself 'your Majesty's most humble but ruined subject').

So it was as the head of a considerable house that Sir John Wemyss of Wemyss was made one of the first Baronets of Nova Scotia by Charles I, and created Lord Wemyss of Elcho in 1628 and Earl of Wemyss in 1633. The second earl, although three times married and having had ten sons and six daughters, had the sorrow of seeing all the sons and four of the daughters die before him. Firmly resolved not to let the family estates be parted from the name—'ane Wemys most have all befor any other name for I will never putt my house out of that antient name for any other in the world'—he secured this by arranging a marriage between his younger daughter and a Wemyss kinsman, son of the Master Gunner. In the marriage contract he bound himself to resign his estates in favour of the couple and their heirs. A grandson appeared in the year before he died in 1679, but Lady Margaret only became Countess of Wemyss in the teeth of opposition from her elder sister (widow of the Marquess of Douglas and wife of the Earl of Sutherland), who challenged her right to both title and estates in the courts and in Parliament itself.

The Wemyss estates were in danger for the third time in the mid-18th century. Family influence seemed to have been strengthened by the earl's elopement with the heiress of Charteris of Amisfield, but his heir Lord Elcho was attainted for his part in the Jacobite Rising of 1745; the second son took the name of Charteris on inheriting the Amisfield property; and it fell to the third son James to succeed under a special entail to the ancient estate of Wemyss (except for the lands of Elcho which went, with the earldom, to his elder brother). James Wemyss of Wemyss, nephew of one Earl of Sutherland and brother-in-law of another, was M.P. first for Fife and then for Sutherland; his son became a lieutenant-general, and raised two Sutherland fencible regiments and the famous 93rd Highlanders. In the next generation the family produced another general and an admiral, and a younger son of the house was Admiral of the Fleet Lord Wester Wemyss, who signed the Armistice on behalf of the Allied Navies after the first world war, when the German fleet surrendered—almost within sight of Castle Wemyss and its famous caves.

FOR FURTHER READING

MOST Scottish historians accept the importance of families and clans in Scottish life, especially in the Highlands and the Borders. 'Much of the history of Scotland can be understood only through a knowledge of family history and family relationships', wrote Professor W. Croft Dickinson. There are admirable summaries in W. R. Kermack's short histories, *The Scottish Highlands* (1957) and *The Scottish Borders* (1967); for more detail Donald Gregory's *History of the Western Highlands and Islands of Scotland* (1836) is still essential, and Dr T. I. Rae's *Administration of the Scottish Frontier* (1966) covers the crucial period before the Union of the Crowns. I have found Professor G. W. S. Barrow's *Robert Bruce* (1965) a valuable key to the emergence of some notable families. The printed records of the Privy Council contain contemporary statements of inter-family disagreements and attempts to curb them.

The Surnames of Scotland: their Origin, Meaning and History, by Dr George F. Black, is a massive compendium of information methodically arranged, published by the New York Public Library in 1946 and since reprinted. Earlier works include Cosmo Innes's essay *Concerning some Scotch Surnames* (1860). *The Scots Peerage*, edited by Sir J. Balfour Paul (1904–14) and modern reference books on titled and landed families are helpful; older books such as Sir Robert Douglas's *Baronage of Scotland* (1798) and William Anderson's *Scottish Nation* (1863) need to be used with caution, but can still provide useful clues. The writings of Sir Walter Scott are an additional quarry from which I have often profited.

Histories of individual families and clans are legion, from the sumptuous volumes of Sir William Fraser to obscure pamphlets. There is a detailed list in *Scottish Family History* (1930) by Margaret Stuart, with an essay on how to write a family history by Balfour Paul; more recent works, including the excellent Johnston clan history series are included in *Scottish Family Histories* (1960) by Joan P. S. Ferguson, with particulars of Scottish library holdings. A number of clan and family societies have published good material, and most books on local history devote some space to genealogy.

A list of 'chiefs of clans and names in Scotland' has been included in *Whitaker's Almanack* in recent years, and in Debrett's *Peerage*, and details are also given in other publications by Messrs Johnston & Bacon. The Standing Council of Scottish Chiefs has published lists of its members. Inquiries regarding descent and family history are dealt with by the Scots Ancestry Research Society, a non-profit-making organisation which charges a fee for registration and has an office at 20 York Place, Edinburgh.

Anyone who knows the field of Scottish family history will realise how much I have borrowed from other writers on the families included in this book. I gladly acknowledge my indebtedness to them, to my wife for constant advice and special research on some of the less well documented families, and to her and to Mr W. D. H. Sellar for reading the book in typescript and making many helpful suggestions.

R.W.M.